THE
SECOND
ATHENIAN
LEAGUE

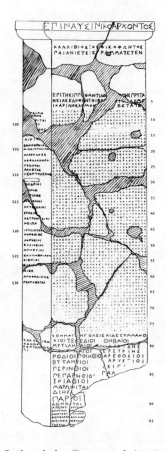

The Stele of the Decree of Aristoteles

FACSIMILE BY J. CARGILL

THE
SECOND
ATHENIAN
LEAGUE

EMPIRE OR FREE ALLIANCE?

JACK CARGILL

UNIVERSITY OF CALIFORNIA PRESS AT
BERKELEY • LOS ANGELES • LONDON

University of California Press
Berkeley and Los Angeles, California
University of California Press, Ltd.
London, England
© 1981 by
The Regents of the University of California

Library of Congress Cataloging in Publication Data

Cargill, Jack L.
  The Second Athenian League.

  Includes index.
  1. Athenian League, Second, 4th cent. B.C.
2. Greece—History—Spartan and Theban supremacies,
404–362 B.C. 3. Greece—History—Macedonian
Expansion, 359–322 B.C. I. Title.
DF231.2.C37   938'.06   80–22532
ISBN 0-520-04069-4

Printed in the United States of America

1 2 3 4 5 6 7 8 9

Το JENNIFER,
ἐλευθέραι οὔσηι καὶ αὐτονόμωι

Καλόν, ὦ ἄνδρες Ἀθηναῖοι, καλὸν
ἡ τῶν δημοσίων γραμμάτων φυλακή.
A good thing, O men of Athens, a good thing
is the preservation of the public documents.

—AISCHINES 3.75

CONTENTS

ACKNOWLEDGMENTS

I must begin by repeating my thanks to those who helped me when this work was at the dissertation stage, including my dissertation committee, Professors Raphael Sealey (chair), R. S. Stroud, and Erich Gruen; Dean Sanford S. Elberg and his staff; the staff of the Epigraphical Museum at Athens; and the personnel of the departments in which I taught while writing it. Further fond thanks are offered to those family members to whom the dissertation was dedicated, not all of whom lived to see this version.

In connection with the present completely rewritten work, I want most particularly to thank Professor Charles W. Fornara, whose corrections and suggestions I always appreciated, even though I did not always heed them. Similar thanks are offered, once again, to Professor Sealey, who aided me in producing the revised version with the same consideration and diligence he showed when overseeing the earlier draft. Professor John Buckler was very helpful in connection with the chapter on which I sought his advice. The anonymous suggestions forwarded to me on the evaluative reading by the University of California Press were most useful; I must also particularly thank August Frugé, Doris Kretschmer, Marilyn Schwartz, and Pericles Georges for their help with my manuscript at various stages. The convenient teaching schedule and excellent collection of Greek sources provided for me at the University of California, Irvine, during the years 1977–78 and 1978–79 helped the revision go smoothly.

CONVENTIONS USED IN THE TEXT

Epigraphical Symbols

[ ]   Surface area completely lost; letters within are editorial restorations.

[. . .]   Definite number of lost letters (one per dot); no restoration suggested.

[---]   Uncertain number of lost letters.

⟨ ⟩   Letters within supply omissions or correct errors of mason.

{ }   Letters within exist on stone, but should be deleted.

⟦ ⟧   Surface area has been erased (still-visible letters and parts of letters are recorded; restorations within the erasure are given single brackets in addition to the double brackets of the erasure).

α, β   Enough of this letter is visible to make it the *only* possible reading.

α̣, β̣   Extant traces are compatible with this letter (which is the most likely one), but also with other(s).

^, ⌐   Trace(s) which could be part of two or more letters; no basis for thinking a particular one is more likely.

α̲, β̲   Letter, or trace(s), seen by earlier editor(s); surface now lost.

v̄   Letter space left blank by mason (one *v* per blank space).

vacat   Remainder of line left blank by mason.

/   End of inscribed line (employed only when quoting short passages; longer texts are printed line by line).

Principles of Greek Translation

All translations are my own, unless credit is given to someone else. Literalness and closeness to the Greek word order are sought, sometimes at the expense of awkwardness in English. Expressions ambiguous in the Greek are left ambiguous in English. Technical terms are generally transliterated, e.g., demos, synedrion, presbeis, boule, and so on. English words added for clarification are placed within parentheses, except (in literary texts) articles and a few very common and universally accepted periphrases. In epigraphical texts, even the article *the*, when supplied for clarity, is put within parentheses, because of the importance of the letter count (and the frequent helpfulness of an extant article's number, gender, and case in restoring nouns and adjectives with which it is associated). Words and parts of words within brackets correspond, as closely as I can make them, to restored elements in the Greek text. Underdotted elements of the Greek text, however, are translated as if they were certain readings.

ABBREVIATIONS USED IN THE NOTES

*Inscriptions, Documents, and
Other Items in Standard Collections*

Cited by item number (not page number) in the collections. Citation followed by "comm." refers to an editorial comment *ad loc.*; in some collections, "intro." has a similar implication.

SV Hermann Bengtson, *Die Staatsverträge des Altertums* II² (München 1975). Primary form of citation for any inscriptions which appear in this collection; literary sources cited via *SV* only when obscure or numerous.

IG *Inscriptiones Graecae* (Berlin 1873–), many editors, many volumes; particularly appropriate for this study are *IG* II, ed. Ulrich Koehler (1877), and *IG* II², ed. J. Kirchner (1913). Inscriptions not in *SV* but in *IG* are cited by their *IG* numbers, though parenthetical notes may indicate employment of more recent texts.

SEG *Supplementum Epigraphicum Graecum.* Successive volumes record the discovery of new epigraphical texts and summarize recent work on inscriptions already published in other collections. I cite some texts not appearing in either *SV* or *IG* by the latest volume of *SEG* in which they are discussed, particularly when access to their original places of publication is difficult.

Syll.³ J. Dittenberger, *Sylloge Inscriptionum Graecarum*³ (Leipzig 1915–24), an old but very large selection (often abbreviated as *SIG*), cited here only for texts not appearing in later collections, or for Dittenberger's comments.

Tod Marcus N. Tod, *A Selection of Greek Historical Inscriptions* II (Oxford 1948), sometimes cited as *GHI*. Never a primary citation, because Tod "regularizes" epigraphic spelling, thus destroying the letter count; but Tod's comments and his improvements in older texts are noted.

ML Russell Meiggs and D. M. Lewis edit the current version of Tod's Vol. I: same title (Oxford 1969).

WV J.Wickersham and G. Verbrugghe, *Greek Historical Documents: The Fourth Century B.C.* (Toronto 1973), inscriptions and a few literary passages, in English translation (with little indication of what is extant, what is restored). Translated phrases and introductions cited as editorial opinions only.

FGrH Felix Jacoby, *Die Fragmente der griechischen Historiker* (Berlin and Leiden 1923–55), some comments in German, some in English. Literary fragments cited via this collection if not accessible in standard texts of extant authors.

DA Decree of Aristoteles (*SV* 257; *IG* II, 17; *IG* II², 43; Tod 123; WV 22), referring to my own text and translation, based on autopsy and squeeze (chapter 2). Certain collections of inscriptions are cited almost solely for their texts and/or translations of this particular document:

Rangabé A. R. Rangabé, *Antiquités Helléniques* II (Athens 1855) 381, 381b.

Pouilloux J. Pouilloux, *Choix d'Inscriptions Grecques* (Paris 1960) 27.

Pfohl G. Pfohl, *Griechische Inschriften* (München 1965) 103.

Ancient Literary Works

Except for works cited only once or twice (and spelled out in full), ancient authors' names are abbreviated as indicated below. Their titles are also abbreviated, unless a standard numerical form of reference exists, in which case it is employed instead of titles. Authors of a single work are cited by name only. Actual texts employed are indicated below by:

1. Text series
   a. OCT = Oxford Classical Texts, Oxford
   b. Teub. = Teubner Classical Texts, Stuttgart and Leipzig
   c. Budé = Budé Texts and French Translations, Paris
   d. Loeb = Loeb Classical Library Texts and English Translations, London and Cambridge, Massachusetts
2. Surname(s) of editor(s)/translator(s)
3. Date(s) of the printing actually consulted

Loeb editions are used only for late or tangential works, cited for general content only. All source quotations, and my translations of source passages, depend on the better OCT, Teub., and Budé editions. Brackets around an author's name or (within the lists below) a work's title indicate the spuriousness of the work cited. "Sch." prior to a citation refers to a scholion to the passage, while "*Hyp.*" is used similarly to refer to the late *Hypothesis* preceding certain works in some manuscripts.

Ain. Takt.   Aineias Taktikos, *Siegecraft* (Budé: Dain, 1967)

Ais.   Aischines, *Orations* (Budé: Martin and Budé, 1962):
1. *Against Timarchos*
2. *On the Embassy*
3. *Against Ktesiphon*

Andok.   Andokides, *Orations* (Budé: Dalmeyda, 1930):
3. *On the Peace*

Aristot.   Aristotle:
Athenaion Politeia (OCT: Kenyon, 1963)
Politics (Loeb: Rackham, 1967)
The "Art" of Rhetoric (Loeb: Freese, 1967)

Dein.   Deinarchos, *Orations* (Loeb: Burtt, 1962):
1. *Against Demosthenes*
3. *Against Philokles*

Dem.   Demosthenes, *Orations* (OCT: Butcher and Rennie, 1955–60):

1. *First Olynthiac*
2. *Second Olynthiac*
3. *Third Olynthiac*
4. *First Philippic*
5. *On the Peace*
6. *Second Philippic*
7. *[On Halonnesos]*
8. *On the Chersonesos*
9. *Third Philippic*
10. *Fourth Philippic*
11. *[Answer to Philip's Letter]*
12. *[Philip's Letter]*
13. *[On Organization]*
15. *For the Liberty of the Rhodians*
16. *For the Megalopolitans*
17. *[On the Treaty with Alexander]*
18. *On the Crown*
19. *On the Embassy*
20. *Against Leptines*
21. *Against Meidias*
22. *Against Androtion*
23. *Against Aristokrates*
24. *Against Timokrates*
40. *[Second Oration Against Boiotos]*
48. *[Against Olympiodoros]*
49. *[Against Timotheos]*
50. *[Against Polykles]*
51. *[On the Trierarchic Crown]*
58. *[Against Theokrines]*
59. *[Against Neaira]*

Letter 3. *[On the Children of Lykourgos]*

Diod.   Diodoros Sikeliotes, *Historical Library* (Teub.: Vogel and Fischer, 1964)

Isok.   Isokrates, *Orations* (Budé: Mathieu and Brémond, 1960–63):

4. *Panegyrikos*
5. *Address to Philip*
6. *Archidamos*
7. *Areopagitikos*
8. *On the Peace*
12. *Panathenaikos*
14. *Plataikos*
15. *Antidosis*

Letter 6. To the Children of Jason
Letter 7. To Timotheos of Herakleia
Letter 8. To the Rulers of Mytilene

Nep.   Cornelius Nepos, *Lives* (OCT: Winstedt, 1952):

Agesilaos	*Epaminondas*
Chabrias	*Iphicrates*
Conon	*Timotheus*

Paus.   Pausanias, *Description of Greece* (Loeb: Jones, Wycherley, and Ormerod, 1965–66)

Philoch. Philochoros, *Fragments* (*FGrH* 328)

Plut.   Plutarch:

Moralia (Loeb: Many titles, editors, dates)

Lives (Loeb: Perrin, 1959–62):

Agesilaos	*Pelopidas*
Alexander	*Perikles*
Aratos	*Phokion*
Artaxerxes	*Solon*
Demosthenes	

Polyain. Polyainos, *Stratagems* (Teub.: Woefflin and Melber, 1970)

Polyb. Polybios, *Histories* (Loeb: Paton, 1967–68)

Theopomp. Theopompos, *Fragments* (*FGrH* 115)

Thuc.   Thucydides, *Peloponnesian War* (OCT: Jones, 1963)

Xen.   Xenophon:

Hellenika (OCT: Marchant, 1961)
Agesilaos (Loeb: Marchant, 1971)
Poroi (Loeb: Marchant, 1971)

Standard Works and Other Books
Cited Frequently

Accame   Silvio Accame, *La lega Ateniese del secolo IV a.C.* (Rome 1941).

ATL   B. D. Meritt, H. T. Wade-Gery, and M. F. McGregor, *The Athenian Tribute Lists* I–IV (Cambridge and Princeton 1939–53).

Beloch   K. J. Beloch, *Griechische Geschichte*[2] 3:1 and 3:2 (Berlin and Leipzig 1922–23).

Bengtson, *G&P* H. Bengtson *et al.*, *The Greeks and the Persians* (London 1969).

Busolt   Georg Busolt, *Der zweite athenische Bund* (Leipzig 1874).

Hammond, *HG*[2] N. G. L. Hammond, *A History of Greece*[2] (Oxford 1967).

Kirchner, *IIA²* J. Kirchner, *Imagines Inscriptionum Atticarum²* (Berlin 1948), cited by item number.

Larsen, *Rep. Govt.* J. A. O. Larsen, *Representative Government in Greek and Roman History* (Berkeley 1955).

Marshall F. H. Marshall, *The Second Athenian Confederacy* (Cambridge 1905).

Meiggs, *AE* Russell Meiggs, *The Athenian Empire* (Oxford 1972).

Rhodes, *Boule* P. J. Rhodes, *The Athenian Boule* (Oxford 1972).

Ryder, *KE* T. T. B. Ryder, *Koine Eirene* (London 1965).

Sealey, *City-Sts.* Raphael Sealey, *A History of the Greek City-States* (Berkeley 1976).

Scholarly Journals

The titles of scholarly journals are abbreviated (if at all) according to the system of *L'Année Philologique*, q.v.

Articles Cited Repeatedly in Abbreviated Form

B&C D. W. Bradeen and J. E. Coleman, "Thera on I.G., II², 43," *Hesperia* 36 (1967) 102–104 and plate 30.

Burnett, "Expans." A. P. Burnett, "Thebes and the Expansion of the Second Athenian Confederacy: *IG* II² 40 and *IG* II² 43," *Historia* 11 (1962) 1–17.

B&E A. P. Burnett and C. Edmonson, "The Chabrias Monument in the Athenian Agora," *Hesperia* 30 (1961) 74–91 and plates 11 and 12.

Cawkwell, "Found." G. L. Cawkwell, "The Foundation of the Second Athenian Confederacy," *CQ* 23 (1973) 47–60.

Cawkwell, "Peace" G. L. Cawkwell, "Notes on the Peace of 375/4," *Historia* 12 (1963) 84–95.

Fabricius E. Fabricius, "Zur Geschichte des zweiten athenischen Bundes," *RhM* 46 (1891) 589–598.

Sealey, "Transf." R. Sealey, "*IG* II².1609 and the Transformation of the Second Athenian Sea-League," *Phoenix* 11 (1957) 95–111.

Woodhead, "Allies" A. G. Woodhead, "Chabrias, Timotheus, and the Aegean Allies, 375–373 B.C.," *Phoenix* 16 (1962) 258–266.

Woodhead, "Inscs." A. G. Woodhead, "Greek Inscriptions," nos. 84–87, *Hesperia* 26 (1957) 221–233.

Woodhead, "Jason" A. G. Woodhead, "IG II² 43 and Jason of Pherae," *AJA* 61 (1957) 367–373.

INTRODUCTION

The period between the end of the Peloponnesian War (404 B.C.) and the defeat of the Greek forces at Chaironeia (338 B.C.) by Philip II of Macedon has sometimes been viewed as an era of Greek self-destruction, which led to a more or less inevitable Macedonian takeover. Popular histories that devote some pages to the period (many virtually omit it) frequently pay slight attention to the existence of the large alliance Athens led from 378 to 338. This Second Athenian League has seemed comparatively dismissable because it has been regarded essentially as an unsuccessful repetition of the first League, that is, the fifth-century Delian League, which metamorphosed over time into the oppressive Athenian Empire. The view that the fourth-century organization's supposedly idealistic beginnings were fairly quickly forgotten, as the so-called second Empire came to exhibit most of the abuses of the first, is essentially shared by the authors of the three monographs heretofore devoted to the League, Georg Busolt (1874), F. H. Marshall (1905), and Silvio Accame (1941).

Lacking the eloquence of Thucydides to immortalize its downfall, leaving no archaeological traces comparable to Perikles' great building projects, the Second Athenian League, thus interpreted, might rightly command little interest. That the Athenians, having failed once in their effort to assume despotic control of Greece, should also fail upon trying again, would seem unsurprising and indeed trivial. This interpretation of the nature of the League has the further effect of trivializing the entire period in which it was an important entity in Hellenic affairs. Some recent scholars, notably T. T. B. Ryder and Raphael Sealey, apparently have sensed something suspicious about the traditional hypothesis as to the nature of the League. But the "second Empire" viewpoint has so entirely permeated most detailed work on the League that authors dealing with larger topics cannot be expected to recognize all of the ramifications of the presupposition. I propose, therefore, to subject the sources on the Second Athenian League to a meticulous reexamination—not, as has so often been done, imposing the second Empire hypothesis, but asking whether it will emerge naturally from the data available.

Information on the League, as on most fourth-century topics, must be laboriously hunted among scattered sources. Xenophon supplies the only extant contemporary narrative history of the first part of the century. But his *Hellenika*, which ends with the battle of Mantineia in 362, concentrates on events involving Sparta or occurring in and around the

Peloponnesos, and is not thorough on the history of Athens or of the Aegean states. The work of Diodoros of Sicily, written in the first century B.C., is broader in scope and draws on some lost fourth-century sources (notably Ephoros), but Diodoros' many obvious mistakes of chronology and of fact throw doubt upon numerous points in his narrative. Published orations abound—by Demosthenes, Isokrates, Aischines, and others—but such sources are frequently uncertain in date and generally tendentious. The biographies of Cornelius Nepos (first century B.C.) and Plutarch (second century A.D.) must necessarily be used with caution because of their genre and their late date. Most other literary sources on the period are fragmentary and/or late.

Inscriptions make up a large proportion of the relevant sources, and their contemporaneity gives them primary importance. These, however, present even greater difficulties than the literary sources. Not only are the dates of many of them conjectural and disputed, but often much of their actual content has been lost through damage to the stones. Restorations are often of dubious value. The monographs of Busolt and Marshall are weakened by their reliance on inaccurate Greek epigraphical texts. Accame, on the other hand, directly consulted many of the inscriptions relating to the League, revised the accepted texts of several, suggested a great many new restorations, and in general laid a firmer foundation under all subsequent study of the topic. Sometimes, however, he appears to have been a bit too ready to re-restore and reinterpret key passages, and too quick to see new letters no one had ever seen before. On the few occasions when other specialists have reexamined some of these stones, they generally have concluded that *less* is visible than supposedly met Accame's eye. I personally can draw such a conclusion from autopsy concerning only one inscription, but it is the most important inscription connected with the League—the decree of Aristoteles of 377 B.C., which invited new states to join the League, setting out the guarantees offered to them, and on whose stele the names of League members were inscribed (chapter 2).

The present work is not a detailed history either of the Second Athenian League or of its period. A strictly chronological treatment could tend to deemphasize important elements of continuity and consistency. Moreover, the necessary digressions to discuss epigraphical and source-critical niceties, and to dispute particular positions taken by modern scholars, would be so numerous that in any case the chronological thread would likely be lost. The organization of my heavily documented chapters 1 to 10, therefore, is essentially topical. Discrete aspects of the League or its period are considered separately, and each aspect is traced through the entire period in which it is a significant factor.

After setting the diplomatic scene (chapter 1) and showing the possibilities and limitations inherent in employing the primary epigraphical source associated with the League (chapter 2), I devote chapters 3 to 5 to the necessary preliminary work (slighted in most treatments) of differentiating League members from Athenian allies of other types. I argue that *only* states listed on the stele of Aristoteles were League members, that *all* members were listed, and that recruitment of League members ended quite early. I suggest that two Athenian allies about whom much controversy has existed—Korkyra and Jason of Pherai—were never members of the League. In chapter 6, I conclude that League membership was not finalized until oaths of the new member states' magistrates at home ratified the oaths exchanged earlier by their ambassadors, and that some League alliances were aborted at this late stage. The legal position of the allied synedrion, I contend in chapter 7, was equal to that of Athens in formulating League policy, and even exclusive in one important area (punishment of Athenians who might illegally hold property in League members' territory). Chapters 8 and 9 examine the promises made to prospective League members in 377 and Athenian performance over the years in fulfilling them. Modern condemnations of Athens's breaches of allied autonomy are characterized as being derived from anachronistic understanding of the concept; scholars' comments about Athenian kleruchies are shown to be irrelevant and misleading; and a new and noncondemnatory appraisal of the sending out of Athenian garrisons and governors is offered. Chapter 10 discusses defections from the permanent League alliance and their motivations, including commentary on the supposedly widespread abuse of League members by Athenian generals. I return to the ancient sources' position of singling out Chares for censure, and reinterpret the meaning and significance even of some of his exploits. The nature of the Social War of 357–355 and of the peace treaty ending it (with careful attention to the phrasing of Isokrates' *On the Peace* and other orations) is reexamined and reinterpreted. A significant but generally disregarded countermovement by dissident states to reestablish friendly relations with Athens is emphasized.

I conclude that the Second Athenian League is most responsibly viewed not as a second Empire, but as the free alliance its organizers proclaimed it to be. Important implications for research in, and evaluation of, fourth-century historical developments arise from this new interpretation. A history of the League, grounded in this reinterpretation but presented as a summary designed only to suggest the direction a more thorough historical treatment might take, rounds out the work.

Part I

CONTEXT AND PRIMARY DOCUMENT

1

THE KING'S PEACE
AND GREEK POWER POLITICS

Sparta had defeated Athens in the Peloponnesian War and crippled Athens as a naval power with the assistance of the Persian King. But relations between the wartime allies did not remain smooth.[1] The Spartan king Agesilaos (399–360 B.C.) entertained ideas of conquering Asia, and did in fact invade the King's domain in 396, keeping an army in the field there for some two years. The Spartans, like the Athenians a century earlier, posed as the defenders of the freedom of the Asiatic Greek cities. Persia's discomfiture was Athens's salvation. The King supplied ships, men, and money, and the Athenian general Konon defeated the Spartans in the important sea battle of Knidos (394). Then he and his helper, the Persian satrap Pharnabazos, sailed along the Asian coast and among the nearby islands, deposing pro-Spartan oligarchies and proclaiming themselves in turn the guarantors of the Greek cities' liberty. The cities in gratitude voted the general and the satrap crowns, titles, special privileges, and honorific statues.

Konon, recently an exile fleeing for his life, returned home to Athens a national hero. Still relying on the assistance of Pharnabazos, he began the rebuilding (394–391) of the long walls linking Athens and Peiraieus, the walls at whose destruction the Spartans and a good many of Athens's former tribute-paying allies had rejoiced not long before. In the meantime, Persian subsidies also strengthened an alliance in mainland Greece directed against the Lakedaimonians: from 395 through 387 Athens, Thebes, Korinth, and Argos engaged in the anti-Spartan struggle known as the Korinthian War. This war bore for the King the hoped-for fruit: the recall (394) of Agesilaos from Asia.

The Athenians were seemingly no more able to restrain themselves during prosperity, or to maintain friendly relations with the King, than the Spartans had been. Konon fell into Persian disfavor when it was realized that he was using the King's money purely to reestablish Athenian sea power. The Spartan Antalkidas, as early as 392, got the ear of the satrap Tiribazos for a suggestion of peace based on recognition of

---

1. This argument draws particularly on Marshall 1–13; Arnaldo Momigliano, "La κοινὴ εἰρήνη dal 386 al 388 a.C.," *RFIC* 12 (1934) 482–514; and Robin Seager, "The King's Peace and the Balance of Power in Greece, 386–362 B.C.," *Athenaeum* 52 (1974) 36–63. See also G. Barbieri, *Conone* (Rome 1955); Ryder, *KE*; and Cawkwell, "Agesilaus and Sparta," *CQ* 26 (1976) 62–84. Sources for events down to the imposition of the King's Peace are primarily Xen. *Hell.* and *Ages.*; Diod.; Plut. *Ages.*; and Nep. *Con.* Now see also Charles D. Hamilton, *Sparta's Bitter Victories* (Ithaca and London 1979).

Persian control of the Greeks in Asia and the autonomy of all other Greek states. Opposed by ambassadors from the other Hellenic powers, Antalkidas' plan did not at this time gain the support of the King. In these few years the Persians found it necessary at times to resist the aggressiveness of both Athens and Sparta. Thrasyboulos of Steiria led the Athenian navy to numerous successes along the Asian and Thracian coasts and among the Aegean islands. He may well have envisioned a new Athenian Empire along the lines of the old. This policy not only provoked Spartan counterstrokes and angered a substantial body of opinion within Athens, but strengthened the resolve of the Great King —particularly since Athens apparently had made the further mistake of supporting the revolt of a Persian client king, Evagoras of Cyprus.[2]

When Antalkidas took his peace suggestion directly to King Artaxerxes II Mnemon at Susa in 388, the response was prompt and positive. Athens was forced to negotiate because Antalkidas himself won control of the Hellespont in 387. Orders for the presence of the Greeks' representatives were issued through Tiribazos. In 386 the satrap had the following rescript read to them, according to Xenophon:

Ἀρταξέρξης βασιλεὺς νομίζει δίκαιον τὰς μὲν ἐν τῇ Ἀσίᾳ πόλεις ἑαυτοῦ εἶναι καὶ τῶν νήσων Κλαζομενὰς καὶ Κύπρον, τὰς δὲ ἄλλας Ἑλληνίδας πόλεις καὶ μικρὰς καὶ μεγάλας αὐτονόμους ἀφεῖναι πλὴν Λήμνου καὶ Ἴμβρου καὶ Σκύρου· ταύτας δὲ ὥσπερ τὸ ἀρχαῖον εἶναι Ἀθηναίων. ὁπότεροι δὲ ταύτην τὴν εἰρήνην μὴ δέχονται, τούτοις ἐγὼ πολεμήσω μετὰ τῶν ταῦτα βουλομένων καὶ πεζῇ καὶ κατὰ θάλατταν καὶ ναυσὶ καὶ χρήμασιν.

King Artaxerxes thinks it just that the states in Asia should be his, and of the islands Klazomenai and Cyprus, and that the other Greek states, both small and great, should be left autonomous, except Lemnos and Imbros and Skyros; and these, as of old, should be (the) Athenians'. But whichever (side) does not accept this peace, upon them I will make war, with those who desire this (arrangement), both by land and by sea, both with ships and with money.[3]

2. Concise descriptions of the career of Thrasyboulos may be found in Marshall 5–8 and Beloch 3:1.90–92; the latter (pp. 150f) insists that Thrasyboulos in this period organized a "second" Athenian League, and consequently he calls the League of 378–338 the "third" League; scholars have generally declined to follow this terminology. See also Cawkwell, "The Imperialism of Thrasybulus," CQ 26 (1976) 270–277. Evagoras was praised as a "Hellene," according to the readings of D. M. Lewis and R. S. Stroud, "Athens Honors King Euagoras of Salamis," Hesperia 48 (1979) 180–193 and plates 60 and 61.

3. Xen. Hell. 5.1.31. A briefer version of the rescript is provided by Diod. 14.110.3.:

τὰς μὲν κατὰ τὴν Ἀσίαν Ἑλληνίδας πόλεις ὑπὸ βασιλέα τετάχθαι, τοὺς δ' ἄλλους Ἕλληνας ἅπαντας αὐτονόμους εἶναι· τοῖς δὲ ἀπειθοῦσι καὶ μὴ προσδεχομένοις τὰς συνθήκας διὰ τῶν εὐδοκούντων πολεμήσειν.

The Greek states of Asia are to be subject to the King, but all the other Greeks are to be autonomous; and upon those not complying and not accepting the agreements, I shall make war through the aid of those consenting.

Cawkwell, "Found." 53, contends: "Clearly the document posted in the national temples (Isoc. 4.180; 12.107) was a very different thing"; he then proceeds to reconstruct his own highly inferential version of the peace agreement.

Except for the concession on Lemnos, Imbros, and Skyros—whose location along Athens's grain supply lifeline would have made their abandonment suicidal[4]—the terms of this "King's Peace" were such that the Athenians rightly lamented their condition "since the King had become an ally of the Lakedaimonians,"[5] and the agreement is called with equal propriety the "Peace of Antalkidas." In the face of the King's threat, desires for a renewed Empire had become untenable. For the foreseeable future, Athenian foreign policy would be conducted in deference to the terms of the King's Peace. Recognition of this changed situation was shown in the bilateral defensive alliance treaty the Athenians signed with Chios in 384. This agreement included a clause directed toward preserving "the p[eace and the frien]dship and the oaths and [the existing agreement]s, which (the) Kin[g] an[d (the) Athenians and] Lakedaimonians and the othe[r Greeks] swore," and a further clause that the alliance was concluded "on the basis of fre[e]dom and autonom[y], not contravening any of the things written on the stelai concerning the peace."[6]

Spartan behavior under color of enforcing the King's Peace is justly notorious.[7] While maintaining unchanged dominance over its own Peloponnesian League, Sparta invoked the "autonomy" clause of the Peace in forcibly breaking up weaker confederacies, a process it had begun even before the actual Peace was established. Sparta's Peloponnesian rival Mantineia was forced to separate into its constituent villages; the Chalkidian League led by Olynthos was dissolved; the Boiotian Confederacy under Thebes was not only broken up, but the Spartan general Phoibidas succeeded in treacherously placing a Spartan garrison on the

4. Xen. *Hell.* 4.8.15 gives fear of losing these islands as the reason for Athens's refusal to agree to Antalkidas' earlier peace proposal (cf. Andok. 3.12). Seager, "Lysias Against the Corndealers," *Historia* 15 (1966) 172 points out that Lemnos and Imbros *themselves* supplied much of Athens's wheat. R. S. Stroud, "Inscriptions from the North Slope of the Acropolis," I, *Hesperia* 40 (1971) 171 and n. 30, comments on an inscription (no. 23 in his article = *IG* II², 30) which appears to relate to Athens's forcible but legally unrecognized possession of Lemnos prior to the adoption of the King's Peace: kleruchs there seem to be mentioned in lines *a*13, 20, and 22; *b*6; and *c*5.

5. Xen. *Hell.* 5.1.29: συμμάχου Λακεδαιμονίοις βασιλέως γεγενημένου. Xenophon is probably speaking more accurately in saying elsewhere (sec. 25) that Antalkidas made an agreement that the King should become Sparta's ally "if the Athenians and their allies were not willing to accept the peace which he suggested" (εἰ μὴ ἐθέλοιεν Ἀθηναῖοι καὶ οἱ σύμμαχοι χρῆσθαι τῇ εἰρήνῃ ᾗ αὐτὸς ἔλεγεν). Aristeides, *Panathenaikos* 293 lists the constraints the peace put on Athens; see also Andok. 3.14–16. Beloch, 3:1.95, however, shows that the terms of the peace were much harder on Athens's chief allies than on the Athenians themselves.

6. *SV* 248, lines 9–12 (τὴν ε[ἰρήνην καὶ τὴν φι]λίαν / καὶ τὸς ὅρκος καὶ [τὰς οὔσας συνθήκα]s, / ἃς ὤμοσεν βασιλεὺ[ς] κα[ὶ Ἀθηναῖοι καὶ] / Λακεδαιμόνιοι καὶ οἱ ἄλλο[ι Ἕλληνες]), and 20–23 (ἐπ' ἐλευθε[ε]ρίαι καὶ αὐτον/ομί[α]ι μὴ παραβαίνοντας τῶν ἐν ταῖς σ/τήλαις γεγραμμένων περὶ τῆς εἰρήνης / μηδέν).

7. Beloch, 3:1.108, provides a clear summary of the dominant position of Sparta at this time.

Kadmeia, the acropolis of Thebes itself, to support a pro-Spartan oligarchy in the city. Another Spartan general, Sphodrias, for reasons about which the sources disagree (chapter 3), actually attempted an overland raid on the Peiraieus, the port of Athens. Athenian outrage was temporarily mollified when Sphodrias was duly brought to trial at Sparta; but it was rekindled when he was acquitted through personal connections. The Athenian assembly thereupon voted that the truce had been broken by the Lakedaimonians.[8]

This vote was very far from signifying that the King's Peace was at an end, however.[9] When the decree of Aristoteles, passed shortly afterward, invited states to join Athens's recently formed confederacy, it invited only those states not belonging to the King, expressed the intent to compel the Spartans to leave the Greeks free and autonomous, promised that the Athenians would themselves do so, and almost certainly made a specific reference to the King's Peace itself.[10] Not much later, the Athenian general Iphikrates, with the official approval of the Athenian demos, led mercenary forces on behalf of the King against rebels in Egypt; his lengthy employment shows that Athens cooperated with the King for several years beyond 377 (one late source even calls this cooperation an alliance, though this is probably an overstatement).[11]

Although Xenophon does not mention any participation by the Persian King in the negotiations leading either to the peace of 375/4 or to the peace of Sparta of 371, Diodoros' statements that the King participated in both have fourth-century support and probably should be believed.[12] The issue is complicated by the apparent doublet in Diodoros'

8. Diod. 15.29.7 (quoted in chapter 3). The account of Xen. *Hell.* 5.4.34 says: "And because of this (i.e., the acquittal) the Athenians put gates on the Peiraieus and were building ships, and gave aid to the Boiotians with all zeal" (καὶ ἐκ τούτου οἱ Ἀθηναῖοι ἐπύλωσάν τε τὸν Πειραιᾶ, ναῦς τε ἐναυπηγοῦντο, τοῖς τε Βοιωτοῖς πάσῃ προθυμίᾳ ἐβοήθουν).

9. Cf. Cawkwell, "Found." 52, who interprets Diodoros' phrase as "the formal denunciation of the King's Peace" (similar phrases on pp. 54, 56, and 60).

10. DA, lines 17f, 9f, 20, and 12–14, respectively. Cawkwell's belief that the Athenians had declared the King's Peace to be abrogated before the passage of the decree compels him ("Found." 60 n. 1) to offer a restoration for the erased line 14 which differs from the version of Accame, which most scholars accept. Cawkwell says that the excised clause may have been "concerned not to assert an intention to maintain the Peace, but to condemn Sparta for acting on behalf of the King under the treaty in a manner improper to the hegemonic power." This interpretation has serious epigraphical problems (chapter 2).

11. The basic source is Diod. 15.29.1–4 and 41.1–44.1. See also Nep. *Iphic.* 2.4 and *Chab.* 2.3. The latter passage says: "*Athenienses cum Artaxerxe societatem habebant. . . .*"

12. Sources for these two peace treaties are quoted in *SV* 265 and 269, respectively. Felix Jacoby, *FGrH*, Part IIIb (Suppl.) I.522f, argues persuasively (quoting the relevant sources) that the Persian King was involved. Cawkwell, "Epaminondas and Thebes," *CQ* 22 (1972) 258 and nn. 4f takes a similar position, specifically on the peace of Sparta of 371; cf. Bengtson, *SV* 269 comm.

account of the two peace agreements.[13] However, even in Xenophon's version of the events, the King is invoked both times as the ultimate author of the peace. Thus the differences between the two historians' stories are not material for the point at issue here: clearly, "the King's Peace" is an accepted catchword of Greek politics throughout the 370s. Moreover, a dated Athenian inscription of 368 refers to "[the K]ing's Pe[a]ce, which [(the) Athenians] and Lakedaimonian[s] a[n]d [the other Greeks] mad[e]."[14] The argument of Accame, to the effect that the Athenians, delighted that the Greeks themselves, without the participation of the King, had concluded a peace in 375 (a point doubtful in itself), thereupon proceeded to erase the reference to the King's Peace from the text of the decree of Aristoteles,[15] disregards this contemporary evidence.

A separate issue is the question of how early "King's Peace" came to be replaced in Greek diplomatic language by "common peace" (κοινὴ εἰρήνη)—a phrase which (unexplicitly and therefore safely) might tend to deny the King a role in maintaining Hellenic tranquillity. Diodoros calls the peace sponsored by the King a common peace in his narratives of both the peace agreements discussed above; Xenophon omits the phrase as well as the King's participation. One of Accame's alternative restorations of the erased provision of the decree of Aristoteles includes an invocation of the common peace, and this restoration has been widely accepted. But it has no epigraphical basis at all (chapter 2). Diodoros' use of the term in the aforementioned passages is probably anachronistic. In his brief account of another Persian-sponsored "common peace" in 366/5, he may be not only anachronistic in terminology but incorrect as to basic facts. His story simply does not ring true in comparison with Xenophon's much more circumstantial narrative, which says that Thebes *attempted* to persuade the other Greeks to accept a very pro-Theban peace plan sent by the King, but failed.[16] In describing the peace concluded in 362/1, after the battle of Mantineia, even Diodorus does not imply that the King participated; the exhausted Greeks themselves are said to have agreed upon a common peace and alliance.[17] Most scholars now connect this peace with an undated inscription found at Argos, in which it is said "[to him who] has come [from t]he satraps"

13. See esp. S. Lauffer, "Die Diodordublette XV 38 = 50 über die Friedenschlüsse zu Sparta 374 und 371 v. Chr.," *Historia* 8 (1959) 315–348.

14. *IG* II², 103, lines 23–26: [---τῆι / βασ]ιλέως εἰ[ρή]νηι ἣν ἐποήσα[ντο Ἀθηνα/ῖοι] καὶ Λακεδαιμόνιο[ι] κ[α]ὶ [οἱ ἄλλοι Ἑλ/ληνες] (brackets as by Accame 154, 157, and 164).

15. Accame 149f.

16. Diod. 15.76.3; Xen. *Hell.* 7.1.39f.

17. Diod. 15.89.1: συνθέμενοι δὲ κοινὴν εἰρήνην καὶ συμμαχίαν; Polyb. 4.33.8f agrees. Demosthenes, ca. 351, refers (in a context that seems to fit the Social War) to actions παρὰ τοὺς ὅρκους καὶ τὰς συνθήκας, ἐν αἷς αὐτονόμους τὰς πόλεις εἶναι γέγραπται (Dem. 15.26).

that the Greeks intend to maintain their "common peace," and that if the King does not interfere with it, "we will also be [peaceful toward (the) Ki]ng."[18] This, if the conjectured date is correct, is the earliest extant certain usage of the phrase "common peace," and at this point the King finds himself virtually excluded from all involvement in the peace originally imposed on the Hellenes by Persian fiat. Even now, as is evident from the last passage quoted, no inherent hostility toward the King is seen as a consequence of an exclusively Greek common peace agreement. The alliance which accompanied this peace had become an accepted part of the arrangement—a development implicit in the original King's Peace itself, and therefore no significant innovation.[19] It remained for Philip of Macedon to convert the "common peace"[20] into an instrument against the Persians.

Quite early, however, the Athenians had significantly altered the meaning of the King's Peace. According to Xenophon, the oath taken by those accepting the peace of Athens of 371 went as follows:

Ἐμμενῶ ταῖς σπονδαῖς ἃς βασιλεὺς κατέπεμψε καὶ τοῖς ψηφίσμασι τοῖς Ἀθηναίων καὶ τῶν συμμάχων. ἐὰν δέ τις στρατεύῃ ἐπί τινα πόλιν τῶν ὀμοσασῶν τόνδε τὸν ὅρκον, βοηθήσω παντὶ σθένει.

I will abide by the truce which the King sent down, and by the decrees of the Athenians and their allies. And if anyone takes the field against any state of those swearing this oath, I will give aid in full strength.[21]

The oath shows two significant developments: (1) policy is to be made by the League and its hegemon, Athens; and (2) only those actually taking the oath are guaranteed its protection. This peace is thus neither "the King's" nor "common," in any but a loose sense.

It is possible to read something cynical and sinister into this sort of development, if one is so inclined. Some scholars who deplore the supposed eventual conversion of the Second Athenian League into another Empire point to the "idealistic" days of its beginning.[22] Some earlier classicists saw the League as the embodiment of the "panhellenic" idealism of Isokrates' *Panegyrikos* (380 B.C.).[23] The attribution of such atti-

18. *SV* 292, lines 3 ([---τῶι παρὰ τ]ῶν σατραπῶν ἥκοντι), 5 ([---κ]οινὴν εἰρήνην; see also line 2: τῆς κοινῆς [εἰρήνης---]), and 11f (ἔξομεν καὶ ἡμεῖς [εἰρηνικῶς πρὸς β/α]σιλέα). This inscription, which is Tod 145 (q.v. for a summary of scholarship on its problems), is cross-referenced as "Tod 154" by the translators of WV 47.

19. Whether the arrangement ending the Third Sacred War in 346 was actually called a common peace (Diod. 16.60.3–5) is subject to debate: see G. T. Griffith, "The So-Called Koine Eirene of 346 B.C.," *JHS* 59 (1939) 71–79.

20. Principal sources for the peace and alliance ("League of Korinth") imposed by Philip are Diod. 16.89.1–3; *SV* (vol. III) 403a; and [Dem.] 17.2 and 4.

21. Xen. *Hell.* 6.5.2.

22. See, e.g., Marshall 20 and 32; Accame 61.

23. Probably implied, e.g., by Marshall 20; cf. Accame 32. See citations of earlier

tudes to a generation of elected politicians has been more recently, and rightly, viewed as unrealistic. But it is equally important to avoid the opposite extreme, i.e., belief in an insatiable desire for empire within the Athenians, temporarily masked by fine words, but ever ready to reassert itself, if given the slightest opening.[24] In reality, one should question these presuppositions, and also the presupposition that Athens's attitude toward the King's Peace was somehow congruent with its attitude toward its allies. Of course the Athenians were cynical about the terms of the King's Peace, just as everybody else was—the King himself, the Spartans, the Thebans, and eventually (the peace having by this time altered its form) the Macedonian conqueror. Meaningful judgments about Athens's relations with its allies must be grounded in more specific evidence.

---

scholars in Phillip Harding, "The Purpose of Isokrates' *Archidamos* and *On the Peace*," *CSCA* 6 (1973) 137 n. 1.

24. Eduard Meyer, *Geschichte des Altertums* V (Stuttgart and Berlin 1902) 394 sees Athenian imperialism at work as early as 375; Marshall, 61 n. 3, cites his statement with apparent approval, and seems to offer similar sentiments of his own, pp. 45–50. Burnett, "Expans." 14, in a context of 373 and earlier, refers to "the ease with which Athens could assume and put off again the cloak of idealism."

2
THE STELE OF THE
DECREE OF ARISTOTELES

The inscribed stele[1] (EM 10,397) is tall (1.93 m.), very slightly taper-
ing (0.44–0.47 m. wide), and of a uniform thickness (0.14 m.). It has
been reconstructed from twenty fragments. The bottom of the stele
is entirely lost, so its exact original height is unknown, but the general
shape of the stele and the content of its inscription indicate that little of
the stone is missing. The text begins on the top molding with the archon
date in large (0.023 m.) letters. The letters of the next two lines are also
rather large (0.015 m.), and these lines are stoichedon with respect to
each other (each containing twenty-one letters and one three-vertical-
dots punctuation mark). A considerable uninscribed area (0.19 m.) follows, then three nonstoichedon lines (letters 0.011 m. high) of further introductory formulae. The main decree (lines 7–77) is inscribed in regular
stoichedon fashion, thirty-one letters per line (minor exceptions in lines
24, 69, and 76). The letters are taller (0.009 m.) than they are wide, but
the stoichedon "checker-unit" is 0.015 m. square. The alphabet is Ionic
(although epsilon occasionally stands for eta), and the diphthong OY is
usually represented by omicron alone (four exceptions).

Below the decree is a one-line heading (line 78, letters 0.012 m. high)
which introduces a list of names (lines 79–90) arranged generally in two
columns, with a few names squeezed in between columns. Part of the
right-hand column has been broken away entirely, presumably taking
with it several names. The names are not stoichedon, except for a small
group within the right column. Immediately under the names comes a
second decree or amendment (lines 91–96), also moved by Aristoteles, in
nonstoichedon script slightly smaller (0.008 m.) than that of the main
decree. On the left lateral face of the stele (called Side B in some texts)
appears another list of names. The entries of thirty-four lines (some indi-

---

1. My text is based on autopsy and on a paper squeeze of the entire inscription generously loaned to me by Prof. W. K. Pritchett. A draft of my text was laboriously compared with the same squeeze by Prof. R. S. Stroud, who offered some helpful suggestions.
Texts consulted: Koehler, *IG* II, 17 (primarily his majuscule); Kirchner, *IG* II², 43; Tod 123;
Pouilloux 27; Pfohl 103; Bengtson, *SV* 257. Photos consulted: Kirchner, *IIA*² 50 (lines
36–57); Accame, figs. 1 (lines 47–96, not very clear), 2 (lines 10–18, squeeze), and 3 (lines
109–115, squeeze); B&C, plate 30 (lines 97–104, squeeze); Sealey, *City-Sts.* 413 (complete,
but small in scale). Letters or parts of letters clearly visible in either Pritchett's squeeze
(made in the 1950s) or any of these photos, but broken away prior to my consultation of
the stone (1974), are treated as extant. For bibliography, see *SEG* XVI, 44; XXI, 229; and
XXIV, 80.

vidual entries occupy more than one line) are more or less evenly spaced, beginning on a level with the opening line of the decree and ending beside line 62. Then comes a long blank space (0.25 m.) and finally one four-line entry, which begins on a level with the first names of the list on the front face. The lines of the left face list are numbered, depending on the editor, either B 1–38 or (as I prefer) 97–134.

The stoichedon text of the decree itself is rather well preserved, and many of its lacunae yield easy and natural restorations. This statement does not apply, however, to the amendment or second decree of lines 91–96, which is very fragmentary and has never been completely restored. About five lines of names would have been inscribed on the broken-away portion of the right-hand column. On the left face, the beginnings of the first few names have been broken off, but no names are entirely missing from the stone—except for the erasure of line 111 (= B 15). The name inscribed here was presumably chiseled away in antiquity. In the decree itself, the extant portions of lines 12–14 also have been erased, though legible traces of several letters remain in the *rasura*. Anyone casually viewing the stone can readily see that the names were not all cut by the same stonemason. The letters differ in size, shape, and closeness. Detailed differentiations in the hands of the inscription are described in the commentary, and some of the more obvious variations are represented by typographical distinctions in the English translation.

Text[2]

Ἐπὶ Ναυσινίκο ἄρχοντος·

Καλλίβιος ⋮ Κηφισοφῶντος

Παιανιεύς ⋮ ἐγραμμάτευεν·

vacat 0.19 m.

ἐπὶ τῆς Ἱπποθωντίδο[ς ἑβδ]όμης πρυτα-

5   νείας· ἔδοξεν τῆι βολ[ῆι κα]ὶ τῶι δήμω-

ι, Χαρῖνος Ἀθμον[εὺς ἐ]πεστάτει,

ΣΤΟΙΧ. 31   Ἀριστοτέλης εἶ[πεν· τύχ]ηι ἀγαθῆι τῆι Ἀ-

θηναίων καὶ [τ]ῶν [συμμ]άχων τῶν Ἀθηναίω-

ν ὅπως ἂν Λακεδ[αιμό]νιοι ἐῶσι τὸς Ἕλλη-

10   νας ἐλευθέ[ρ]ος [κα]ὶ αὐτονόμος ἡσυχίαν

ἄγειν, τὴ[ν χώραν] ἔχοντας ἐμ βεβαίωι τὴ-

[ν ἑαυτῶν·[. ⁴. .]] [[. . .ʼ. . .ΩΣ . . .ʼ^HIʼ. ʼ^I]]

Erased: [[. . . .¹⁰. . . .:]] [[. . . . . .²⁰. . . . . ^]]

Traces   [[. . . .¹⁰. . . .]] [[. . ⋮⋮. .Σ ⋮. Ε. Σ ⋰Α ⋮ Α⋮. . . ⋮N]]

15   [[. .⁵. .]] ἐψηφί]σθαι τῶι δήμωι· ἐάν τις βόλ-

2. Underlined letters depend upon Koehler's majuscule for the level of certainty indicated: (1) those recorded as certain would be underdotted but for Koehler's traces;
(2) those underdotted would have been bracketed but for Koehler's traces. An asterisk
over a letter, or over a space, indicates that the majuscule of Koehler shows traces incompatible with what I think I see on the stone—traces for which I cannot account and that I
cannot definitely overrule. In line 125, there seems actually to have been no room on the
stone for the final iota. Pointed brackets within this text usually mark incompletely cut letters, e.g., Λ for A or ΙΙ for Η, etc. In line 72, T was erroneously cut instead of Γ.
In line 130 the letters in pointed brackets were initially omitted; the mason began cutting

Translation

1-3　**IN THE ARCHONSHIP OF NAUSINIKOS (378/7 B.C.).**

KALLIBIOS (SON) OF KEPHISOPHON

OF (THE DEME) PAIANIA WAS SECRETARY.

4-6　*IN THE [SEV]ENTH PRYTANY, OF (THE TRIBE)*

HIPPOTHONTI[S] (SPRING, 377). RESOLVED BY THE

BOUL[E AN]D THE DEMOS. CHARINOS OF

ATHMON[E P]RESIDED.

7-12　Aristoteles mo[ved]: To the good [fortu]ne of the Athenians
and of [t]he [all]ies of the Athenians, so that (the) Lake-
d[aimo]nians shall leave the Greeks fr[e]e [an]d autonomous, to
enjoy tranquillity, possessing th[eir own territory] in safety . . .

12-15　(Traces within the erasure may permit restoration of the closing
phrase:)

[------------------------King, according to the agreements.]

15-20　[Decr]eed by the demos:

---

the next two letters (TA), and had incised TΛ when he saw his error; at this point, he cut
the proper letters over the almost complete incorrect ones (so that what actually appears
on the stone is 𝕄), and completed the name. In inscribing the consecutive words
ἀποδόμενοι ἀποδόντων in lines 44f, the mason cut the first five letters of the prior word.
Then, confused by the fact that the next word begins with exactly the same five letters, he
followed immediately with that word's final four letters. Discovering his error, he inserted
the ending of the first word and the beginning of the second word between lines, as close as
possible to the place of their omission.

[ηται τῶν Ἑλ]λήνων ἢ τῶν βαρβάρων τῶν ἐν

[ἠπείρωι ἐν]οικόντων ἢ τῶν νησιωτῶν, ὅσ-

[οι μὴ βασι]λέως εἰσίν, Ἀθηναίων σύμμαχ-

[ος εἶναι κ]αὶ τῶν συμμάχων, ἐξεῖναι αὐ̇[τ]-

20   ῶ[ι ἐλευθέρ]ωι ὄντι καὶ αὐτονόμωι, πολι-

τ[ευομέν]ωι πολιτείαν ἣν ἂν βόληται, μή-

τε [φρορ]ὰν εἰσδεχομένωι μήτε ἄρχοντα

ὑπο[δεχ]ομένωι μήτε φόρον φέροντι, ἐπὶ

δὲ τ[οῖ]ς̣ αὐτοῖς ἐφ' οἷσπερ Χῖοι καὶ Θηβαῖ-

25   οι κα[ὶ] οἱ ἄλλοι σύμμαχοι. τοῖς δὲ ποιησ-

αμέν[οι]ς συμμαχίαν πρὸς Ἀθηναίος καὶ

τὸς συμμάχος ἀφεῖναι τὸν δῆμον τὰ ἐγκ-

τήματα, ὁπόσ' ἂν τυγχάνηι ὄντα ἢ ἴδια ἢ [δ]-

ημόσια Ἀθ[η]ναίων ἐν τῆι χ[ώραι τῶν ποιο]-

30   μένων τὴν συμμαχίαν, κ[αὶ περὶ τούτων π]-

ίστιν δôναι ˄͜ ³[.....¹²..... τ]υγχάν[η]-

ι τῶν πόλεων [τῶν ποιομένων] τὴν συμμαχ-

3. It is possible, though not certain, that a tiny portion of the upper arc of the round letter Koehler drew is still visible on the stone (squeeze is no help here). In any case, there seems to be a bit of blank space extant at the top of the stoichos, indicating that some small letter—such as an omicron—occupied the space. Upsilon, which is rather tall in this inscription, would appear to be a very unlikely restoration. Therefore I prefer Koehler's traces over the restoration α[ὑτοῖς], which is adopted by IG II², Tod, Pouilloux, Pfohl, and SV. Koehler's suggested restoration of the passage (Ἀθ[ηναίος. ἐὰν δὲ τ]υγχάν[η]/ι) was, as

If anyone wis[hes, of the Gr]eeks or of the barbarians [l]iving on
[(the) mainland], or of the islanders, whoe[ver do not] belong to
(the) [Ki]ng, [to be] an all[y] of (the) Athenians [a]nd of their
allies, it shall be permitted to h[i]m,

20   Being [fre]e and autonomous,

20f   Gov[ernin]g (himself according to the) constitution which he
        prefers,

21–23   Neither receiving a [garris]on nor ac[cep]ting a governor nor
        paying tribute,

23–25   But on t[h]e same (terms), just like (the) Chians and Thebans
        an[d] the other allies.

25–31   For those maki[n]g alliance with (the) Athenians and their allies,
        the demos shall give up the possessions, however many there
        happen to be, either private or [p]ublic, of Athenians in the
        l[ands of those mak]ing the alliance, a[nd concerning these mat-
        ters] give [as]surance . . .

31–35   [. . . If there h]appe[n] to be stelai at Athens unfavorabl[e] to
        the states [making] the alliance with (the) Athen[ians, t]he boule

---

Tod points out, one letter too short. This, however, seems to be an inadequate reason to
reject his drawing of what he saw. I am grateful to R. S. Stroud for suggesting a simple im-
provement: Ἀθ[ηναῖος. ἐάν τωι τ]υγχάν[η]/ι. Omission of δέ is hardly fatal; cf. ἐάν τις in line
15. Stroud's restoration would yield the translation: " . . . (the) Ath[enians] shall give
[as]surance. [If there h]appe[n] to be stelai at Athens unfavorabl[e to any] of the
states. . . . " I refrain from putting this conjectural restoration in my Greek text, but since
some phrase with an ἐάν must have appeared here, I do include an "if" in my translation.

ίαν πρὸς Ἀθην[αίος] στῆλαι ὅσαι Ἀθήνησ-

ι ἀνεπιτήδειο̣[ι, τ]ὴμ βολὴν τὴν ἀεὶ βολε-

35 ύοσαν κυρίαν ε[ἶν]αι καθαιρεῖν. ⟨ἀ⟩πὸ δὲ Ν-

αυσινίκο ἄρχογ[τ]ος μὴ ἐξεῖναι μήτε ἰδ-

ίαι μήτε δημοσ[ί]αι Ἀθηναίων μηθενὶ ἐγ-

κτήσασθαι ἐν τ[α]ῖς τῶν συμμάχων χώραι-

ς μήτε οἰκίαν μήτε χωρίον μήτε πριαμέ-

40 νωι μήτε ὑποθε[μ]ένωι μήτε ἄλλωι τρόπω-

ι μηθενί· ἐὰν δέ [τ]ις ὠνῆται ἢ κτᾶται ἢ τι-

θῆται τρόπωι ὁτωιον, ἐξεῖναι τῶι βολο̣-

μένωι τῶν συμμάχων φῆναι πρὸς τὸς συν-

έδρος τῶν συμμάχων· οἱ δὲ σύνεδροι ἀπο-

Between lines   μενοι ἀ̲π̲ο̲δ̲ό̲

45 [δ]ό̲ᴧντ̲ω̲ν̲ [τὸ μὲν ἥ]μυσυ τῶ[ι] φήναντι, τὸ δὲ ἄ-

[λλο κοι]νὸν [ἔσ]τ̲ω τῶν συμ̲[μ]άχων. ἐὰν δέ τι-

ς ἴ[ηι] ἐπὶ πολέμωι ἐπ̲ὶ τ[ὸ]ς ποιησαμένος

τὴν συμμαχίαν ἢ κατὰ γ[ῆ[ν ἢ κατὰ θάλαττ-

αν, βοηθεῖν Ἀθηναίος καὶ τὸς συμμάχος

50 τούτοις καὶ κατὰ γῆν καὶ κατὰ θάλαττα-

ν παντὶ σθένει κατὰ τὸ δυνατόν· ἐὰν δέ τ-

ις εἴπηι ἢ ἐπιψηφίσηι, ἢ ἄρχων ἢ ἰδιώτη-

ς, παρὰ τόδε τὸ ψήφισμα ὡς λύειν τι δεῖ τ-

sitting at the time shall [b]e empowered to destroy (them).

35-46   From the archon[sh]ip of Nausinikos, it shall not be permitted to any Athenian, either privately or publ[i]cly, to possess in t[h]e territories of the allies either a house or an estate, neither by purchasing nor by mort[g]aging, nor by any other means. And if [an]yone buys or acquires or takes on mortgage (such properties) by any such method, it shall be permitted to anyone of the allies who wishes to give evidence to the synedroi of the allies. Let the synedroi, auc[t]ioning (the offender's property), give [the one h]alf to th[e] informer, and let the r[est b]e [com]mon (property) of the al[l]ies.

46-51   If anyone co[mes] for war against t[ho]se making the alliance either by l[an]d or by sea, (the) Athenians and the allies shall give aid to them both by land and by sea, in full strength so far as possible.

51-63   If anyone, either magistrate or private person, proposes or puts to the vote, in violation of this decree, (a measure) such as would necessarily abrogate anything that is bei[ng] said in this

ὧν ἐν τῶιδε τῶι ψηφίσματι εἰρημέν[ων, ὑ]-

55 παρχέτω μ[ὲν] αὐτῶι ἀτίμωι εἶναι, καὶ [τὰ]

[χρ]ήμα[τα αὐ]τô δημόσια ἔστω καὶ τῆς θ[εô]

[τ]ὸ ἐπιδ[έκα]τον, καὶ κρινέσθω ἐν Ἀθην[αί]-

[ο]ις καὶ τ[οῖς] συμμάχοις ὡς διαλύων τὴν

συμμαχία[ν, ζ]ημιόντων δὲ αὐτὸν θανάτω-

60 ι ἢ φυγῆι ὅ[περ] Ἀθηναῖοι καὶ οἱ σύμμαχο-

ι κρατôσι[ν· ἐὰν] δὲ θανάτο τιμηθῆι, μὴ τα-

φήτω ἐν τῆ[ι Ἀττ]ικῆι [μ]ηδὲ ἐν τῆι τῶν συμ-

μάχων. τὸ δ[ὲ ψήφι]σμα τόδε ὁ γραμματεὺς

ὁ τῆς βολῆ[ς] ἀν[αγρ]αψάτω ἐν στήλη λιθί-

65 νηι καὶ καταθέ[τω] παρὰ τὸν Δία τὸν Ἐλευ-

θέριον· τὸ δὲ ἀρ[γύ]ριον δôναι εἰς τὴν ἀν-

αγραφὴν τῆς στ[ήλη]ς ἑξήκοντα δραχμὰς

ἐκ τῶν δέκα ταλ[άν]των⁴ τὸς ταμίας τῆς θε-

ô· εἰς δὲ τὴν στήλην ταύτην ἀναγρά-

70 φειν τῶν τε ὀὺσ[ῶ]ν πόλεων συμμαχίδων τ-

ὰ ὀνόματα καὶ ἥτις ἂν ἄλλη σύμμαχος γί-

⟨γ⟩νηται. ταῦτα μὲν ἀναγράψαι, ἑλέσθαι δ-

ὲ τὸν δῆμον πρέσβεις τρεῖς αὐτίκα μάλ-

α εἰς Θήβας, [ο]ἵτινες πείσοσι Θηβαίος ὅ,

---

4. This was apparently a special fund, administered by different officers during different periods of Athenian history, for the inscribing of stelai; see Rhodes, *Boule* 103 n. 7.

decree, let (this) [s]uffice for him to be without civic rights, and let [hi]s [g]oo[ds] be public (property), and [t]he ti[th]e (be the property) of the go[ddess], and let (him) be judged among (the) Athen[ian]s and t[he] allies as destroying the allianc[e], and let them [p]unish him by death or exile from wh[erever] (the) Athenians and the allies contro[l. If] he is condemned to death, let him not be buried in [Att]ica [n]or in the (territory) of the allies.

63–69   Let the secretary of the boul[e] have this [dec]ree ins[cri]bed on a marble stele and let it be se[t] up beside the (statue of) Zeus Eleutherios. The treasurers of the goddess shall give the mo[n]ey for the inscription of the st[ele], sixty drachmas out of the Ten Tal[en]ts.

69–72   And on this stele he shall inscribe the names both of those (al-ready) bei[n]g allied states and whatever other becomes an ally.

72–77   He shall inscribe these things; and the demos shall choose at once three ambassadors to Thebes, [w]ho will persuade (the) Thebans to whate[v]er good they can. These were chosen: Aris-

75   [τ]ι ἂν δύνωγται ἀγαθόν. οἴδε ἡιρέθησαν·

    Ἀριστοτέ<u>λ</u>ης Μαραθώνιος, υ Πύρρανδρο‐

    <u>ς</u> Ἀναφλύσ[τ]ιος,[5] Θρασύβολος Κολλυτεύς.

    Ἀθηναίων πόλεις αἴδε σύμμαχο<u>ι</u>·

Names in several hands	Χῖοι	Τενέδιοι	Θηβαῖοι	
80	Μυτιληγαῖοι		<u>Χ</u>α<u>λ</u>κιδῆς	
	[Μ]ηθυ[μ]γαῖοι		Ἐρετριῆς	
	Ῥόδιοι	Ποιήσσιο<u>ι</u>	Ἀρεθόσιοι	ΣΤΟΙΧ.
	Βυζάντιοι		Καρύστιοι	
	Περίνθιοι		Ἴκι<u>οι</u>	
85	Πεπαρήθιοι		Παλ^[-----]	
	Σκιάθιοι		[----------]	
	Μαρωνῖται		[----------]	
	Διῆς		[----------]	
	Πάρ[ι]οι	Ο[---------]	[----------]	
90	Ἀθηνῖται	<u>Π</u>[---------]	[----------]	

NON-ΣΤΟΙΧ.   Ἀριστοτέ<u>λ</u>ης εἶπ<u>ε</u>·[--------------ἐπει]‐

    δ⟨ὰ⟩ν πρῶτ<u>ο</u>[ν----------------------------]

    ἑκόντες π[ρο]σχωρῶσι [----------ἐψη]‐

    φισμένα τῶι δ⟨ή⟩μωι κα<u>ὶ</u> <u>τ</u>[--------------]

5. Lacking room for another skipped space between names (cf. line 76), the mason achieved the desired visual effect by placing the theta of Thrasyboulos at the extreme right of its stoichos.

toteles of Marathon, Pyrrandros of Anaphlys[t]os, (and) Thrasyboulos of Kollytos.

78	THESE STATES (ARE) ALLIES OF (THE) ATHENIANS:		
79–90	CHIANS	*TENEDIANS*	THEBANS
80	MYTILENAIANS		80 *CHALKIDIANS*
	[M]ETHY[M]NAIANS		*ERETRIANS*
	RHODIANS	Poiessians	*ARETHOUSIANS*
	BYZANTINES		*KARYSTIANS*
	Perinthians		*IKIANS*
85	Peparethians		85 Pal[------------]
	Skiathians		[---------------]
	Maroneians		[---------------]
	Dians		[---------------]
	PAR[I]ANS	O?[-----------]	[---------------]
90	Athenitai	P[-------------]	[---------------]

91–96   *Aristoteles moved:* [--*sin*]*ce*

firs[*t* ---]

they a[*g*]*ree in coming* [---]

the things [*v*]*oted by the demos and t*[*he* ----------------------------]

> 25 <

95 ν⟨ή⟩σων εἰς τὴν συμμ[αχίαν -----------------]

τοῖς τῶν ἐψ⟨η⟩φι[σμένων --------------------]⁶

On left side of stele	[2 or 3]ραιων		'Ερέσιοι
	[ὁ δ]ῆμος		'Αστραιούσιοι
	['Αβδη]ρῖται		Κείων
100	[Θάσι]οι	120	'Ιουλιῆται
	[Χαλκι]δῆ⟨ς⟩		Καρθαιὲς
	ἀπὸ [Θράικης]		Κορήσιοι
	Αἴνιοι		'Ελαιόσιοι
	Σαμοθρᾶικες		'Αμόργιοι
105	Δικαιοπολῖται	125	Σηλυμβρι⟨α⟩νο[?]*
	'Ακαρνᾶνες		Σίφνιοι
	Κεφαλλήνων		Σικινῆται
	Πρῶννοι		Διὲς
	'Αλκέτας		ἀπὸ Θράικης
110	Νεοπτόλεμος	130	Νεοπο⟨λῖ⟩ται
Erased	⟦ ca. 6 ⟧		vacat 0.25m.
	Ἄνδριοι		Ζακυν[θ]ίων
	Τ̣ήνιοι		ὁ δῆμος
	['Εσ]τιαιῆς		ὁ ἐν τῶι Νήλλ–
115	Μυκόνιοι		ωι
	'Αντισσαῖοι		

6. Eugene Schweigert, "Epigraphical Notes: 2. A Duplication of Texts," *Hesperia* 8 (1939) 171f shows that the fragmentary text *IG* II², 883 is in reality a duplication of lines 93–96.

of islands to the all[iance---]

to those of the things vot[ed---]

97f	Of [--]raians:		Eresians
	[the d]emos		Astraiousans
99–130	[Abde]rites		Of Keans:
100	[Thasi]ans	120	Ioulietans
	[Chalki]dians		Karthaians
	from [Thrace]		Koresians
	Ainians		Elaiousians
	Samothracians		Amorgans
105	Dikaiopolitans	125	Selymbrian[s]
	Akarnanians		Siphnians
	Of Kephallenians:		Sikinetans
	Pronnoi		Dians
	Alketas		from Thrace
110	Neoptolemos	130	Neapolitans
	[erased]		
	Andrians		
	Tenians	131–134	*OF ZAKYN[TH]IANS:*
	[Hes]tiaians		*THE DEMOS*
115	Mykonians		*IN THE NELL-*
	Antissans		*OS*

Commentary

Lines 12–14. The Erased Provision: Readings

I restore an unerased area in line 12 and an erased portion in line 15, on the assumption that the intent was to erase certain phrases, not simply whole lines. Within the double brackets which signify an erasure, I print entire letters where the traces are sufficient to exclude every reading but one; where a letter would have to be underdotted, I simply draw the traces. The following chart compares Koehler's majuscule and his text (there are differences between them, which he does not explain) with the readings and restorations of Accame and with my text. Kirchner in these lines simply follows Koehler's text (*not* his majuscule), while Tod, Pouilloux, Pfohl, and *SV* accept Accame.

Lines 12–14. Variant Readings

Line 12

	St. 15	20	25	30	
IG II Majuscule		⌐ ˉ	˛ ˄ H I	˛ Δ	I
IG II & II² Text	I K	O Σ	H I	A	I
Accame	Ạ I Q Π Ω Σ Ḳ		Ṛ I Ạ H I K A I Ạ		I
My Text	˛	Ω Σ	˛ ˄ H I ˛	˛ ˄	I

Line 13

All editors read A in the last (31st) stoichos (see my questions, infra). Accame alone reads Σ in stoichos 30. All agree that everything else is completely erased.

Line 14

	St. 15	20	25	30	
IG II Majuscule	\ Π	◂ ˛ ʟ	◂ ⋀ ˛ ⋀	-- ◂	N
IG II & II² Text	A Π	Σ E	Σ	Ω Σ	N
Accame	K A I B A	Σ I Λ E Y	Σ K A T A	T A Σ Σ Y	N
My Text	˛ ˛	Σ ˛ E	Σ ˎ A ˛ A	˛ ˛	N

Accame's full restoration of the erased provision (including alternative suggestions for line 13):

```
11                                                  τή-
12 [ν ἑαυτῶν πᾶσαν κ]αὶ ὅπως κ[υ]ρία ἦι καὶ δι-
              ⎧ εἰς ἀεὶ ἡ κοινὴ εἰρήνη ἦν  ⎫
13 [αμένηι ⎨                                  ⎬ ὤμο]σα-
              ⎩ ἡ εἰρήνη καὶ φιλία ἥμπερ   ⎭
```

14 [ν οἱ Ἕλληνες] καὶ βασιλεὺς κατὰ τὰς συν-
15 [θήκας, κτλ]

Accame misspells the first word of his line 13: διαμήνηι.

Line 12

In the area broken away at the left end of the line, there would surely have been no reason for anyone ever to erase the final letter of the article τήν which begins on the preceding line, nor to erase any of the six letters of the very likely restoration ἑαυτῶν. If this same sentence was continued and completed with the word πᾶσαν ("all"), that too should not have been erased; the erasure would logically begin with the first word of the next clause. But only eleven letter spaces have broken away. The twelfth space, in which the final letter of πᾶσαν is often restored, is extant—and the letter in that space was erased. This fact, I submit, makes πᾶσαν a very unlikely restoration. Consequently, any restoration of the entire line that includes this word must also be suspect. No one doubts that stoichoi 18 and 19 contain definite traces of the top of a round letter and a sigma. On the stone (but not squeeze), I see faint traces of the bottom half of the letter in space 18 which lead me to prefer Accame's omega to the omicron of the *IG* texts. In stoichoi 25 and 26, ηι is equally obvious to all; likewise the iota at the end of the line. In stoichoi 14 and 15, Koehler draws no traces at all on his majuscule, yet restores ικ in his text; Accame, in contrast, reads ᾳι. Squeeze and Accame's squeeze photo show some trace of the upper part of letter number 15—the end of a vertical stroke, compatible with either iota or kappa. But I can see nothing on stone or squeeze to support either Accame's alpha or *IG*'s iota in stoichos 14. Any trace which would have allowed these incompatible readings must have been tiny and/or ambiguous indeed. Accame's restorations in stoichoi 23, 24, 27, and 29 are all compatible with visible traces, but none are necessary readings. I can see no bases at all for his "certain" pi in space 17 or alpha in space 28, nor for his under-dotted omicron (stoichos 16), kappa (20), or rho (22). In the penultimate letter space, I agree with Accame that the crossbar of Koehler's alpha cannot be seen; Accame's underdotted delta is equally—but not more —acceptable. Accame's bold "reading" of line 12 turns out to be mostly an adventurous restoration: [ν ἑαυτῶν πᾶσαν κα]ὶ [ὅπ]ως [κυρ]ίᾳ ἦι κ[α]ὶ δ[ι]. Given the aforementioned unlikelihood of πᾶσαν having been erased, the restoration of the remainder of the line becomes even more suspect.

Line 13

Accame does not seem to suggest any preference between the alternative restorations he offers for this line (he does mention, and reject, a third[7]). Tod, Pouilloux, Pfohl, and *SV* all adopt the first restoration, which, if correct, would make the decree of Aristoteles the first known epigraphical source employing the expression "common peace" (κοινὴ εἰρήνη). The translations of WV and Adcock and Mosley follow these texts; that of Hammond follows the other alternative.[8] But Accame's entirely speculative restorations of this line can provide support for nothing whatever. Moreover, the end of the line is not as certain as is generally believed. The sigma which Accame reads in the next-to-last space is invisible to me, as it was also to Koehler; and even the final alpha is doubtful. A break line on the stone may have been taken for a crossbar, and the upper part of the letter—all that is actually visible—is rather narrow and sharply pointed: it could be the second point of a mu. Therefore I simply draw the sharp point, and I decline to restore a line of which only one ambiguous trace of one letter is extant.

Line 14

Here Koehler and Kirchner, in their texts, print less than Koehler, in his majuscule, indicates that he saw. At the opposite extreme, Accame "reads" the entire erased line (beyond the 10 broken-away spaces on the left) without bracketing or even underdotting a single letter. Cawkwell[9] would put a rho in stoichos 13 (not suggesting it is a certain reading) and would restore an omega in stoichos 20, thus arriving at the phrase ὑπὲρ βασιλέως where Accame has καὶ βασιλεύς. The trace in stoichos 12, however—which Cawkwell does not discuss—would permit the alpha of Accame's καί, but not the epsilon of Cawkwell's ὑπέρ. Although the genitive βασιλέως is just as possible as Accame's nominative βασιλεύς, the phrase ὑπὲρ βασιλέως is therefore impossible, and Cawkwell's rho in space 13 has no contextual support. Koehler had read a certain pi in that space, which, if accepted, would make either the nominative *or* genitive form of βασιλεύς impossible—since neither could be preceded by a word ending in pi. But Koehler's "certain" reading is mistaken. One vertical hasta is quite definitely extant, but it could belong to Koehler's pi, Accame's iota, or even Cawkwell's rho. The surface is lost where the top horizontal stroke of pi might have been. A second vertical stroke —clearly visible even in Accame's squeeze photo—is obviously what led Koehler to his pi reading. But this mark is too close to the other vertical stroke to have been part of pi, unless this pi were far narrower than all others on the stone; it must be simply a chisel mark made in the process of erasing these lines. Thus Accame's iota, while not a necessary reading, is nonetheless possible, and therefore his phrase καὶ βασιλεύς is also

7. Accame 51 n. 4: διαμένηι ἐς ἀεὶ ἐρήνη καὶ φιλία ἦν, κτλ ("non sembra probabile").

8. F. E. Adcock and D. J. Mosley, *Diplomacy in Ancient Greece* (London 1975) 259f; Hammond, *HG²* 486 and n. 1.

9. Cawkwell, "Found." 60 n. 1.

possible—though it should properly be rendered as [κ]αὶ [βα]σῐ[λ]ε[ύ]ς. In stoichos 22, Koehler's traces (he prints nothing in his text) would be more appropriate to alpha, delta, or lambda than to the kappa Accame prefers. Stone and squeeze reveal that the right-hand stroke is not as vertical as Koehler draws it: it could be a stroke of Accame's kappa (or of chi). On the left, there does appear to be a slanting chisel mark, but its slant is slight enough that it could have been part of the "vertical" of a kappa (in this inscription the verticals are not all perfectly plumb); it could also have been just another mark made by the erasing chisel. I record only the stroke that seems sure. Most of stoichos 27, all of 28 and 29, and part of 30 were on a bit of stone that was lost before Pritchett made his squeeze, but present when Accame made his. I cannot see any traces of Accame's sigma in stoichos 28 on his squeeze photo, and Koehler clearly thought he saw the "feet" of an omega there (which he and Kirchner accordingly printed as certain in their texts). Having no basis for choosing, I cannot express a preference for either letter. The reading is obviously critical for Accame's phrase κατὰ τὰς συν/θήκας. If one overrules Koehler and accepts it, one should print the phrase thus: κατὰ τ[ὰς σ]υν/[θήκας].

Lines 12–14. Content and Significance

Although I have argued that most of Accame's readings in these lines are in fact restorations, I do agree that the King was mentioned, and that some sort of reference to the King's Peace was erased. The decree as a whole reveals Athens's intent to set its League within the context of that peace. But this basic fact is *all* the stone tells us. Debates about whether the King's Peace was already being described as a "common peace" or whether it was said to be established "for all time" or whether "friendship" between the King and the Greeks was invoked or whether anyone "swore" anything are all based on phrases within Accame's alternative restorations. When and why the reference to the King's Peace was erased, however, remains a legitimate and important question. Cawkwell, who argues that the clause dealt not with the King's Peace *per se* but with Sparta's role as its "enforcer," says that it was erased when Athens and Sparta agreed to share the Hellenic hegemony in the short-lived peace of 375/4. That hypothesis is ruled out by the non-erasure of phrasing in lines 9–12 which dedicates the League to the general purpose of controlling the Spartans. The same lines militate against the suggestion of Marshall that lines 12–14 were removed when Athens became Sparta's ally around 370–369. Accame's suggestion, which Cawkwell describes as "similar" to his own, is actually similar only as to date. The weakness of his theory that in 375 the Athenians excised the reference because they had made a peace without the participation of the King has been pointed out (chapter 1). One may further ask, if the occasion for the erasure was this early redefining of the general peace, why excise the reference to the peace *in toto*, rather than simply the reference to the King's participation in it? Following either of Accame's restorations, a complete and coherent statement of principles that were (in Accame's interpretation) still relevant could be left on the stone simply by erasing everything in the clause after εἰρήνη in line 13—or even only everything beyond οἱ Ἕλληνες in line 14. In sum, the occasion Accame suggests for the erasure serves to weaken the likelihood of his own restoration(s) of what was erased. A considerably later occasion, one upon which the erasure of the clause would in fact declare the King's Peace entirely abrogated, makes far more sense. Consequently, I prefer the suggestion of Ryder, that the Athenians erased the clause when the King threw his support behind Thebes in response to the arguments of Pelopidas in 367.[10]

Line 17. Europe?

There is no reason to adopt Εὐρώπηι in preference to the ἠπείρωι which most editors prefer (cf. WV). Aristophanes, *Acharnians* 534 shows that the latter word requires no article. In the context of the King's Peace, both restorations would have the same meaning in any case: all Asia was recognized as the King's territory.

Lines 78–83. The First Group of Names[11]

All recent editors agree that line 78 and the names of Chios, Thebes, Mytilene, Methymna, Rhodos, and Byzantion were inscribed by the mason who inscribed the decree itself. This is a reasonable conclusion, but not *entirely* a necessary one. Certain minor differences in letter forms can be seen when the text of the decree is compared with these names and their heading. While such differences are probably due entirely to the letters' size (i.e., more room for niceties of cutting), nevertheless the forms do not exactly correspond to those of the large letters in lines 1–6 above the decree. It is accordingly possible that some time (obviously brief) *could* have elapsed between the inscribing of the decree and the cutting of the first group of names. Any problems about the order of these six names[12] should be eliminated by this possibility.

10. Marshall 16f; Accame 149f; Ryder, *KE* 81f, n. 9 (see chapter 10).

11. In the translation of WV, the spatial relationships of the names are not indicated, nor would one even know that some names appear on the left side of the stele. Parenthetical statements (presented as facts, but often highly conjectural) divide the names into groups according to their supposed dates of joining the League. Pouilloux's translation simply divides the two columns of front-face names into "paragraphs," lumping the names between columns with the left. Pfohl provides a text and translation of the decree only, not the lists of names.

12. See, e.g., Victor Ehrenberg, "Zum zweiten attischen Bund," *Hermes* 64 (1929) 322–338; cf. Marshall 56 n. 3; Tod 122 comm.; and Accame 44–47. The major supposed "problem" arises from a provision of Methymna's alliance treaty (quoted in chapter 6).

Line 79. Tenedos

Names between the right and left columns were probably squeezed in after both columns had been filled, and after the amendment of lines 91–96 had been inscribed. The single name of Tenedos may, however, provide an exception.[13] The *first* line of the list of allies would be honorific, regardless of how much space was available below (thus Thebes is placed on a level with Chios,[14] though Thebes clearly became an Athenian ally later than Chios). Athens's high regard for the Tenedians is well documented,[15] so it would not be unreasonable to suppose that Tenedos' name was added to the first line at any point after the inscribing of the first group (who were already League members when the decree was passed). The letter forms of the name show, however, that it was not itself part of the first group. WV omit Tenedos entirely.

Lines 80–84. The Second Group of Names

The Euboian cities of Chalkis, Eretria, Arethousa, and Karystos, along with the nearby small island of Ikos, have long been recognized as a distinct group of names because of their neat stoichedon arrangement. Accame, essentially following Beloch, argues that Euboian Arethousa (not a member of the Delian League) did not exist at the time of this inscription, and says that the League member was instead a city of the Thracian Chalkidike, listed here near its mother city Chalkis.[16] But Euripides, *Iphigeneia at Aulis* 170 provides a clear, late fifth-century reference to Euboian Arethousa. Probably it was a small place, treated as part of Chalkis during the period of the Delian League, but "autonomous" under provisions of the King's Peace, which the Second Athenian League recognized.[17] The group as a whole is dated before the names be-

13. Suggested by Fabricius 598. Tenedos provides an excellent example of the way in which the analysis of Busolt frequently was undercut by his reliance on inadequate texts (in this case, ultimately the text of Rangabé). Knowing nothing about the existence of different hands in the name lists, Busolt, 740ff, puts Tenedos in the first group of names and Thebes in a later group (Koehler, with far less excuse, makes the same mistake with respect to Thebes). Elsewhere (p. 768), Busolt actually posits the loss of some 18 names on the "mutilated" *right* side of the stele, which is and always has been simply uninscribed. Incredibly, Cawkwell in 1963 ("Peace" 91 n. 61) fell into a similar error, later retracting the statement (*SEG* XXI, 229).

14. Cf. Beloch, 3:2.156, who says that the most powerful (mächtigsten) allied states' names were put at the top of columns—including Korkyra in lines 97f (v. infra, comm.).

15. *IG* II², 232 and 233; Ais. 2.20, 97, and 126. Marshall, 57, suggests that Tenedos was added to the League even earlier than the Euboian cities listed below Thebes (but see next comm.).

16. Accame 72f (Beloch, 3:2.158f, actually says the city was in Macedonia); cf. Sealey, *City-Sts.* 412. See E. Ziebarth, *IG* XII (9), pp. 148f, for sources and literature.

17. B. D. Meritt, "Greek Inscriptions," *Hesperia* 32 (1963), 1f and plate 2, publishes a very fragmentary inscription which includes the word Ἀρεθοσίοις, and which he dates to ca. 377, saying it may have been connected with Arethousa's League alliance. The fragment actually gives no clue as to the location of the city, despite Meritt's connecting it with

low Byzantion because Diodoros says the Euboian cities (except Hestiaia) were first to join the established League.[18] A concrete date (377 B.C.) is provided by the extant Athens-Chalkis treaty.[19]

Line 82. Poiessa

No clues, beyond its position on the front face of the stele and between columns, exist for dating the accession of this city of Keos, whose other cities are listed on the left side of the stele (lines 119–122). Poiessa, like Tenedos (line 79), is omitted from WV's list.

Lines 84–88. Perinthos, Peparethos, Skiathos, Maroneia, and Dion

Tod calls these "a third group, inscribed in a crude and thick script," and both editors of IG regard these names as a group. But Fabricius divided the five names into subgroups—Perinthos, then Peparethos and Skiathos, then the other two—on the basis of letter forms, and Accame's detailed descriptions support his divisions. Neither, however, would separate these subgroups very much in time—Accame in fact says that the names were all inscribed by the same mason, but during different prytanies of the Attic year 377/6.[20] Both the dating and the assertion that there was a single stonecutter are speculative.

Line 85. Pal-

The fourth letter of Παλ- was definitely either lambda or alpha; its trace, though invisible to me on the stone, was clear both on Pritchett's squeeze and in Accame's photograph. Accame, rejecting the common restoration of Παλλ[ηνῆς], suggests Παλα[ισκιάθιοι],[21] and considerations of letter spacing may strengthen his argument. The 13 letters of Παλαισκιάθιοι would be more than occur in any extant name in the right-hand column (the closest being the 9 letters of Ἀρεθόσιοι and Καρύστιοι, which fill the space nicely). The three extant letters and one partial letter of line 85 seem to be cut considerably closer together than the letters of other names in this column—as would be necessary for a long name, but not for Παλληνῆς or other commonly suggested restorations such as

---

the Euboian city and its title in SEG XXI, 230: Foedus Atheniensium cum civitate Arethusa Euboeae.

18. Diod. 15.30.1; Ikos may reasonably be interpreted as included in this statement, because of its closeness to Euboia and its unimportance. Marshall, 58, takes this passage as indicating the accession of Ikos somewhat later than that of the Euboian cities, but Fabricius, 597, had already shown that its name was at least listed at the same time as theirs.

19. SV 259, line 3; see Accame 70f and n. 4.

20. Fabricius 597; Accame 76f, n. 3.

21. Accame 79 (citing Dittenberger, Syll.³ 147 n. 4); cf. WV's "Pallene" without comment. Though the confederacy of Pallene would be unattested, Beloch, 3:2.157, suggests that such a confederacy may well have been organized after the Spartans broke up the Chalkidian League; he too, however, seems to prefer Palaiskiathos.

Παλλῆς and Παλαιῆς. None of these states is listed among members of the Delian League,[22] but Palaiskiathos might have been subsumed under Skiathos at the time (cf. Arethousa, line 82). Accame's date for this member's adherence to the League—namely, at the same time as Peparethos and Skiathos—depends both on acceptance of his restoration (Old and New Skiathos joining simultaneously) and on the names being in the same hand (which Accame himself admits is uncertain).

Line 86. Anaphe?

I can see no traces on stone or squeeze to support Accame's restoration of Ἀγ[αφαῖοι] in the right-hand column.[23]

Line 88. Between Columns

Without expressing much certainty, my impression based on the stone is that enough uninscribed surface is extant here to rule out the possibility that a name was once inscribed in this space.

Line 89. Paros and the Lost Name between Columns

Just to the right of the large letters of Πάρ[ι]οι, a round letter with its center missing once began the name of some League member. Most editors suggest names beginning with omicron, e.g., Οἰναῖοι or Ὀλιάριοι,[24] but Pouilloux prefers Θάσιοι—which is generally restored in line 100 on the left side of the stele. Pouilloux's argument is that Thasos would have joined the League at the same time as its mother city Paros, and that the two cities practiced consistent political cooperation during the period of the League. He demonstrates Thasos' consistent loyalty to Athens, but the same cannot be claimed for Paros, which apparently rebelled and was forcibly restored to the League in the 370s.[25] Moreover, Πάριοι is written in the largest letters of any name anywhere on the stele, whereas the round letter which began the lost name is quite small: simultaneity of inscription is unbelievable. When both cooperation and simultaneity are so doubtful, there is no more reason to look for Thasos with its metropolis (line 89) than with its neighbors (line 100)—probably less.

22. The only appropriately named Delian Leaguers—Παλαιπερκώσιοι and Παλαμήδειον—are ruled out by their location in Asia. Apparently, residents of Palaiskiathos always had difficulty persuading the Athenians to recognize their town's separate existence (IG I², 118).

23. Accame, 82, with a description of the "traces." Presumably this description is the basis of the large "trace" drawn in the text of SV.

24. Beloch, 3:2.158 (citing Busolt 748), says that Ο[ἰναῖοι] is a very likely restoration, whereas Oliaros was never an independent state. See comm. (infra) on lines 85–90 for other possible restorations.

25. Pouilloux's restoration (which he follows with a question mark) is supported by his arguments in Recherches sur l'histoire et les cultes de Thasos I (Paris 1954) = École Française d'Athènes, Études Thasiennes III.428–433 (esp. 428 n. 7). Thasian loyalty: IG II², 1441; Parian rebellion: SV 268 (text of Accame 230).

Line 90. Pyrrha?

Ἀθηνῖται were citizens of Athenai Diades, on Euboia; no clues exist for dating their adherence to the League. Most scholars would agree with Beloch and Accame that Πυρραῖοι once appeared between columns in this line, because an inscription of 369–367 mentions the synedroi of Mytilene, Methymna, Antissa, and Eresos—all other cities of Lesbos, all listed here as League members—and of Pyrrha.[26] The name could, of course, have been among those broken away from the right-hand column, and a different name beginning with pi could have appeared in this spot.

Lines 85–90. Lost Names of the Right Column

The wholly lost names occupied probably five lines (four, if one accepts Accame's Anaphe in line 86). Since two short names conceivably could have been inscribed side by side on some of these lines, we may reasonably take five names as a minimum. Certain clues exist for identifying the lost names, beginning with geographic, political, and ethnic patterns within the extant names. With the sole exception of Thebes, all the League members listed on the front face are Greek πόλεις (not barbarians, factions, confederacies, or kings—all of which are represented in the list on the left side) located either on Aegean islands or along the coasts of the Northern Aegean or Propontis. Again with Thebes as the exception (if the arguments, supra, on lines 82 and 85 be sound), all had been members of the Delian League. Except for Dorian Rhodos, all are either Ionians or Aiolians (though the presence of names of Dorian states among those on the left side of the stele makes this a weak determinant, as will immediately be seen). All states of Asia are excluded by the provisions of the decree of Aristoteles itself, and there is no solid evidence that the territory of the League ever extended as far south as Krete and the nearby islands.[27] Thus in its initial phase, before the passage of the amendment of lines 91–96 (v. infra) and before the expansion of membership indicated by the list on the left side of the stele, the Second Athenian League was essentially an Aegean, European, and Ionian subset of the Delian League, and states falling under such rubrics are the most likely candidates for the lost names of the right-hand column. Some initially attractive names must be eliminated at once, however. Delos itself, in both the fifth and the fourth centuries, was not an Athenian ally, but an Athenian possession;[28] the same is true of Skyros. Lemnos and Im-

---

26. *IG* II², 107 (passage quoted in chapter 6); Beloch 3:2.158; Accame 83.

27. *SV* 296 seems to show friendly Athenian relations with some Kretan city whose name is lost, but this is no evidence for the city's League membership (chapter 5).

28. Beloch, 3:1.144, correctly points out that Athenian possession of Delos was a breach of the terms of the King's Peace. The connection was so ancient that it hardly would have caused much outcry; there is no indication it ever did.

bros, though Delian League allies, were recognized under the terms of the King's Peace as Athenian possessions, so they too must be eliminated. Samos, a very loyal fifth-century ally, was dominated by Persia when the fourth-century League was established; when eventually it came under Athenian influence again, it was not an ally but a possession.[29] The same applies to Poteidaia. Olynthos would not have had a separate listing because that city would have been subsumed under the membership of the Chalkidian league which it led (lines 101f, on the left side). Euboian Oreos may (though not necessarily) have been treated as part of the same city as Hestiaia (line 114).[30] Other known fourth-century Athenian allies are likely to have been allies of non-League types (chapters 4 and 5). Certain strong *positive* clues exist. The best-attested name is that of Dorian Kos, because Kos is mentioned as one of the allies who revolted from the League during the Social War of 357–355; the names of all the other rebels mentioned are extant on the stele.[31] The so-called Sandwich Marble, which records monetary transactions with the Athenian-controlled amphictyony at Delos during the years 377–373, mentions Athenians, Delians, several listed League members, and Syros, Seriphos, Ios, Naxos, and two cities of the island of Ikaros: Oine and Thermai.[32] Either of the last-named pair could have been the state whose name began with the round letter between columns in line 89, and either or both could have appeared among the wholly lost names. Soldiers at Syros were involved in the awarding of a crown to the Athenian general Chabrias.[33] One may reasonably doubt whether Naxos, the site of Chabrias' victory over the Spartan navy in 376, was treated as a conquered enemy (i.e., became an Athenian possession) or was added to the League as an ally.[34] Pyrrha on Lesbos was certainly a member; if it was not listed in line 90, it was listed among these lost names. A similar statement may be made concerning Thasos, if its name did not appear either in line 89 or line 100. From the map at the end of *ATL* I, it is possible to suggest other Aegean island candidates, e.g., Delian League members Kythnos, Astypalaia, Patmos, Leros, the Dorian islands of Anaphe

29. Beloch 3:2.163; Accame 61 n. 1.

30. Diod. 15.30.3f seems to equate Hestiaia and Oreos.

31. Diod. 16.7.3: οἱ δ' Ἀθηναῖοι Χίων καὶ Ῥοδίων καὶ Κῴων, ἔτι δὲ Βυζαντίων ἀποστάντων ἐνέπεσον εἰς πόλεμον τὸν ὀνομασθέντα συμμαχικόν, ὃς διέμεινεν ἔτη τρία. The same names are listed when the narrative is resumed after a digression (*ib.* 16.21.1).

32. *IG* II², 1635, accepted as evidence on this point by, e.g., Busolt 748; Marshall 58 n. 5; Beloch 3:2.161; and Accame 81, 83, and 105.

33. B&E 81.

34. Sources sometimes cited on this issue (none decisive) include Diod. 15.35.2; Dem. 20.77; and *SV* 321. Busolt, 757–760, argues that Naxos was not a League member. Most believe that it was, e.g., Marshall 60; Beloch 3:1.153 n. 2 and 3:2.161; Accame 81–85; and Woodhead, "Allies" 264. The weight of scholarly opinion, however, cannot make vague sources any the less vague.

(which Accame restores in line 86), Nisyros, and Telos, plus perhaps several small islets. Possible allies among cities of the Thracian coast are simply too numerous to list; none is supported by any evidence. In sum, the strongest candidates are Kos and Syros (virtually certain), Oine and/or Thermai (one of the two probably having been inscribed between columns in line 89), and Ios and Seriphos. Naxos and Oreos are possible, but less likely.[35]

Dating the Names of the Front Face

The cities whose names constitute the first group (Chios, Mytilene, Methymna, Rhodos, Byzantion, and Thebes) clearly were already members of the alliance when the decree of Aristoteles was passed in early 377. The second group (Chalkis, Eretria, Arethousa, Karystos, and Ikos) joined very soon afterward. After Chabrias left Euboia, says Diodoros, "he, sailing to the Cyclades islands, won over Peparethos and Skiathos and some others which had been subject to the Lakedaimonians."[36] If, as Fabricius and Accame have argued, the names of Maroneia and Dion were cut later than those of Peparethos and Skiathos, it is difficult to see how Diodoros' vague phrases can apply to very many simultaneously inscribed names on the stele: perhaps only Παλα[ισκιάθιοι] and the first lost name (which Accame insists was Anaphe) under it in the right column, but even this much is doubtful. We would certainly not expect the simultaneous listing of two names in the left column and as many as six in the right column—though Accame's argument really does seem to suggest acceptance of this epigraphical monstrosity.[37] In truth, clues for any precision in dating Tenedos, Poiessa, Maroneia, Dion, Paros, Athenai, the partially preserved names to the right of the latter two, and the wholly lost names of the right-hand column simply do not exist. Accame wishes to date all the names of the lists of the front face of the stele prior to Chabrias' victory at Naxos in the autumn of 376, but the inscribing of some of these names after the battle cannot be ruled out, because of the vagueness of the sources. Demosthenes, e.g., says of Chabrias: "Then he defeated (the) Lakedaimonians in a sea battle . . . and he took many of those islands and gave (them)

---

35. On Naxos see preceding note. On Oreos ('Ωρεός with an omega, i.e., not a candidate for the name between columns in line 89) see Ais. 3.94 and 101. League membership for Aigina would be an overbold inference from Xen. *Hell.* 5.4.61. Prokonnesos (see [Dem.] 50.5) probably was a bilateral Athenian ally (chapter 5). I do not think that Accame, 82 and 124 (echoing Beloch 3:2.161), makes a strong case for the membership of Dorian Melos on the basis of [Dem.] 58.56.

36. Diod. 15.30.5: . . . αὐτὸς δὲ ταῖς Κυκλάσι νήσοις ἐπιπλέων προσηγάγετο Πεπάρηθον καὶ Σκίαθον καί τινας ἄλλας τεταγμένας ὑπὸ Λακεδαιμονίοις.

37. Accame 78 and 81.

over to you, and made friendly (those) formerly being hostile."[38] The only real epigraphic evidence for any significant historical event intervening between the listing of the names on the front and on the side of the stele is the existence of the amendment below the names of the front face. Even this consideration puts no restriction on the lateness of the names written between columns. Accame's attempt at determining the prytanies of the Athenian year in which various groups of names were inscribed on the front face was the assumption of an impossible task.

Lines 91–96. Amendment or Second Decree

This amendment or rider, also moved by Aristoteles, must have been inscribed after at least all of the names of the left-hand column above it. The presence of "afterthought" names between columns makes it highly unlikely that there were ever any names *below* the amendment; the small script of these lines is a further indication that they were quite near the bottom of the stone (everything below line 96 is now broken away). It is reasonable to see the amendment as, in a sense, a heading for the list of names subsequently added on the left side of the stele. Some important military and/or political development(s) may have occurred, leading to a large increase in League membership. If so, the battle of Naxos is an appropriate, even if not certain, occasion. The content of the amendment is so fragmentary that one can offer little in the way of reconstruction. "Islands" are mentioned (line 95), along with some resolutions of the Athenian demos (in line 94 at least). Whether the synedrion of the League concurred in these resolutions cannot definitely be known, though Busolt's restoration for the end of line 94, καὶ τ[οῖς ουμμάχοις---], is certainly possible (see also chapter 6).[39]

Lines 97–134. Preliminary General Comment on Names of the Left Side of the Stele[40]

Several detailed studies have concentrated on epigraphical and historical problems associated with the names of the left side. Key areas of disagreement include the total number of hands involved (all agree, how-

38. Dem. 20.77 (quoted in chapter 6). Beloch, 3:2.156, suggests that the names on the front face were all listed before or immediatley after the battle of Naxos.

39. Busolt 740 (without brackets). The restoration καὶ τ[ῆι βολῆι---] must be ruled out; Rhodes, *Boule* provides no examples of any such formula from Athenian inscriptions of any period.

40. Koehler's majuscule of the list on the left side is less accurate than his majuscule of the front face; possibly his squeeze did not include the left side. As Fabricius, 598, observes, the levels of the names there in relation to the lines of the front face do not correspond to their actual levels on the stone. Fortunately, the left side of the stele has suffered no damage since Koehler's time, and Pritchett's squeeze is complete. I do not rely on Koehler's majuscule for any readings within this list.

ever, that the hand which cut lines 131–134 cut no other names on the stele), the sequence in which different groups of names were inscribed, the dates of the first and last entries, and the content and significance of the erased line 111.[41]

Lines 97f. The Restored Faction

The invariable restoration of these lines in every text, translation, and discussion since Rangabé suggested it in 1855 has been [Κερκυ]ραίων / [ὁ δ]ῆμος. This has seemed so fitting and obvious that even scholars who meticulously examined the stone and quarrelled over other readings and restorations never thought to question it. Yet the restoration is definitely erroneous. In 1967, illustrating the inaccurate facsimile of the *editio princeps* (the source of Rangabé's incorrect idea of epigraphic possibilities) beside a clear photograph of a squeeze of the relevant portion of the list, and recording precise measurements, D. W. Bradeen and J. E. Coleman showed conclusively that only two or three letters could possibly have been inscribed in the area supposedly occupied by the five restored letters of [Κερκυ]ραίων. They added the further point, also not generally recognized, that lines 97f are not in the same hand as the lines below. Thus the faction apparently was not listed on the stele at the same time as these states, and the question of its proper chronological position arises. Of possible new restorations, Bradeen and Coleman strongly prefer [Θη]ραίων / [ὁ δ]ῆμος. They contend that a democratic faction on the island of Thera was admitted to the Athenian League, and that the faction joined the League earlier than any of the states whose names are listed below it.[42] The position of the entry—on a level with the beginning of the decree on the front face (line 7)—supports this suggestion.

41. Pouilloux, in his translation (without mentioning dates), groups the names of lines 97–121 and then those of lines 122–134; these divisions correspond to no conceivable epigraphical or historical considerations. WV say that the names listed in lines 131–134, 97f, 106–111, and 99–105 (in that order!) were "added about 375"; those of lines 112–130 are said to have been "added about 375/4 or 373."

42. Eustratiadis, in the *ed. prin.* (which I have been unable to consult directly), had restored ['Ερυθ]ραίων, which is ruled out by Erythrai's location in Asia. B&C reject [Αἱ]-ραίων (Hairai is also in Asia) and [Δει]ραίων (Thracian Deire is too insignificant). The mention of an "assembly" on Thera in *IG* XII (3), Suppl., p. 280, no. 1289, indicates to B&C that a democratic faction took control of this normally oligarchic state at some point in the fourth century. Thera had already been suggested as a member of the Second Athenian League by Beloch, 3:2.161 (of "unlisted" type, however), and by Accame, 82 (as one of the names lost from the front face of the stele). The side-by-side photos of Eustratiadis' inaccurate facsimile and their own squeeze in B&C, plate 30, make inescapable their point about the possible number of lost letters. Autopsy further convinces me; it also confirms the statement of B&C that the letters of lines 97f are "slightly smaller, more deeply cut and more widely spaced" than the letters of the lines below. I would add that the omega is lower and wider than the rather tall omegas of the other names. The publication of this important article was announced by *SEG* XXIV, 80 (1969), and it is cited in the supplementary section of the second edition of *SV* (1975). Yet Bengtson's text is unchanged, and the

But one must also take the amendment of lines 91–96 into consideration. If it served in some sense as a heading for the list of names on the left side of the stele, as has been suggested, surely it envisioned a substantial group of names to be listed. One additional name, e.g., the democratic faction of Thera(?), could have been squeezed in between columns on the front face, just as other names were. A name in a unique hand at the top of a list could even have been cut *last*, and the entry of lines 97f would make sense as a late addition, precisely because it was a faction. All of the extant entries of the front face appear in the form of simple ethnics; most of the names of lines 99–130 are in similar form. In the decree itself (lines 20f), the Athenians promise to avoid tampering with member states' internal political systems. The only other faction listed (lines 131–134) probably should be dated rather late (v. infra). Thus, the admission of a faction in the League's very early days seems unlikely; and it is suggested by no other epigraphic or literary source. In sum, the position of this faction's name on the list puts little restriction on its date of accession.

Lines 99–130. Abdera through Neapolis

Woodhead describes himself as one in a long line of scholars who contend that the names of lines 99–110 were inscribed in 375 and those of lines 112–130 (below the erased line 111) in 373 B.C. His argument is that the names of lines 99–110 are "more generously spaced, especially the shorter names, . . . in order to give them a better proportion in relation to the longer names," than those of what he calls his "Aegean" group of lines 112–130. In the latter group, he says, "the engraver preferred to begin all the names as far to the left as he could, and to preserve a quasi-stoichedon arrangement of the letters."[43] My observation convinces me, however, that the only shorter name whose letters are widely spaced is Αἴνιοι (line 103), and the group to which Woodhead assigns it has so many long names that his generalization is undemonstrable. He himself concedes that Σίφνιοι (line 126) is an exception within the group he calls "quasi-stoichedon." The same letter forms are employed throughout all these lines (notably epsilon, kappa, nu, and phi), and the variations in spacing indicate no pattern I can see. Epigraphically, all the names appear to have been cut by the same hand, and it is reasonable to infer from this that they were all cut at the same time. Either of the years suggested by Woodhead (375 or 373) might be acceptable—depending on other evidence—but there is no epigraphic reason to divide the names into two groups. (I assume that the erased name in line 111 was not cut

---

translation of WV 22 (1973) follows the discredited restoration. One scholar who seems to be aware of the problem is Sealey, *City-Sts.* 422 n. 5 (cf. "Transf." 105).

43. General statement in Woodhead, "Allies" 359 (cf. B&E 82f); quotation from "Jason" 371f.

in a unique hand.) A firm, uncontradicted date for the listing of any one of the names should logically date them all, but the inference that date of *joining* equals date of *listing* is unjustified. On the front face of the stele, the multiplicity of hands does indeed make it likely that not much time elapsed between the accession and the listing of the members whose names appear there. But the sameness of hand for so many names here has the contrary implication. Nothing proves that any of these states were listed immediately upon joining the League, and the convoluted geographical order of these lines lends credence to scholars' suggestions that names were "saved up" for shorter or longer periods of time, then all listed at once.[44] But reasons suggested to account for such time lapses are often themselves suspect.

Line 99. Abdera

The implication of Diod. 15.36.4 is that Abdera joined the League in 375.

Line 100. Thasos?

This traditional restoration is obviously not epigraphically necessary. But since Philip of Macedon said that Athens could compel Thasos and Maroneia (a listed League member, line 87) to arbitrate territorial claims, it would seem that both recognized Athens's hegemony, so Thasos probably *was* a League member.[45] If the name is not to be restored here, it should be restored somewhere else on the stele (e.g., in line 89).

Lines 101f. The Chalkidian League

Schaefer believed that the Chalkidians of these lines were dwellers in some town on the peninsula of Mt. Athos, on the basis of a definition in Stephanos of Byzantion: Χαλκίς· ἔστι καὶ ἐν Ἄθῳ ἄλλη Χαλκίς, ὡς Εὔδοξος τετάρτῳ· μετὰ δὲ τὸν Ἄθῳ μέχρι Παλλήνης, ἣ ἐπὶ θάτερα πεποίηκε κόλπον βαθὺν καὶ πλατὺν Χαλκίδα ἐπονομαζόμενον. Tod appears to accept this interpretation. But Marshall, Beloch, and Accame have the stronger case in identifying the League member with the revived Chalkidian confederacy, led by Olynthos, whose breakup had been part of Sparta's imperialist policy under color of "enforcing" the King's Peace (chapter 1).[46]

---

44. See the suggestions of, e.g., Accame 103 and Sealey, "Transf." 105.

45. [Dem.] 12.17; see also sec. 2. Dem. 4.32 is less decisive, since Thasos is there grouped with both a League member (Skiathos) and an Athenian possession (Lemnos), and in the context could be classed with either.

46. Schaefer as reported by Marshall 61 n. 5; Steph. Byz. as quoted by Beloch 3:2.159 and Accame 87 n. 4; Tod 123 comm.; see also F.C. Thomes, "Il trattato con i Calcidesi nella prima attività diplomatica di Filippo II," *PP* 8 (1953) 343–355. Beloch, 3:2.160, insists that *SV* 250 is the Athenian alliance with the Chalkidian confederacy (dated 376/5 or 375/4), but the text is really too fragmentary for a decision pro or con.

Lines 106–110. Akarnania, Pronnoi of Kephallenia, Alketas, and Neoptolemos

The accession of the Akarnanian confederacy and the Kephallenian city of Pronnoi (lines 106–108) is clearly somehow related to an inscription, securely dated to 375 B.C., which to all appearances is the League membership treaty of the Korkyraians, Akarnanians, and Kephallenians.[47] The adherence of Alketas, the Molossian king of Epeiros, and his son Neoptolemos is generally connected with that of these states because literary sources seem to indicate that Timotheos recruited these kings for the League in his western expedition of 375.[48] But the striking facts in connection with these names are the following: (1) that (given the observations, *supra*, on lines 97f) Korkyra was *not* listed along with the other names, and (2) that *only* Pronnoi, one of four cities of Kephallenia, was listed. These inescapable problems are addressed elsewhere (the status of Korkyra in chapter 4, the problem of the Kephallenians in chapter 6), but there is no real reason to reject 375 as the accession date of the allies that *are* listed in these lines—especially since this date is consistent with that suggested for Abdera (line 99), whose name appears to have been inscribed by the same hand.

Line 111. Jason of Pherai?

Fabricius first suggested the restoration of the Thessalian tyrant's name in this erased line: ['Ιάσω]ν. His lead has been almost universally followed. If Fabricius' position be strictly accepted, the final nu of the name should be regarded as certain, though some editors underdot it.[49] Both Jean Hatzfeld and A. G. Woodhead have shown, however, that the restoration has no epigraphical basis.[50] The possible stroke of the right vertical hasta of nu at the end of the *rasura* could just as easily be an iota —a letter with which many of the names on the stele end—or simply a chisel mark made in erasing. Woodhead, who unnecessarily attributes the names above and below line 111 to different hands, is thereby influenced to suggest that the erased name probably had six letters if inscribed with one group or seven if inscribed with the other. M. P. Roussel (who looked at the stone for Hatzfeld) and Beloch (claiming autopsy[51]) are on firmer ground in concluding that the erased area probably held six letters. Of course, since the erasure could have been longer

47. *SV* 262, date in lines 2f. Korkyra's case is complicated by the existence of a further alliance treaty (undated), *SV* 263 (see chapter 4).

48. Xen. *Hell.* 5.4.64; Isok. 15.107f; Diod. 15.36.5; Nep. *Timoth.* 2.1.

49. Fabricius, esp. 590 and 594; Kirchner and Pouilloux treat nu as certain; Tod and *SV* underdot it. The most extreme overstatement is to be found in the parenthetical comm. of WV: "the name Jason is discernible here, but was deleted. . . . "

50. Hatzfeld, "Jason de Phères a-t-il été l'allié d'Athènes?" *REA* 36 (1934) 441–461; Woodhead, "Jason" *passim*. See Accame's fig. 3.

51. Beloch 3:1.165 n. 2 and 3:2.158.

than the name erased, epigraphic considerations do not rule out ['Ιάσων], among possible total restorations. But support for it must be sought elsewhere; the stele provides none. In chapter 5, I argue for rejecting the restoration, and the League membership of Jason. For all the stone reveals, the mason could have simply excised a mistake—perhaps a name accidentally inscribed twice. Moreover, he could have discovered such an error midway through the erroneous recutting of a long name, so even the length of the *rasura* does not definitely provide any clue to the identity of the erased name.

Lines 131–134. The Zakynthian Faction

This entry is in a unique, and very sloppy, hand. From its position at the bottom of the list on the left side, some scholars contend that it was the last member listed, and that consequently a firm date for the faction's adherence to the League would provide a terminus for the list as a whole. Others infer from the fact that the entry begins on the same level as the first names of the front face that it was the *first* entry of the left side, citing the long gap between lines 130 and 131 in support of this suggestion. Epigraphically, neither alternative is preferable to the other.[52] The same uncertainties apply here as apply to the faction of lines 97f: the Zakynthians were not listed at the same time as the names of lines 99–130, but they could have been listed *either* before or after, and the temporal relationship between the inscribing of the two factions remains undeterminable through epigraphic considerations. The accounts of Xenophon and Diodoros concerning events following the signing of the peace of 375/4 provide the only clues for dating the enrollment of the Zakynthian demos.[53] But problems abound: the peace itself is not precisely datable;[54] neither author specifically says that the Zakynthians were made League members, but only that Timotheos established them on their home island, provoking hostilities with the Spartan-supported oligarchy then in power there; and Diodoros calls the exiles' stronghold not Nellos but "Arkadia."[55] See the discussion of these problems in chapter 3.

---

52. Last name listed, e.g., Accame 86; first, e.g., Cawkwell, "Peace" 88; Sealey, "Transf." 105 and *City-Sts.* 418; aware of problem but neutral, e.g., Woodhead, "Jason," 371 n. 15.

53. Xen. *Hell.* 6.2.2f; Diod. 15.45.1–46.3.

54. Xen. *Hell.* 6.2.1; Diod. 15.38.1–4 (these and other sources on this peace are quoted in *SV* 265—though Ais. 2.32 and Dem. 19.253 and 9.16 are probably mistakenly included, since they appear to refer to a peace, or peaces, of different date). For suggestions as to the exact date of the peace of 375/4, see Beloch 3:1.156 n. 1 and 3:2.235; Sealey, "Transf." 99–104; Cawkwell, "Peace" *passim*; and Buckler, "Dating the Peace of 375/4 B.C.," *GRBS* 12 (1971) 353–361.

55. Cawkwell, "Peace" 88, correctly points out that Nellos (or Nellon—the toponym is otherwise unattested) need not even have been on Zakynthos: cf. Samian exiles at Anaia, Thuc. 2.32.2.

Total Names and Total League Membership

The number of names originally inscribed on the stele can be computed fairly accurately. On the front face twenty certain names are preserved, plus parts of three others. The lost part of the right-hand column must have been filled with names; otherwise there would have been no need to squeeze names in between columns. None of the extant entries of the front face occupies more than one line, so probably the lost names did not, either. Spacing between lines here could have varied, of course, from the spacing of lines in the extant left-hand column, and two short names could have been cut on one line. But a figure of five or six wholly lost names must be roughly correct. Therefore the front face of the stele originally held about twenty-eight or twenty-nine names. The list of the left side of the stele is better preserved, which is fortunate, because there some entries occupy more than one line and a large uninscribed space intervenes between the penultimate and final entries. Since at least part of every originally inscribed line is extant, however (except the erased line 111), no doubt exists about the original number of entries. All or part of twenty-nine names appear in this list; if the erased line bore another name (i.e., if the erasure was not simply the correction of a mistake), the total would be increased by one; if Alketas and Neoptolemos, as co-regents, are counted together as one member, the total would be decreased by one. An overall total of fifty-eight members would not err by more than one or two in either direction. Only about sixty allies, then, were listed. The decree of Aristoteles (lines 69–72) gives specific, exact instructions: states already in alliance and those which subsequently become allies are all to be listed on the stele. Extant alliance treaties echo this provision, as applied to the individual states concerned.[56] The stone-cutters certainly did not run out of room for members' names: the aforementioned large gap on the left side of the stele and its completely uninscribed right side attest to this. Was not, then, the full membership of the League about sixty states? I know of no scholar who is willing to say so. This reluctance is based on two literary passages. In 343 B.C., Aischines, condemning Athens's war with Philip over Amphipolis, says:

. . . συνέβαινε δ' ἡμῶν τὸν στρατηγὸν ἐν τῷ πολέμῳ ἑβδομήκοντα μὲν καὶ πέντε πόλεις συμμαχίδας ἀποβεβληκέναι, ἃς ἐκτήσατο Τιμόθεος ὁ Κόνωνος καὶ κατέστησεν εἰς τὸ συνέδριον. . . .

. . . It came to pass that our general in the war caused the loss of seventy-five allied states, which Timotheos (son) of Konon acquired and established in the synedrion. . . .[57]

---

56. SV 258, lines 9–11; SV 262, lines 13f (see chapter 6 for discussion of steps involved in joining the League).

57. Ais. 2.70 (the general is Chares; see chapter 10). Beloch, 3:2.163, cites this source erroneously as "gKtes.," i.e., Ais. 3.

Diodoros, writing in the Augustan period, follows his description of the organization of the League with a summary statement:

. . . τοῖς Ἀθηναίοις εἰς συμμαχίαν συνέβησαν ἑβδομήκοντα πόλεις καὶ μετέσχον ἐπ' ἴσης τοῦ κοινοῦ συνεδρίου. . . .

. . . To (the) Athenians for alliance came seventy states, and they participated on equal terms in the common (or League) synedrion. . . .[58]

These (discrepant) statements have led some scholars to assume that the Athenians came to disregard the decree's provision for listing all League members and denied some or all of the privileges of League membership to such unlisted allies.[59] But these testimonia may be misleading. Aischines' rhetorical statement, certainly, is manifestly false, for Timotheos did not win over seventy-five states. Isokrates, who was Timotheos' teacher, admirer, and defender, surely was not diminishing his pupil's fame when he told the Athenians that Timotheos had made them masters of *twenty-four* cities. This figure has contemporary support from Deinarchos.[60] Though both these authors seem to be counting cities captured rather than allies enrolled, Aischines' statement remains unbelievable, if only for its implication that the League's *entire* membership was recruited by Timotheos.[61] Many League allies, on the contrary, are known to have been recruited by Chabrias.[62] The slightly lower total of Diodoros is no more to be trusted. Where would Diodoros' source (probably Ephoros) get a total League membership figure? The most obvious place, I should think, would be the lists of the stele of Aristoteles, in the Athenian agora. He would walk up to the stele and count the names, and record either an exact or a rounded-off figure: in the latter case, sixty. Surely Ephoros' history had been recopied before Diodoros

58. Diod. 15.30.2.

59. See the theories of, e.g., Busolt 768; Marshall 74f; Accame 104–106; Sealey, "Transf." 107 (but expressing doubts in *City-Sts.* 438f); Cawkwell, "Peace" 91 n. 61; and Ryder, *KE* 55. Beloch's estimates of the total geographical area and total population of the League (3:1.310f), based on similarly doubtful theories about who the League members were, are themselves therefore unreliable.

60. Isok. 15.113; Dein. 1.14 and 3.17. Diod. 15.47.2 says that on one expedition (see chapter 3 for problems concerning its date) Timotheos added thirty ships to the League's fleet, but of the number of allied *states* then recruited, he gives us only the vague πολλὰς πόλεις.

61. I make the inference (the same inference is made by Beloch 3:2.163) on the basis that Aischines' figure is larger than Diodoros', which in turn is explicitly a League membership total. On the status of the cities mentioned by Isokrates and Deinarchos, see chapter 4. S. I. Oost, "Two Notes on Aristophon of Azenia," *CPh* 72 (1977) 240 offers the intriguing suggestion that Aischines may have used "seventy-five" to express any vague large number: his statement that Aristophon was acquitted in seventy-five trials (Ais. 3.194) is equally unbelievable.

62. *IG* II², 404; Dem. 20.80; Diod. 15.30.5. See Beloch 3:1.154 and n. 1.

used it; just as surely, his own work was recopied prior to the production of the earliest extant manuscript. At any point, ἑξήκοντα (sixty) could easily have become ἑβδομήκοντα (seventy), and the next copyist would have no way of noticing and correcting the error.[63] Only independent outside evidence could have led anyone to make the correction, and it was lacking. But the reassembly of the stele makes that information available to us. Scholars have preferred to invent unattested categories of unlisted League members, and to infer large and ominous shifts in Athenian policy toward the League allies on very frail evidence, rather than to accept the testimony of the original, primary document of the League. I prefer to accept the *best* ancient evidence, and conclude that the total membership of the Second Athenian League was around sixty states—the states whose names were listed on the stele of the decree of Aristoteles, and only those states.

63. This argument assumes that Ephoros' original figure was at least approximately accurate. The assumption itself is not necessarily warranted, to judge from that writer's general numerical perversity: see Meiggs, *AE* 13, 60, and 447–457.

Part II

LEAGUE ALLIES AND OTHER ALLIES

3

MEMBERS OF THE LEAGUE

The alliances of Athens in the years 378–338 B.C. fit with fair consistency into divisions as to period and type.[1] The 370s, down to the battle of Leuktra and the peace of Athens of 371, were the days of League membership alliances. The present chapter deals with the evidence for Athens's alliances with states identified in chapter 2 as members of the Second Athenian League. It may be true (though I think it is unlikely) that in the period of its struggle with Sparta (378–371), Athens made no alliances except these. During the period roughly bounded by the peace of 371 and the peace of 362/1 (after the battle of Mantineia), when the chief enemy of Athens was Thebes, the main form of alliance it made with Greek cities and groups of cities seems to have been the "alliance with Athens and its League" (chapter 4). Simultaneously, in its relations with kings and tyrants on the fringes of Hellas, Athens seems generally to have made bilateral alliances to which the League was not a party. After the emergence of Philip II of Macedon as a serious threat to Athenian interests in the middle 350s, the Athenians appear almost invariably to have concluded bilateral alliances, no matter what types of allied states were involved (chapter 5).

Even after the breakup of the League by Philip in 338, Athens maintained friendly relations with many of its loyal members. Long before, however, certain factors had tended to lessen the importance of the League in Athenian foreign policy—most significantly the defections (chapter 10), first of Thebes and then of states enticed away by the Thebans, or by the Persians, or by Philip, or rebelling for other reasons of their own. Athens and its loyal allies forcibly returned some of these to the League, but the rebels of the crucial Social War of 357–355 B.C. seem to have been more successful. Some non-League membership alliances sworn by Athens in later years were actually concluded with former members of the League.[2]

Sometimes hostile cities simply were conquered and taken over without alliance—notably in Athens's struggles with the Persian King in the 360s and subsequently with Philip. Such territorial acquisitions must receive brief comment, for scholars often have assumed that every hamlet

---

1. The existence of different types of fourth-century Athenian alliances has been recognized by most scholars, e.g., Marshall 87, 94, and 103–105; Beloch 3:2.164; Accame 128 and 130f; Marta Sordi, "La pace di Atene del 371/0," *RFIC* 29 (1951) 40f; Hammond, *HG²* 488; and Woodhead, "Jason" 373 and "Inscs." 225. No general agreement exists, however, on which alliances are to be listed in the respective categories.

2. Beloch, 3:2.164, recognizes this.

taken by Timotheos or Chares became a member of the Second Athenian League, and the treatment of such conquered territories has been taken as evidence for Athenian attitudes toward the members of the League.

The first group of names listed below the decree of Aristoteles— Chios, Mytilene, Methymna, Rhodos, Byzantion, and Thebes— clearly fits the rubric of line 70 of the decree: "those (already) bei[n]g allied states." The alliance treaties of Byzantion and Methymna are extant.[3] They are chiefly interesting, however, for the light they shed on the structure and mechanics of the League, so my discussion of their provisions will be reserved for Part III. Chios and Thebes, whose names appear at the top of the two columns of names below the decree, are used in the text itself (lines 24f) as paradigms of the equal status of members of the League. Inscribed Athenian alliance treaties with both of these states exist, but controversy and uncertainty mark scholarly discussion of each.

Both Tod and Bengtson combine two separate fragmentary inscriptions to produce a composite text which they call the Athens-Chios treaty of 384 B.C.[4] Both cite Accame's discussion of the Chian treaty, without describing or commenting upon his argument itself. Yet Accame contends that the two fragments (IG II², 34 and 35) from which these editors' composite text is derived are not identical copies of one treaty. Rather, he says, IG II², 34 is the Athens-Chios treaty of 384, and the other is a different treaty modeled upon it. The name of the allied state in this second treaty is not extant and not restorable with any certainty. Accame believes that the ally is in fact Chios, but that this is a new, revised treaty which takes the existence of the recently established League into account.[5] The suggestion is plausible, though speculative. We do not have any clear-cut examples of inscribed pre-League and post-League Athenian alliances. The Methymna treaty, however, is a League membership alliance which refers to a preexisting alliance with Athens[6]—which may have been inscribed, though now lost.

A fragmentary inscription (IG II², 40) which seems to refer to an Athenian-Theban alliance has been the subject of much scholarly controversy. The main body of the inscription is lost; we have only the bottom part of the stele, which held mostly an amendment to whatever was in-

---

3. SV 256 and 258. See Beloch, 3:1.149 and n. 4, for the circumstances of Rhodos' joining the League (no treaty is extant).

4. Tod 118; SV 248.

5. Accame 9–13 and 34f.

6. SV 258, lines 4–11: "Since (the) Methymnaians are allies and well disposed toward the city of (the) Athenians, so that also with the other allies of (the) Athenians they may have the alliance, list them, etc." (ἐπειδ/ὴ σύμ⟨μ⟩αχοί εἰσιν καὶ εὔνοι τῆι πόλη/ι τῆι Ἀθηναίων Μηθυμναῖοι, ὅπως ἂν / καὶ πρὸς τὸς ἄλλος συμμάχος τὸς Ἀθ/ηναίων ἦι αὐτοῖς ἡ συμμαχία, ἀναγρ/άψαι αὐτός, κτλ).

scribed above—and only approximately the right-hand half of this. Unfortunately, all published texts of this inscription are marred by excessive restoration, grounded in the historical theories which the respective editors are attempting to propound. The following text[7] omits contentious restorations:

(After an unknown number of lost lines)

[. . . . . .20. . . . .]ων ἑπτακαίδεκα [. .]
[. . . .14. . . . . καλέσα]ι δὲ καὶ τὼ Θηβ[αίων]
[. . . . . .20. . . . .]ον ἐπὶ ξένια ἐς τὸ [π]-
[ρυτανεῖον ἐς αὔριον. Στέ]φανος εἶπε· περὶ ὧν
5 [λέγοσιν οἱ ἐς τὸς συμμά]χος πρεσβεύσαντες,
[τὰ μὲν ἄλλα καθάπερ τῆι] βολῆι, ἐπαινέσαι δέ
[. . . . . .18. . . . .]ντα καὶ Θεόπομπον κα-
[ι?. . . .8. . . . καὶ τὸν τρι]ήραρχον Ἀριστόμ[α]χο-
[ν καὶ καλέσαι ἐπὶ δεῖ]πνον ἐς τὸ πρυτανεῖ[ον]
10 [ἐς αὔριον. ἐπαινέσαι] δὲ καὶ Ἀντίμαχον τὸγ Χ-
[ίον καὶ . .6. . . τὸν Μυ]τιληναῖον καὶ καλέσα-
[ι ἐπὶ δεῖπνον ἐς τὸ πρ]υτανεῖον ἐς αὔριον. κ[α]-
[ι?. . . . .16. . . . .]αι αὐτῶν τὸ[γ] γραμματέ-
[α τῆς βολῆς . . . .8. . . .]λει κατὰ τὸ ψήφισμα τῆ-
15 [ς βολῆς τὸ περὶ τῶν συν]θηκῶν τῶν ἐν τῆι στήλ-
[ηι . . . . . . .16. . . . . . . φ]αίνεται διάφορος ἡ
[. . . . . . . .17. . . . . . . π]όλει στήληι, προβολε-
[ύσασαν τὴν βολὴν περὶ] αὐτῶν [ἐ]ξενεγκὲν ἐς τ-
[ὸν δῆμον . . . . .11. . . .]το το[ῦ] Μυτιληναίο τὴ-
20 [ν βολὴν προβολεύσασα]ν ἐξεν[εγκ]ὲν ἐς τὸν δῆ-
[μον. ὑπὲρ δὲ τῆς ἀναγρα]φῆς τῶν στηλῶν μερίσ-
[αι . . . .16. . . . . .]κοντα δραχμὰς ἑκατέ-
[ρας, καὶ ἀναγραψάτω ὁ γ]ραμματε[ὺς] τῆς [β]ολῆ[ς].
                    vacat

The apparent reference to Thebans in line 2, the invitation to ξένια (hospitality for foreign visitors) in line 3, and the mention of persons serving as ambassadors in line 5 combine to make it very likely that the subject matter of the lost upper portion of the stele was indeed a Theban alliance. It also has been plausibly argued that seventeen (line 1) was an appropriate number of oath-takers on each side for such an important treaty at this time.[8] In the amendment by one Stephanos (line 4),[9] com-

7. SV 255. My text is based upon that of Burnett, "Expans." 4, including her underlining of letters read by Kirchner but no longer visible.

8. Buckler, "Theban Treaty Obligations in IG II² 40: A Postscript," Historia 20 (1971) 506–508 suggests that seventeen Thebans would correspond to seventeen League oath-takers: one synedros from each of the five pre-Theban allies, plus the ten Athenian strategoi and two hipparchoi. Cawkwell, "Found." 49 n. 2, finds this hypothesis attractive.

9. Early editors restored [Κέ]φαλος here, the name of the proposer of a pro-Theban resolution mentioned in Dein. 1.39 (see SV 254). Accame, though directly discussing only

mendation is offered (lines 6–10) to a Theopompos, to a trierarch called Aristomachos, and to one or two others whose names are lost—all presumably being Athenian citizens, since the hospitality to which they are invited is called δεῖπνον rather than ξένια. A further commendation (lines 10–12) is offered to certain foreigners: Antimachos the Chian and a Mytilenaian whose name is lost. But since these too are invited to δεῖπνον (the letter count in line 12 requires this restoration), they appear at some time to have been granted Athenian citizenship (an Antimachos of Chios who meets this description is attested).[10]

Several restorations have been suggested for lines 13f. The version of SV (and Burnett) combines Velsen's [.τὰ ὀνόματα ἀναγράψ]αι in line 13 with Kirchner's [---ἐν τῆι στή]λει in line 14. Wilhelm had instead restored [.τὰς στήλας ἀναγράψ]αι and [---ἐν ἀκροπό]λει, respectively. Accame differs from Wilhelm's restorations only in substituting [ἀναθεῖν]αι for [ἀναγράψ]αι. A fundamental problem is the reference of αὐτῶν in line 13. If, following the ὀνόματα restoration, it refers to the inscribing of names, one cannot tell exactly whose names are meant—only Antimachos and the Mytilenaian, or also the Athenians of lines 6–10? But if the reference is to the inscribing (Wilhelm) or erecting (Accame) of stelai, the antecedents of αὐτῶν are equally unclear. In line 14, the spelling [στή]λει would be highly unusual. This ending for the dative is extant only once in IG II², 1–140, and it is inconsistent with the spelling στήληι in line 17 of this very inscription. Therefore the restoration [---ἐν ἀκροπό]λει seems to be stronger epigraphically. If we accept it, however, we still cannot tell what is said to be on the acropolis.[11] Possible differences between stelai

elements of the inscription beginning with line 10, accepts the older restoration in an introductory paragraph, p. 39. Yet Kirchner had already shown the preferability of the other name. After autopsy, Burnett, "Expans." 5 n. 5, concludes that the nu of Stephanos does not require underdotting (cf. SV).

10. Both Accame 39 (claiming autopsy) and Burnett, "Expans." 4, testify to the correctness of A. Wilhelm's reading of the letter at the end of line 10 (the first letter of the city of Antimachos) as chi. Bengtson, though citing Wilhelm, Accame, and Burnett in his comm., does not even mention this particular suggestion, and prints the gamma of IG II², 40 in his text (the second edition of SV makes no changes). Antimachos of Chios, an Athenian citizen, is mentioned in IG II², 1604, line 79 (cited by Accame 39 and nn. 1f). IG II², 1, lines 37, 51, 54, 63, and 74, throws some suspicion on the δεῖπνον-for-citizens-ξένια-for-foreigners interpretation, however; cf. the alternative interpretation of David G. Rice, "Xenophon, Diodorus and the Year 379/378 B.C.: Reconstruction and Reappraisal," YClS 24 (1975) 95–130, who suggests (p. 125) that the League members' representatives were entitled to δεῖπνον, but the Thebans only got ξένια because their alliance was not yet of the League membership type (but see IG II², 107, lines 26–30, quoted in chapter 6).

11. My comments on lines 13f draw on the apparatus criticus of SV 255, and especially on a private communication from Prof. John Buckler, who adds that he also distrusts the restoration of [σ]τ[ήλει] in IG II², 116, line 43. At the time of this writing, the publication of Buckler's The Theban Hegemony has been announced, though I have not had the opportunity to consult it.

and procedures for eliminating them seem to be the subject matter of lines 16–19. The use of ἑκατέρας, rather then ἑκαστάς, in lines 21–23 indicates that only two stelai are to be inscribed.[12] The stele of lines 15f and the stele of line 17,[13] which appear to have been different stelai, seem already to have been inscribed and set up. If a stele is in fact mentioned in line 14, upon which names(?) are to be inscribed, it may be a fifth stone, though it could just as easily be one of the two new stelai of lines 21–23. The boule is empowered to take some sort of preliminary action (in one case involving a Mytilenaian—perhaps the same one mentioned in connection with Antimachos the Chian), preparatory to action by the demos (lines 17–21).

From these ambiguous remains several conflicting theories emerge. Kirchner calls the inscription *Foedus cum Thebanis et Mytilenaeis*, presumably only because a Mytilenaian is mentioned in lines 11 and 19. Early editors restored a reference to τῆι στήλ/[ηι τῶν συμμάχων---] in lines 15f. There is no reason to accept this restoration, but if one should do so, "the stele of the allies" would obviously refer to the stele of the decree of Aristoteles, which is unambiguously cited in an inscription of 375 as τὴν στήλην τὴν κοινὴν τῶ[ν συμμάχων].[14] Accame, while accepting the restoration, nevertheless denies the clear reference the phrase would have, positing instead the existence of a different, otherwise unattested, stele of the allies. He restores a reference in lines 16f to a treaty with Chios: [---ἐπειδὴ] φαίνεται διάφορος ἡ / [(στήλη) πρὸς Χίος τῆι ἐν ἀκροπ]όλει στήληι, κτλ. He also infers that each of the men commended in the inscription is to be given a separate commemorative stele.[15] Burnett rightly censures this wholesale creativity. Yet the earlier Theban treaty which she restores in lines 15f (τῆι στήλ/[ηι τῆιδε πρὸς Θήβας, εἰ φ]αίνεται, κτλ) has no firmer basis.[16] Despite the ingenious efforts of edi-

12. Various sums for the inscribing have been restored in line 22, the relative appropriateness of which I cannot evaluate. Upon the length of the restored number depends the length of the name of the board of magistrates involved (or perhaps the converse). Currently, most editors prefer the 'Αποδέκται (Aristot. *Ath. Pol.* 48.1f, 50.1, and 52.3), a choice which Rhodes, *Boule* 101 n. 2, regards as certain.

13. The lost phrase probably ended with [---τῆι ἐν ἀκροπ]όλει στήληι, as most commentators suggest, but I do not see how one can *absolutely* (cf. Accame 42f) rule out a slightly anachronistic use of the term "polis" to mean "acropolis," as occurs frequently in fifth-century Athenian inscriptions, including very *late* fifth-century inscriptions: note ἐς πόλι[ν] in *IG* II², 1, line 39—a resolution of 405/4, inscribed in 403/2. Little support for this possibility is provided, however, by the restorations of *IG* II², 13, line 10; 55, lines 7f; and 56, line 3. The length of the last restored word naturally would affect the restoration of what precedes it. If [---ἐν ἀκροπό]λει is a correct restoration in line 14, we certainly would not expect the shorter form here.

14. *SV* 262, line 14.

15. Accame 41–46.

16. Burnett, "Expans.," has criticisms of the excessive restoration of Accame (pp. 7 and 12 n. 15; cf. Cawkwell, "Found." 49 n. 5), and she certainly is correct in pointing out (p. 6

tors, in the end this fragmentary inscription really tells us very little about Thebes' connection with Athens. Whatever we can know about the chronology and circumstances of the Theban adherence to the League must be derived from literary sources.

The Athenian alliance with "Boiotia" of 395 B.C.[17] had been terminated by the Greeks' acceptance of the King's Peace. Many Athenians nonetheless remained decidedly pro-Theban, a feeling that was greatly strengthened when the Spartans occupied the Kadmeia in 382. All sources agree that the Theban liberators received Athenian support in 379, though they differ as to the nature of that support. Xenophon says the Thebans were assisted by troops under two Athenian generals, and that later the Athenians, fearing Spartan retaliation, punished these generals with death and exile; there is no implication that the assistance was given by order of the Athenian state. Diodoros, however, says that the liberators sent an embassy to request full-scale Athenian intervention, and that the demos voted for the sending of as large a force as possible immediately, while mobilization began for intervention πανδημεί; he says nothing about any generals being punished. Plutarch gives the most discreditable version of Athenian actions: though there had been an actual "alliance" (συμμαχίαν) with Thebes, he says, the Athenians in their fear renounced it and prosecuted Boiotian sympathizers (τῶν βοιωτιαζόντων) in their city; nothing is said about any generals or any specific events.[18] The earliest version (Xenophon's) seems most believable. What probably happened is that two Athenian generals of "Boiotizing" sympathies, relying on popular support, led their troops against the Spartans at the time of the Theban exiles' liberation of the Kadmeia. The Athenian demos, fearing Spartan retaliation, punished the generals—quite properly and untreacherously—for having acted without official orders.[19]

---

n. 7) that Accame's restoration of line 16 not only records one letter (phi of φαίνεται) as certain which all other editors have bracketed, but is also one letter too long. Her own suspicious restoration appears on p. 8.

17. SV 223 (the inscription is dated through literary sources).

18. Xen. Hell. 5.4.9 and 19; Diod. 15.25.4–26.2; Plut. Pelop. 14.1. For whatever such a late source may be worth, Aristeides, Panathenaikos 294 says that Athens had no alliance with Thebes when this aid was given to the liberators.

19. Burnett, "Expans." 16, chastizes scholars who have chosen the interpretation under which the Athenians appear most treacherous. Cawkwell, "Found." 56–60, hedges on the problem by combining the sources, suggesting that the Athenians followed up the two generals' unofficial aid, for which they were punished (Xen.), with a formal decree of assistance (Diod.). Such a position would appear to be supported by Dein. 1.38f, but this rhetorical source is difficult to trust—it refers, e.g., to the Thebans as having long been enslaved (πολὺν χρόνον δουλεύουσαν) in 379. Rice (supra n. 10) almost indiscriminately picks and chooses from the accounts of Xenophon and Diodoros items consistent with his own highly creative interpretation of these events, and cavalierly describes Athenians hostile to Sparta's domination as being ipso facto "imperialists" (see, e.g., pp. 101, 103, and 110f).

The fullest account of subsequent events is that of Diodoros.[20] The elements of his narrative are as follows:

1. The Boiotians, having formed a league alliance (οἱ μὲν Βοιωτοί . . . κοινὴν συμμαχίαν ποιησάμενοι), expected a Spartan invasion.

2. The Athenians sent ambassadors to states dominated by the Spartans, calling on them "to hold on to the common freedom" ('Αθηναῖοι δὲ πρέσβεις . . . ἐξέπεμψαν ἐπὶ τὰς ὑπὸ {τοὺς} Λακεδαιμονίους τεταγμένας πόλεις, παρακαλοῦντες ἀντέχεσθαι τῆς κοινῆς ἐλευθερίας).

3. Because the Spartans treated them harshly, many of their allies were won to the Athenian side (πολλοὶ τῶν ὑπ' αὐτοὺς τεταγμένων ἀπέκλινον πρὸς τοὺς 'Αθηναίους), first Chios and Byzantion, then Rhodos and Mytilene and "some of the other islanders" (πρῶτοι δέ . . . Χῖοι καὶ Βυζάντιοι, καὶ μετὰ τούτους 'Ρόδιοι καὶ Μυτιληναῖοι καὶ τῶν ἄλλων τινὲς νησιωτῶν). As the movement gathered force, many states (πολλαὶ πόλεις) joined the Athenians.

4. The delighted Athenian demos established a League synedrion of all the allies, and appointed synedroi for each state (ὁ δὲ δῆμος . . . κοινὸν συνέδριον ἁπάντων τῶν συμμάχων συνεστήσαντο, καὶ συνέδρους ἀπέδειξαν ἑκάστης πόλεως).

5. The organization of the new League—said to have been adopted "by common consent"—is briefly described: the synedrion will meet at Athens, states both large and small will each have one vote, all will remain "autonomous," and the Athenians will hold the hegemony (ἐτάχθη δ' ἀπὸ τῆς κοινῆς γνώμης τὸ μὲν συνέδριον ἐν ταῖς 'Αθήναις συνεδρεύειν, πόλιν δὲ ἐπ' ἴσης καὶ μεγάλην καὶ μικρὰν μίας ψήφου κυρίαν εἶναι, πάσας δ' ὑπάρχειν αὐτονόμους, ἡγεμόσι χρωμένας 'Αθηναίοις).

6. The Spartans attempted by various means to win back their lost allies, and prepared for a major and extended Boiotian war, "since the Athenians and the other Greeks leagued together in the synedrion were allied to the Thebans" (συμμαχούντων τοῖς Θηβαίοις τῶν 'Αθηναίων καὶ τῶν ἄλλων 'Ελλήνων τῶν κοινωνούντων τοῦ συνεδρίου).

[A digression follows here on Athenian involvement with an Egyptian rebellion from the Persian Empire (chapter 1).]

7. The Spartans and Athenians were still at peace up to this point (μένειν τὴν εἰρήνην μέχρι τῶνδε τῶν καιρῶν), but now "Sphodriades" was persuaded by the Spartan king Kleombrotos to attack the Peiraieus. Failing, he was put on trial before the Spartan council, but "having the kings for supporters, he was unjustly acquitted" (συναγωνιστὰς ἔχων τοὺς βασιλεῖς, ἀδίκως ἀπελύθη). The Athenians, incensed at this, "voted that the truce had been broken by the Lakedaimonians" (ἐψηφίσαντο λελύσθαι τὰς σπονδὰς ὑπὸ Λακεδαιμονίων). Planning to make war, they chose Timotheos, Chabrias, and Kallistratos as generals, levied troops, and manned the ships.

20. Diod. 15.28–30.

8. "They also took the Thebans into the League synedrion upon entirely equal terms" (προσελάβοντο δὲ καὶ τοὺς Θηβαίους ἐπὶ τὸ κοινὸν συνέδριον ἐπὶ τοῖς ἴσοις πᾶσιν).

9. They also voted to restore the existing kleruchies to the former owners, and passed a law that no Athenian could cultivate land outside of Attica (ἐψηφίσαντο δὲ καὶ τὰς γενομένας κληρουχίας ἀποκαταστῆσαι τοῖς πρότερον κυρίοις γεγονόσι, καὶ νόμον ἔθεντο μηδένα τῶν Ἀθηναίων γεωργεῖν ἐκτὸς τῆς Ἀττικῆς).

10. Now many other states inclined toward the Athenians, "and those dwelling on Euboia, besides Hestiaia, first and most eagerly made alliance" (πρῶται δὲ καὶ προθυμότατα συνεμάχησαν αἱ κατὰ τὴν Εὔβοιαν οἰκοῦσαι χωρὶς Ἑστιαίας). A digression explains Hestiaia's loyalty to Sparta. Seventy states, summarizes Diodoros (cf. chapter 2), eventually joined the Athenian alliance "and participated on an equal basis in the League synedrion" (καὶ μετέσχον ἐπ' ἴσης τοῦ κοινοῦ συνεδρίου).

Item 1 refers to a reconstitution of the Theban-dominated Boiotian confederacy, formerly broken up by Sparta as being contrary to the "autonomy" provision of the King's Peace. The Athenian appeal of item 2 seems to invoke the terms of that peace. In item 3, the phrase "other islanders" must look to the League's future expansion, just as does "many states," because (except for Thebes) only Methymna is listed on the stele of the allies in the same hand as the names mentioned.

Item 4 is, of course, the establishment of the League, i.e., the conversion of the individual alliances of item 3 into a multilateral organization with a governing council (on the choosing of synedroi, see chapter 6). Item 5 must describe action taken simultaneously with, or immediately subsequent to, item 4. The "autonomy" of the King's Peace, it is asserted, is compatible with Athenian hegemony.

Item 6 is easy to translate but, for some scholars,[21] difficult to accept. However, I see no good reason to doubt that Athens and its new League made an alliance with Thebes—an alliance that at this stage did *not* involve Theban membership in the League itself. This short-lived alliance would have been made after the unofficial aid given to the Theban liberators of the Kadmeia in 379 and the punishment of the generals involved. The combination of items 1 and 5 can provide a reason for Thebes' wishing to remain outside the Athenian League: the Thebans intended to follow their traditional policy of dominating the other Boiotian cities, and they had no desire to pledge themselves to recognize the "autonomy" clause of the King's Peace.

I agree with Cawkwell that there is no reason to reject Diodoros' implication (item 7) that Sphodrias' raid came *after* the establishment of

21. See, e.g., the denials or omissions of Marshall 13 and n. 2; Beloch 3:1.146f n. 3; Cawkwell, "Found." 58 n. 3; and Ryder, KE 54 and n. 4.

the Second Athenian League. Cawkwell speculates that it was in fact the establishment of the League that prompted the raid.[22] Several suggestions—ancient and modern—have been offered for Sphodrias' motive. Perhaps Diodoros' attribution of the idea to Kleombrotos is no more than an inference from the king's known support for Sphodrias' acquittal. Xenophon, a contemporary, and one with far greater knowledge of Spartan royal intrigues—and very little love for Klemobrotos, rival of his hero Agesilaos—tells a quite circumstantial story that does not blame Kleombrotos. Instead, he reports that Sphodrias was persuaded by the Thebans—bribed, it was suspected—to make the raid.[23] There is nothing implausible about this interpretation. Athens and its League, though allied with the Thebans, would have been more interested in deterring Spartan aggression through an appearance of solidarity than in actually fighting Sparta. The Thebans knew, however, that nothing could stop Sparta from waging war on them, so they had every incentive to draw their allies into active participation. If so, their scheme worked.[24]

Item 8 indicates that a *quid pro quo* was exacted for this direct involvement. Thebes, up to this point an ally of Athens and its League, now became one of six equal members of the League itself. Contrary to the implication of Cawkwell's phrase "full membership,"[25] this was not an advancement in status for Thebes. Rather, Thebes now had to recognize Athens as its hegemon for the first time. Moreover, the Athenian League's explicit acceptance of the "autonomy" clause of the King's Peace would have compelled the Thebans—at least officially—to abandon their assertion of special status among the Boiotians.[26] The Thebans

22. Cawkwell, "Found." 51 and 55. Cf. Marshall 14; Ryder, *KE* 55; and Rice (supra n. 10) 109f, n. 34.

23. Xen. *Hell.* 5.4.20: οἱ δ' αὖ Θηβαῖοι ... πείθουσι τόν ... Σφοδρίαν, χρήματα δόντες, ὡς ὑπωπτεύετο, κτλ. Plut., *Pelop.* 14.2f and *Ages.* 24.5, essentially agrees. Xenophon's quite believable story of the maneuvering leading to Sphodrias' acquittal appears in *Hell.* 5.4.25–34.

24. Cf. Marshall 12: "It is probable that neither the Thebans nor Kleombrotos were the instigators of the attempt. The example of Phoebidas and his success were quite sufficient to induce a second Spartan commander to seek to emulate his feat." Hammond, *HG²* 483, and Ryder, *KE* 54 n. 2, make similar suggestions. Beloch, 3:1.147 n. 1, seems to think that Kleombrotos was in fact responsible, a position explicitly taken by Alexander MacDonald, "A Note on the Raid of Sphodrias," *Historia* 21 (1972) 38–44, and by Rice (supra n. 10) 109 and n. 34 and 112–115.

25. Cawkwell, "Found." 48.

26. Athens did not "enforce" the King's Peace in Spartan style by breaking up leagues, and in fact accepted the Akarnanian confederacy and the Chalkidians of Thrace into its alliance, but all sources agree that the Athenians were disturbed by Thebes' subjugation of the smaller Boiotian cities. The Boiotian Confederacy on its border was of considerably greater concern to Athens than the more distant and weaker leagues with which it was allied. Perhaps the three-man embassy to Thebes of 377 B.C. (DA, lines 72–77) was sent to dissuade the Thebans from flouting the terms of the Athenian League alliance by thus forci-

were never happy with either of these concessions; no doubt only fear of reconquest by Sparta prompted them to acquiesce. Their entire association with the Athenian League was one long process of shirking responsibilities and seeking maximum advantages for themselves. As soon as they felt strong enough (371 B.C.), they abandoned the League—a breach of the terms of this permanent alliance—and pursued the independent course they had wished to pursue all along (chapter 10). Athens in 378, however, had good reasons for negotiating with this troublesome ally. The Thebans had shown some signs of contemplating a Spartan alliance in preference to Spartan reconquest. What would be the Athenians' position if the two strongest land powers in Greece were united against them? This fear[27] explains the initial Theban alliance; Athenian desire to inhibit Theban assertiveness explains Athens's subsequent insistence on converting this alliance into Theban League membership.

I have omitted mention of the above-discussed Athenian-Theban alliance treaty (*IG* II², 40) in connection with either item 6 or item 8. The inscribed fragment probably comes from *one* of these alliances, but its condition makes it impossible definitely to determine *which*. My guess is that the fragment is from the second alliance, i.e., the Theban League membership treaty of 378. The guess is based on the fragment's apparent reference to a process for reconciling differences in inscribed stelai (lines 16f)—though if this treaty supplants the other, I see no reason why the former treaty's stele would not simply be destroyed.[28]

As Burnett cogently observes, the island allies of Athens had little to gain from the admission of Thebes to their League. The Thebans could provide them no significant naval protection, and their presence in the League would draw it into a war with Sparta. Therefore Athens had to offer the islanders something to make Thebes' entry into their synedrion palatable. That something was item 9, which appears to be a slightly confused reference to the decree of Aristoteles of spring, 377.[29] The League already had its organizational structure (items 4 and 5), but apparently only the vague "autonomy" of the King's Peace had been guaranteed to its members. Now much more specific and detailed guarantees and protections for current and prospective members were spelled out, inscribed, and publicized.

---

bly incorporating the Boiotian towns, as is suggested by Accame, 69, and Cawkwell, "Found." 49. This theory is certainly preferable to that of Burnett, "Expans." 13, which holds that specific terms of the Theban alliance were at this late date yet to be worked out.

27. Isok. 14.29 mentions the possibility of this Theban-Spartan alliance; sec. 38 shows that the same fear was operating ca. 373 B.C.

28. Note the provision of DA, lines 31–35, and see SV 293, lines 39f.

29. Burnett, "Expans." 11f. Cf. Cawkwell, "Found.," who, though agreeing that item 9 refers to the decree and showing (p. 48) that Diod. uses both the terms "kleruchy" and "law" imprecisely here, denies (p. 50 n. 1) that there is any connection between the decree and Thebes' entry into the synedrion.

Item 10 reports the success of this offer, which Burnett calls a "single, admirably conceived, Athenian diplomatic manoeuvre": the League's great period of growth ensued. As has been shown (chapter 2), Diodoros' identification of the first group of adherents after the passage of the decree is supported by the epigraphic evidence, namely, the states on (or very near) Euboia listed in lines 80–84 of the right-hand column of names below the decree, and the dated (377) League membership treaty of one of those states, Chalkis.[30] What little literary and epigraphical evidence there is for the adherence of the other allies listed on the front face of the stele of Aristoteles would allow, but would not require, the conclusion that the states listed here joined the League prior to the victory of Chabrias at Naxos in the autumn of 376. A possible problem for the generalization might seem to arise from the listing of the Kean city of Poiessa on the front face (line 82). The three other cities of the island (Ioulis, Karthaia, and Koresos) are listed together on the left side of the stele (lines 119–122), which—if the generalization just suggested is accurate—would imply that they joined the League after the battle of Naxos. Yet an Athenian inscription which looks back to earlier events apparently refers to the entry into the League of all the cities of Keos. The alternative probabilities are, either this undated inscription (most editors prefer a date in the mid-350s) loosely includes a pre-Naxos alliance with Poiessa within its reference to the post-Naxos treaty involving the other Kean cities, or Poiessa joined the League at the same (post-Naxos) time as its neighbors, but for some now unknown (honorific?) reason had its name squeezed into the space between columns on the already-filled-up front face of the stele.[31] Either alternative would allow the generalization to stand, though it remains unprovable.

All scholars agree that some of the allies listed on the left face of the stele of Aristoteles were recruited by Chabrias and Timotheos in voyages of 375 b.c. Literary or epigraphical evidence (chapter 2) for adherence during this year exists for Abdera (line 99), Akarnania (106),

30. SV 259. Schweigert, "Epigraphic Notes: 1. A Duplicate of the Treaty between Athens and Chalkis, I.G., II².44 (378/7 b.c.)," Hesperia 7 (1938) 626 says that the fragment IG II², 155 comes from a copy of SV 259. Accame, 71f, suggests that the fragment is, instead, part of a treaty of almost identical wording signed simultaneously between Athens and another Euboian city. Epigraphically, either theory is possible; Accame's seems to make better sense historically—it is difficult to see why the Athenians would want two copies of the Chalkis treaty.

31. IG II², 404 (cited by line-numbers of the text as improved by F. G. Maier; see SEG XIX, 50) refers to αἱ πόλεις αἱ ἐγ Κέω[ι] (line 8) and includes the statement that someone ἀνεγράφη [τῶν πόλ]εων ἑκάστης τὰ ὀ[νόματα ἐν τῆι στή]ληι (line 10). D. M. Lewis, "The Federal Constitution of Keos," ABSA 57 (1962) 1–4 shows reasons to suspect the existence of a Kean federation that included the other three cities while excluding Poiessa, but offers no certainty about the dates of its operation. On this inscription and others relating to Keos, see chapter 8.

Pronnoi on Kephallenia (107f), and the Epeirot kings Alketas and Neoptolemos (109f). Serious controversy exists, however, over the question of whether Timotheos added some of the listed allies to the League in 373. I have insisted that there is no epigraphic reason to believe that the names of lines 99–130 were listed at two or more times. No epigraphic considerations prevent the belief that *all* of these names (including those of some states which joined the League in 375) were listed in 373. Such a long delay, however, would seem to be unlikely (cf. the apparent rapid sequence of names listed in different hands on the front of the stele), and would itself call for an explanation. But certain literary accounts have seemed to most scholars to make necessary the positing of the listing of at least some of the names no earlier than 373. We must now examine these sources critically.

Xenophon and Diodoros agree that when Timotheos, in 374/3, was appointed general and assigned to bring aid to the Korkyraians,[32] he did not immediately set out around the Peloponnesos to reach Korkyra. Xenophon says: "Not being able to man his ships on the spot, sailing to the islands, he attempted to complete his crews there . . . ." Diodoros describes Timotheos' commission and goes on to say: "But he . . . , having sailed toward Thrace, and having summoned many states to alliance, added on thirty triremes."[33] Both accounts agree that Timotheos angered the Athenians by delaying the voyage to Korkyra. Xenophon says that he was therefore removed from his command and replaced by Iphikrates; Diodoros says that he was initially deprived of his command, "but as he sailed along to Athens, bringing a great number of ambassadors of states concluding the alliance, and having added thirty triremes . . . , the people repented and again bestowed the command on him." When Iphikrates arrives at Korkyra, Diodoros consistently has Timotheos commanding alongside him.[34]

It has always been recognized that elements of Diodoros' account are incorrect. Apollodoros, son of the banker Pasion, who had loaned Timotheos sums at various times, laid an accusation in his oration *Against Timotheos* (ca. 362), which is preserved in the Demosthenic corpus. Drawing upon written contemporary records, Apollodoros cites

32. It is routinely assumed that this aid was given because Korkyra was a member of the League and under attack, but the sources do not say so (chapter 4). I do not rule out the possibility, however, that Athens had some sort of alliance with Korkyra at about this time.

33. Xen. *Hell.* 6.2.12: ὁ δ' οὐ δυνάμενος αὐτόθεν τὰς ναῦς πληρῶσαι, ἐπὶ νήσων πλεύσας ἐκεῖθεν ἐπειρᾶτο συμπληροῦν. . . . Diod. 15.47.2: οὗτος δέ . . . πλεύσας ἐπὶ Θρᾴκης, καὶ πολλὰς πόλεις ἐπὶ συμμαχίαν προκαλεσάμενος, προσέθηκε τριάκοντα τριήρεις.

34. Xen. *Hell.* 6.2.13; Diod. 15.47.3 and 7. The translated passage is Diod. 15.47.3: ὡς δὲ παρέπλευσεν εἰς τὰς 'Αθήνας, ἄγων πρέσβεων πλῆθος τῶν τὴν συμμαχίαν συντιθεμένων καὶ τριάκοντα τριήρεις προστεθεικώς . . . , μετενόησεν ὁ δῆμος καὶ πάλιν αὐτῷ τὴν στρατηγίαν ἀποκατέστησεν.

precise Attic dates for several events connected with Timotheos' expedition. The general was at Peiraieus, ready to sail, in spring of 373. He was definitely removed from his command and subsequently tried, but (unlike his luckless treasurer) he escaped punishment because of the intercession of many relatives and friends, and of Alketas and Jason. Apollodoros also mentions one definite place which Timotheos visited prior to his recall for the trial: Kalaureia, an island off the east coast of the Peloponnesos.[35] Therefore Xenophon is right, and Diodoros is wrong, about Timotheos' fate and proabably about his direction of sailing—at least Xenophon's ἐπὶ νήσων seems more consistent with his appearance at Kalaureia than Diodoros' ἐπὶ Θρᾴκης.[36]

The question is, how much of Diodoros' account is faulty? The narrative of Xenophon does not necessarily imply any recruitment of new allies in 373. It would be more logical, as Burnett and Edmonson have suggested, to seek crew members among the citizens of existing allies.[37] Should Diodoros' "many" new allies and his twice-repeated thirty triremes be simply dismissed as fictional? Accame thinks so,[38] but a less extreme alternative seems to me preferable. Diodoros' source was, after all, probably correct in attributing the recruitment of many League allies to Timotheos. Contemporary authors seem to include this among his accomplishments, though their phrasing cannot be certainly said to require it.[39] The points that are more doubtful are exact numbers, geographical area(s) of recruitment, and reliable dates for the adherence of all except the few allies definitely connected with his western expedition of 375. Aside from the cited Diodoran passage, no source would require

35. [Dem.] 49.6 (date when ready to sail, i.e., Mounychion, tenth month of the Attic year 374/3), 9f (intercession; see also Nep. *Timoth.* 4.2f, and chapter 5), and 13f (Kalaureia). Plut. *Dem.* 15.1 says that Apollodoros won his case and that Demosthenes himself wrote the speech; scholars generally doubt the latter statement.

36. Marshall, 68f, combines the accounts of Xenophon and Diodoros without trying to reconcile their differences (but note the apologetic tone in p. 69 n. 3). Sealey, "Transf." 100, attempts to reconcile the accounts by arguing that Timotheos made *two* voyages in 373, citing the phrase of [Dem.] 49.6: "this man Timotheos, being about to sail on his second voyage . . . " (μέλλων ἐκπλεῖν τὸν ὕστερον ἔκπλουν Τιμόθεος οὑτοσί . . .). But Woodhead, "Allies" 261, is surely correct in insisting that the "first" expedition was Timotheos' original voyage around the Peloponnesos in 375; Sealey, *City-Sts.* 416–419, seems to have abandoned the "two voyages" position.

37. B&E 82.

38. Accame 101 and n. 3.

39. Xen. *Hell.* 5.4.64 says that Timotheos' generous treatment of Korkyra made all the nearby states more friendly (εὐμενεστέρας) toward Athens. Isok. 15.107 says that in several regions, Timotheos' conquest of key cities compelled all the surrounding territory to become connected (οἰκεῖος) with Athens. Both these passages can be given a less "friendly" reading, drawing the inference that only the acquisition of subject territories is being discussed, and not also the addition of new allies. Ais. 2.70 definitely credits Timotheos with bringing seventy-five allied states (πόλεις συμμαχίδας) into the synedrion, but the excessively large number (chapter 2) casts some doubt on this source as well.

acceptance of the suggestion that Timotheos (or Chabrias) recruited any of the states listed in lines 99–130 later than 375. No evidence exists, either, for the later recruitment of any of them by anyone else. The cities of Kephallenia which Iphikrates "subdued" (καταστρεψάμενος) in 373/2 did not become League members: their names do not appear on the stele. After another stop at Kephallenia, where some cities were still unfriendly, Iphikrates "prepared to do harm to the territory of the Lakedaimonians and, of the other enemy states being in that region, to win over those that were willing, and to make war on those which were not persuaded." These plans were clearly never carried out, because Athens and Sparta made peace in summer, 371.[40] All the names inscribed (apparently by a single hand) in lines 99–130 of the stele of Aristoteles, therefore, can be believed to have been inscribed in 375 B.C., without calling into question any of the ancient testimonia except the date of one passage in Diodoros. It has been suggested that in this episode he is following an unreliable apologetic life of Timotheos.[41] Even if he is following his usual source for the period, Ephoros, that author apparently did not organize his history according to strict chronology. Known examples abound of Diodoros' placing of events in the wrong years. Others, where parallel accounts are lacking, must have gone undetected.[42] Probably this is one such passage.

Since Athens and Sparta made peace in 375/4, it seems entirely logical that the adherence of new League members would slow to a trickle thereafter. I suggest that in fact only two more members were ever added: two democratic factions, those of (probably) Thera and of Zakynthos, inscribed in different unique hands in lines 97f and 131–134 on the left face of the stele of Aristoteles, respectively. Both these islands had historic connections with Sparta, yet both had been Athenian allies at times within the fifth century.[43] Diodoros, after describing the peace agreement of 375/4 and then commenting on aggressive Theban activities, turns to a description of general unrest and internal strife in Greece, especially in the Peloponnesos. After a digression on events in Egypt, he resumes this narrative, observing that in the states troubled by internal disorders, "the Lakedaimonians gave aid to those establishing oligarchies and the Athenians fought on behalf of those holding to democ-

---

40. Xen. *Hell.* 6.2.33 (cities subdued) and 38 (translated passage: παρεσκευάζετο τήν τε τῶν Λακεδαιμονίων χώραν κακῶς ποιεῖν καὶ τῶν ἄλλων τῶν κατ᾽ ἐκεῖνα πόλεων πολεμίων οὐσῶν τὰς μὲν ἐθελούσας προσλαμβάνειν, τοῖς δὲ μὴ πειθομένοις πολεμεῖν); the effect of the peace on Iphikrates' plans is made explicit in 6.3.3 (see Plut. *Ages.* 28.5 for the date of the peace). Cf. the interpretations of Beloch, 3:2.161, and Sealey, "Transf." 108 (perhaps modified in *City-Sts.* 419).

41. B&E, 82 n. 21, commenting: "his entire treatment of the events of 373 is filled with falsehoods."

42. Another such episode may appear in Diod. 15.95.3 (chapter 10).

43. Xen. *Hell.* 6.2.3; Diod. 15.45.4; Thuc. 2.9.4; *ATL* I.285; Meiggs, *AE* 321.

racy." This general situation appears, at first glance, to be presented as the cause of renewed war. The democratic uprising on Zakynthos is mentioned in Diodoros' narrative after the general breakdown of the peace, and could be seen as a consequence, rather than as a principal cause of that breakdown. But Diodoros goes on to say that Timotheos aided the popular faction and established its partisans at a base on the island (which, he says, they named "Arkadia"), and that when the Spartans heard of this (from the ruling Zakynthian oligarchs), "they first, sending ambassadors to Athens, accused Timotheos, but as they saw that the demos inclined toward the exiles," they sent a fleet to assist their Zakynthian allies.[44] If Athens and Sparta were already at war, there would have been little point in the Spartans' sending ambassadors (not heralds, incidentally) to Athens to complain of Timotheos' conduct. No doubt, then, his actions on Zakynthos provided the specific occasion for the renewal of hostilities—his actions and whatever action by the Athenian demos is implied by Diodoros' phrase "inclined toward the exiles." What he probably means is the admission of the Zakynthian democrats to the Second Athenian League, and presumably the fairly immediate listing of the faction in lines 131–134 of the League stele.

Xenophon, though mentioning no series of internal conflicts, nor in fact any other events after the signing of the peace of 375/4, explicitly attributes the renewal of war to Timotheos' giving assistance to certain Zakynthian exiles. In his account, the Spartans are not said to have sent any complaint to Athens, but to have decided immediately (εὐθύς) that the Athenians were guilty of wrongdoing; their military response follows directly.[45] Though the terseness of the contemporary account of Xenophon may create some misgivings, and some problems in dating the peace of 375/4 itself with precision (chapter 1), there seems to be no good reason to deny the identity of the Zakynthian factions of Diodoros, Xenophon, and the stele of Aristoteles. The most reasonable date for its League membership, and its listing (a lapse of time between them would serve no apparent purpose), would appear to be sometime in 374.[46]

Both narrative sources describe Athenian and Spartan participation in factional strife on Korkyra as being roughly simultaneous with their

44. Diod. 15.40 and 45.1–4; translations from 15.45.1 (τοῖς μὲν τὰς ὀλιγαρχίας κατασκευάζουσιν ἐβοήθουν οἱ Λακεδαιμόνιοι, τοῖς δὲ τῆς δημοκρατίας ἀντεχομένοις συνεμάχουν οἱ Ἀθηναῖοι) and 4 (τὸ μὲν πρῶτον εἰς τὰς Ἀθήνας ἀποστείλαντες πρέσβεις κατηγόρουν τοῦ Τιμοθέου· ὡς δ' ἐθεώρουν τὸν δῆμον ἀποκλίνοντα πρὸς τοὺς φυγάδας, κτλ).

45. Xen. Hell. 6.2.2f.

46. See the various theories of, e.g., Marshall 66; Beloch 3:2.156; Accame 86; Sealey, "Transf." 105f; and Cawkwell, "Peace" 88. It seems pointless to argue whether the outbreak of war in the west would contradict the phrase εἰρήνης οὔσης in a Boiotian context in 373 (Isok. 14.1 and 5). Acceptance of a date of 373, or even 372, for the events on Zakynthos would cause no problems for the general hypothesis advanced here, namely, that the

conflict on Zakynthos. Having argued (chapter 2) that the Korkyraians were not listed on the stele and were not members of the League, I deal with this conflict elsewhere (chapter 4). Neither Xenophon nor Diodoros —nor any other extant source—mentions similar strife on Thera. Since, however, the most likely restoration of lines 97f of the League stele seems to be [Θη]ραίων / [ὁ δ]ῆμος, a date for the accession and listing of this faction must also be suggested. The only clue is quite indirect, namely the observation that the Athenians' acceptance of the Zakyn-thian faction into their League prompted the above-described strong reaction from Sparta. One would expect that such a reaction would follow from the enrolling of the *first* democratic faction of a state whose oligarchical government was loyal to Sparta, not from the second. The adding of the Theraian(?) faction, which seemingly elicited no notice from contemporary historians, must have occurred in the wake of the enlisting of the Zakynthians, probably very soon afterward, as part of the same general movement. Under this interpretation, which does no violence to the epigraphic evidence, both factions probably would have been listed as League members within the year 374 B.C.

The fact that *only* two factions apparently joined the League also ac-cords well with the literary evidence. The Athenian League had over-played its hand.[47] Sparta had been compelled to agree to the peace of 375/4, and to recognize Athens as joint hegemon of Greece. But the Spartans had no intention of watching the League subvert the friendly oligarchies of its traditional client states one by one, giving recognition, League membership, and support to the democratic factions in these states. So the peace in which Athens had greatly rejoiced[48] came to a premature end. Once again, however, the Athenians proved capable of learning from their mistakes. No more factions were added to the League, and in fact no more additions were made at all. The Athenians and their allies might still resist the Spartans in factional struggles when called upon, as at Korkyra, but a retreat was made from rhetoric and provocation. Even if one or more new alliances were signed at this time (chapter 4), they were no longer League membership alliances. Athens and its League might pledge to defend a friendly state if attacked, but the Spartans were not further affronted by the adding of more members to the confederacy organized against them. This lowering in tone, no doubt

---

League's membership was complete before the cessation of conflict with Sparta in 371. The problem such later dates cause for those who suggest them is that Timotheos is known to have been in western waters in 375/4, whereas he had already been removed from com-mand when Athenian forces reached the area in 373 or 372—unless one is willing to believe Diodoros' story about his reinstatement.

47. The summary here has certain features in common with the account of Ryder, *KE* 60f.

48. Isok. 15.109f; Nep. *Timoth.* 2.2f.

partly promoted by Athens's growing uneasiness about the increasing pretensions of its refractory ally Thebes, helped the Athenians and the Spartans agree on peace in 371. Henceforth Athenian and Spartan policy would be largely in accord; the danger posed by Sparta to Athenian interests had passed. The Second Athenian League had fulfilled its original purpose.

The Thebans' surprise victory at Leuktra in the summer of 371 removed even the possibility of a further Spartan threat to Athens's position. When Athens hosted the second peace conference of 371, it acted as the unquestioned hegemon of Greece, and claimed for itself and its League the kind of authority the Great King had assumed in 386 (chapter 1). The members of the League now constituted the privileged inner circle of Greek politics. In succeeding years, friendly states would ally themselves with Athens and the League, but they would no longer be invited to join it. The League members had no need to share their authority and privileges. The Athenians had no need to offer concessions and make promises to prospective allies, as had been necessary in the dark days of Spartan assertiveness. Trouble loomed with rebel League member Thebes, but in the peace of Athens of 371 the first period of the history of the League ended on a triumphant note.

4

ALLIES OF ATHENS
AND THE LEAGUE

The nature of the connection of the island state of Korkyra with the League is problematical. An Athenian inscription definitely dated to 375 B.C. directs the secretary of the boule to inscribe the names of the Korkyraians, Akarnanians, and Kephallenians on the common stele of the allies and to administer the proper oaths to their ambassadors and to Athenian and League officials, and calls on the three states to send synedroi. In short, it definitely deals with the process of their joining the League. Moreover, a second inscription, extremely well preserved, is explicitly an "Alliance of (the) Korkyraians and Athenians for all time." Finally, an inscription in letters appropriate to the first half of the fourth century on a stele in the Kerameikos cemetery in Athens commemorates two Korkyraian ambassadors who died during their mission and were given a public funeral by the Athenians.[1] The combination of these inscriptions and the putative listing of the demos of Korkyra in lines 97f of the stele of the decree of Aristoteles made it an inevitable conclusion that the Korkyraians joined the Athenian League in 375.

But the observations of Bradeen and Coleman (chapter 2), which show conclusively that [Κερκυ]ραίων / [ὁ δ]ῆμος is an impossible restoration in the list of names on the left side of the stele, have thrown the entire supposition of Korkyra's League membership into doubt. For geographical and chronological reasons, Korkyra should not have been one of the names lost from the front face of the stele,[2] nor could it have been the name erased in the list on the left side.[3] Consequently, the Korkyraians were not listed at all, which means that they did not become members of the League. Furthermore, although "the Kephallenians" were in the process of joining the League, only Pronnoi, one of the four cities on the island, is listed on the stele of Aristoteles (lines 107f). The necessary inference from these omissions is that the treaty of 375 was partially aborted (chapter 6). The connection of the epitaph of the Korkyraian ambassadors with their state's joining the League in 375 has also now been quite literally undermined. Recent excavations have

---

1. *SV* 262 and 263 and *IG* II², 5224, respectively.

2. DA, lines 85–90 comm.; cf. B&C 102 n. 6: "With the elimination of Kerkyra from the left side, it seems most likely that Marshall was right and that an earlier treaty with Kerkyra was recorded on the front of the stele. Otherwise we must assume that for some unknown reason the city was not listed even though the alliance was made."

3. Κορκυραῖοι or Κερκυραῖοι would be too long for the *rasura* of approximately 6 spaces in line 111.

shown that the fourth-century commemorative stele is a refurbished version of a monument to two *fifth*-century ambassadors buried under it.[4]

One must still explain the Athens-Korkyra treaty of perpetual alliance. It has been described conventionally as one of three separate treaties envisioned by the agreement made between the Athenians and the three western states in 375 (the Kephallenian and Akarnanian alliance treaties having been lost). Supposedly the Korkyra treaty spells out the "precise conditions" of Korkyra's membership in the League; its date is also a direct inference from its supposed connection with the 375 agreement, since the alliance treaty itself lacks any notation of date.[5] But all these inferences are weak. The phrasing of the Korkyra-Akarnania-Kephallenia agreement would not in any way call for the drawing up of such separate treaties for the three states. It encompasses within itself the necessary elements of their League membership, provided only that the required procedures are carried to completion; in the cases of Korkyra and the Kephallenian cities other than Pronnoi, they apparently were not. Nor is there anything very "precise" or unique about the terms of the extant Korkyraian treaty, if indeed it should be a League membership treaty. Its virtually complete text includes only pledges of mutual defense and promises to be guided by the resolutions of the Athenians and a majority of their allies, followed by oaths confirming these mutual obligations and appropriate blessing and curse formulae; no proposer, ambassador, or any other person is mentioned. The alliance would in fact have been essentially redundant and pointless if it were signed at the same time as the 375 treaty. The consensus date is therefore perhaps the least appropriate date of all. To find a date and a context for this alliance, we must turn to the literary sources.

The sources that specifically describe the accomplishments of the Athenian general Timotheos in the area of Korkyra in 375 use phraseology the precision of which is significant. Xenophon's account goes as follows:

ὁ μέντοι Τιμόθεος περιπλεύσας Κέρκυραν μὲν εὐθὺς ὑφ' ἑαυτῷ ἐποιήσατο· οὐ μέντοι ἠνδραποδίσατο οὐδὲ ἄνδρας ἐφυγάδευσεν οὐδὲ νόμους μετέστησεν· ἐξ ὧν τὰς περὶ ἐκεῖνα πόλεις πάσας εὐμενεστέρας ἔσχεν.

4. The connection is suggested, e.g., in Tod 126 comm., but nothing about the text of the epigram makes the connection necessary:

> Ἐνθάδε Θέρσανδρον καὶ Σιμύλον, ἄνδρε ποθεινὼ
> πατρίδι Κερκύραι, δέξατο γαῖα τάφωι·
> πρέσβες ἐλθόντας, κατὰ συντυχίαν δὲ θανόντας,
> παῖδες Ἀθηναίων δημοσίαι κτέρισαν.

Ursula Knigge, "Untersuchungen bei den Gesandtstelen im Kerameikos zu Athen," *AA* (1972) 591–602 shows that the fourth-century memorial commemorates two men who probably formed part of the embassy described in Thuc. 1.31ff; artifacts found in the graves establish the fifth-century date.

5. See, e.g., Tod 127 comm.; *SV* 263 comm.; *WV* 26 intro.

Now Timotheos, having sailed around (the Peloponnesos), immediately made Korkyra subject to himself; he did not, however, enslave the people or send men into exile or alter the laws, for which (reasons) he made all the states around it more friendly.[6]

Xenophon is hardly describing the recruitment of a League ally. If he were, it would not have occurred to him to point out that Timotheos did not enslave or banish citizens of the allied state or change its government. The decree of Aristoteles, published two years earlier, had guaranteed potential members of the League that they would suffer no such treatment, and many states had already joined the League on this understanding. Xenophon's point can only be that Timotheos was showing unusual generosity to a *conquered* state.

Isokrates, another contemporary, supports this interpretation, as he summarizes Timotheos' accomplishments in *Antidosis* (ca. 354–3 B.C.):

... τοσαύτας ᾔρηκεν πόλεις κατὰ κράτος ὅσας οὐδεὶς πώποτε τῶν ἐστρα-
τηγηκότων ..., καὶ τούτων ἐνίας ὧν ληφθεισῶν ἅπας ὁ τόπος ὁ περιέχων οἰκεῖος
ἠναγκάσθη τῇ πόλει γενέσθαι· τηλικαύτην ἑκάστη δύναμιν εἶχεν. τίς γὰρ οὐκ οἶδεν
Κόρκυραν μὲν ἐν ἐπικαιροτάτῳ καὶ κάλλιστα κειμένην τῶν περὶ Πελοπόννησον, Σάμον
δὲ ἐν Ἰωνίᾳ, Σηστὸν δὲ καὶ Κριθώτην τῶν ἐν Ἑλλησπόντῳ, Ποτείδαιαν δὲ καὶ Το-
ρώνην τῶν ἐπὶ Θράκης;

. . . He has taken so many states by force, such as no one ever of those who have been generals . . . , and upon some of these being taken, all the area around was compelled to become connected with the city (i.e., Athens), each had such importance. For who does not know that Korkyra was most strategically and best situated of those (states) around the Peloponnesos, and Samos in Ionia, and Sestos and Krithote of those on the Hellespont, and Poteidaia and Torone of those toward Thrace?[7]

It could have been considered rather anomalous that this passage grouped "League member" Korkyra with all these states "taken by force" and not listed on the stele of Aristoteles; this problem now disappears.

Later sources mostly share the careful language of the contemporary authors. Cornelius Nepos describes Timotheos' accomplishments of 375 as follows:

. . . circumvehens Peloponnesum, . . . Corcyram sub imperium Atheniensium redegit sociosque idem adiunxit Epirotas, Athamanas, Chaonas omnesque eas gentes, quae mare illud adiacent.

. . . Sailing around the Peloponnesos, . . . he brought Korkyra back under the control of the Athenians, and he also added as allies the Epeirots, Athamanes, Chaones, and all those people who live next to that sea.[8]

6. Xen. *Hell.* 5.4.64.
7. Isok. 15.107f; see also [Dem.] 13.22.
8. Nep. *Timoth.* 2.1.

Diodoros' account of Timotheos' expedition says:

Τιμόθεος δὲ παραλαβὼν τὴν ναυαρχίαν καὶ πλεύσας εἰς τὴν Κεφαληνίαν, τάς τ' ἐν αὐτῇ πόλεις προσηγάγετο καὶ τὰς κατὰ τὴν 'Ακαρνανίαν ὁμοίως ἔπεισεν ἀποκλῖναι πρὸς 'Αθηναίους. 'Αλκέταν τε τὸν Μολοττῶν βασιλέα φίλον κατασκευάσας, καὶ καθόλου τὰς πλείστας τῶν περὶ τοὺς τόπους ἐκείνους πόλεων ἐξιδιοποιησάμενος, ἐνίκησε ναυμαχίᾳ τοὺς Λακεδαιμονίους περὶ Λευκάδα.

Timotheos, taking over the naval command and sailing to Kephallenia, won over the cities on it and likewise persuaded those in Akarnania to be favorable toward the Athenians. Having made Alketas, king of the Molossians, a friend, and generally having won over most of the states around those places, he defeated the Lakedaimonians in a sea battle near Leukas.[9]

The omission of any mention of Korkyra from this account, which has caused scholars to discount its reliability,[10] is, on the contrary, the proverbial exception that proves the rule: Diodoros is discussing new League members recruited by Timotheos, and Korkyra was not one of them. Only Polyainos describes Korkyra as an Athenian ally in a context which appears to fit 375 B.C., referring to Timotheos as having fought a sea battle "with (the) Korkyraians and the other allies."[11] It is easier, however, to believe that Polyainos made a careless slip than that the other cited sources are united in error.

Apparently the Athenians gave the conquered Korkyraians the opportunity to join the Athenian League in 375, but for some reason the agreement fell through, and the island remained under rather loose Athenian domination until after the signing of the peace of 375/4. After a period of widespread internecine strife, and after Athenian involvement in factional politics on Zakynthos, both Xenophon and Diodoros describe Spartan intrigues directed against Korkyra, which apparently was governed by an Athenian-imposed democracy. Again, the phrasing of both accounts is significant. Xenophon says that the Spartans appealed to their ally Dionysios of Syracuse for aid in this enterprise by arguing that "it would also be advantageous to him that Korkyra should not be under Athenian control." The Korkyraians themselves, in his account, did not appeal to Athens for help on the basis of any alliance, but warned "that they (the Athenians) would throw away a great advantage if they should be deprived of Korkyra."[12] Diodoros, in telling of the Athenians' send-

9. Diod. 15.36.5.
10. See, e.g., Accame 90: "Riguardo alla spedizione di Timoteo nell' Ionio Diodoro sunteggia malamente la fonte; non parla di Corcira. . . . "
11. Polyain. 3.10.16: Τιμόθεος μετὰ Κερκυραίων καὶ τῶν ἄλλων συμμάχων πρὸς Λακεδαιμονίους ναυμαχῶν. . . . Ais. 3.243 says only that Timotheos had been honored διὰ τὸν περίπλουν τὸν εἰς Κέρκυραν. Dein. 1.14 and 3.17 says he won a victory at Korkyra.
12. Xen. Hell. 6.2.4: καὶ ἐκείνῳ χρήσιμον εἴη τὴν Κέρκυραν μὴ ὑπ' 'Αθηναίοις εἶναι; and sec. 9: ὡς μέγα μὲν ἀγαθὸν ἀποβάλοιεν ἄν, εἰ Κερκύρας στερηθεῖεν. Cf. Beloch 3:1.157: "Kerkyra wandte sich . . . um Bundeshilfe nach Athen. . . . "

ing aid to Korkyra, likewise omits any mention of a preexisting alliance. Very possibly, however, this crisis did prompt Athens to make an alliance with the Korkyraians. Diodoros' statement that after the Korkyraian appeal Timotheos sailed toward Thrace πρὸ τῆς συμμαχίας ταύτης generally has been translated in some roundabout way, e.g., the Loeb edition's "before intervening in their favour," probably on the assumption that Korkyra had been an Athenian ally since 375. But the phrase could mean, more literally, "before this alliance," i.e., a new non-League membership alliance of 374/3, had been concluded.[13] Such an interpretation would be consistent with the statement of Apollodoros that, at about the time Timotheos was recalled for trial in 373, "the allies around the Peloponnesos were being besieged by the Lakedaimonians."[14]

The foregoing discussion should finally make it possible to examine the Athens-Korkyra alliance treaty in full perspective. Omitting the oaths of the Athenians (lines 16–26) and of the Korkyraians (lines 27–38), the complete, well preserved text says:

Συμμαχία Κορκυραίων καὶ 'Αθηναίων εἰς
τὸν ἀεὶ χρόνον. ἐάν τις ἴηι ἐ[πὶ] πολέμωι ε-
[ἰ]ς τ[ὴ]γ χώραν τὴγ Κορκυραίων ἢ ἐπὶ τὸν δῆμον τὸγ Κορκυραίων, βοηθεῖν 'Αθηναίος π-
5   αντὶ σθένει, καθότι ἂν ἐπαγγέλλωσιν Κορκυραῖοι, κατὰ τὸ δυνατόν· καὶ ἐάν τις ἐπ-
ὶ τὸν δῆμον τὸν 'Αθηναίων ἢ ἐπὶ τὴγ χώραν
τὴν 'Αθηναίων ἐπὶ πολέμωι ἴηι ἢ κατὰ γῆν
ἢ κατὰ θάλατταν, βοηθεῖν Κορκυραίος πα-
10   ντὶ σθένει κατὰ τὸ δυνατόν, καθότι ἂν [ἐ]π-
αγγέλλωσιν 'Αθηναῖοι. πό[λ]ε[μ]ον δὲ καὶ εἰρήνην μὴ ἐξεῖναι Κορκυραίοις ποιήσασθαι [ἄ]νευ 'Αθηναίων καὶ [τοῦ π]λήθους τῶν σ-
υμμάχων· ποιεῖν δὲ καὶ τἆλλα κατὰ τὰ δόγ-
15   ματα τῶν συμμάχων. Ὅρκος·

Alliance of (the) Korkyraians and Athenians for all time. If anyone comes f[or] war i[nt]o t[h]e territory of the Korkyraians or against the demos of the Korkyraians, (the) Athenians are to give aid in full strength, just as (the) Korkyraians request, so far as possible. And if anyone comes for war against the demos of the Athenians or against the territory of the Athenians either by land or by sea, (the) Korkyraians are to give aid in full strength so far as possible, just as (the) Athenians [r]equest. W[a]r and peace are not permitted to be made by the Korkyraians [wi]thout (the) Athenians and [the m]ajority of the allies. They are also to do other things according to the dogmata of the allies. Oath:[15]

13. Diod. 15.46.1–3 and 47.1–7 (quoted phrase in 47.2).
14. [Dem.] 49.13: πολιορκεῖσθαι δὲ τοὺς περὶ Πελοπόννησον συμμάχους ὑπὸ Λακεδαιμονίων.
15. SV 263, lines 1–15.

It is quite possible that this exact phrasing was employed in the non-League membership alliance which, as suggested above, the Korkyraians and Athenians may have signed in 374/3. But the unusual absence of any dating formula may suggest another interpretation. The omission of date was not due to haste, for this inscription is cut on a rather ornate stele topped by a relief sculpture.[16] The phrasing of the treaty itself provides a clue. In the early days of their League, the Athenians consistently paid deference to the terms of the King's Peace. That settlement permitted the signing of defensive alliances, such as those made with members of the League. But the King's Peace as originally understood probably would not have allowed Athens and a majority of its allies to presume to determine when an allied state should make war, or to forbid it to make peace—as this treaty provides (lines 11–14). This provision and the general clause recognizing the League's authority which follows it (lines 14f) show the same subtle shift in emphasis and meaning as was shown in the phrasing of the oath associated with the peace of Athens of 371 (quoted in chapter 1). An agreement including such phrasing might reasonably be dated to about the same time.

Consider the following scenario. The Athenians, having seen that granting League membership to democratic factions on Zakynthos and Thera(?) provoked renewed war with Sparta, would not permit the demos of Korkyra to join their League (as had earlier been contemplated), but they did respond to Korkyraian requests for assistance against Spartan incursions with a non-League defensive alliance in 374 or 373. This alliance treaty either was not inscribed, or was hastily, and perhaps sloppily, inscribed on a stone not now extant. In 371, Korkyraian representatives presumably came to Athens, along with representatives from many other states, to take the oath associated with the peace. At this time, these representatives may have hired a mason to inscribe a neat copy of their alliance with Athens and its League on a new, decorative stele; perhaps the terms of the alliance and its oaths were slightly updated to take account of the new hegemonic position asserted by Athens and the League in connection with the peace they were sponsoring. Since the Korkyraian alliance (even if thus slightly updated) was not new, it may not have seemed appropriate to date the text as of the time of inscribing it; but it may have seemed equally inappropriate to put an old date on the neat new stele. The alliance being

16. The omission of date is rare but not unique; cf., e.g., *SV* 223. A photograph of the entire stele of *SV* 263 appears in J. N. Svoronos, *Das Athener Nationalmuseum: Phototypische Wiedergabe seiner Schätze mit erläuterndem Text* II (Athens 1913?) plate CIII, mus. no. 1467; the stele is described in *ib.*, I.588–591, entry no. 240. The form of the stele does not help in dating it very precisely: it closely resembles both *IG* II², 212 (346 B.C.) and *IG* II², 1392 (398/7 B.C.); Svoronos has photos of these in plates CIV (mus. no. 1471) and CVIII (mus. no. 1482), respectively.

both current and permanent, it might have seemed perfectly reasonable simply to omit the date, and all other "extraneous" limiting matter, entirely. One could (but need not) take this scenario even further, and suggest that the visiting Korkyraian ambassadors took this same occasion (371) to refurbish the monument dedicated to their fifth-century predecessors, commissioning another similar ornate stele.[17]

Many inferences are obviously involved in the foregoing reconstruction, though, unlike other published reconstructions, it at least uses all the epigraphic and literary evidence (save only one date implicit in Polyainos) in an organic and consistent way. In any event, the fundamental conclusion is irrepressible: the sources do not show that Korkyra joined the Second Athenian League; in fact, they imply the contrary.

This conclusion has certain direct consequences for an interpretation of the history of Athens's relations with the members of its League. Cawkwell, e.g., dates the renewal of war between Athens and Sparta after the peace of 375/4 to the sending of a Spartan expedition against Korkyra, "since an attack on a member of the Second Athenian Confederacy must have been regarded in Athens as constituting a state of war between Athens and Sparta." Xenophon's account, which describes this incident, therefore makes the duration of the peace too short, Cawkwell thinks, and so he is led to revise Xenophon's chronology. In point of fact, however, neither Xenophon nor Diodoros indicates that the Spartan attack on Korkyra is the event which reopens hostilities.[18] The interpretation is purely a modern inference from the supposed League membership of Korkyra. Similarly, the misconduct of the Athenian general Chares on Korkyra, often cited as evidence of Athenian abuse of League members and perhaps as a direct cause of the outbreak of the Social War, now also requires reinterpretation.[19] The alliance undoubtedly signed between Athens and Korkyra[20] was, I believe, the first of a new type of which we have several later examples, an "alliance with Athens and its League." Let us turn now to survey, in much less detail, these other examples.

In 373, says Xenophon, Iphikrates sailed to Korkyra, "having subdued the cities in Kephallenia." This summary statement probably excludes Pronnoi, a League member. Somewhat later, Xenophon tells us that Iphikrates, having gathered a fleet elsewhere, "sailing first to Keph-

17. The commemorative stele (see Pfohl, plate 5, for a clear photo) does not have a carved relief, but includes a large flat panel above the inscription, upon which some scene was probably painted.

18. Cawkwell, "Peace" 85f (quotation from p. 85). The Korkyra campaign is described in Xen. *Hell.* 6.2.2–38 and Diod. 15.45–47; both authors attribute the renewal of war to events on Zakynthos (chapter 3).

19. Diod. 15.95.3; I believe the incident may also be misdated (see chapter 10).

20. To the sources already cited, add Dem. 24.202 and 18.234 and 237.

allenia, exacted money, some from the willing, some from the unwilling."[21] The cities described as "willing" probably included Pronnoi and one or more of the other three towns (Same, Kranioi, and Pale) on the island, which by this time (372) perhaps had made some sort of alliance with Athens. A very fragmentary inscription has long been connected with this probable alliance. Accepting the scholarly consensus that this inscription is a treaty with some or all of the Kephallenian cities, it is nevertheless necessary to deny the customary deduction that the inscription and the Xenophontic passages cited above provide evidence that these cities entered the Athenian League. Their absence from the stele of Aristoteles is decisive against that interpretation, and the suggested date of their alliance (373 or 372) falls at a time when all additions to the League apparently had ceased (chapter 3). Though contextual support is lacking for Wilhelm's commonly accepted restoration of a provision within the treaty that in certain circumstances the "[---Kephall]enians [are to give aid] just like [the other allies]," it does seem likely that this agreement was not a bilateral treaty, but an alliance with Athens and the League, comparable to the one signed with Korkyra in this same general period.[22]

Leukas fought on the Spartan side against the Athenians as late as 373 B.C.[23] A fragmentary inscription exists, however, which indicates a friendly relationship between Athens and Leukas. The upper part of the stele is broken away, leaving a text beginning with the names of certain Athenian magistrates and Leukadian oath-takers. Then, starting in the sixth extant line, a formula yielding a date of 368 introduces a separate resolution whose content is almost entirely lost. As editors admit, we cannot tell whether this mutilated inscription deals with a peace treaty or an alliance.[24] It is not even certain that the agreement involving the oaths was made prior to the resolution of 368 that follows it on the stone: an Athenian inscription is extant in which a decree dated to 367 provides for inscribing *below* it a resolution of 369/8 on a similar subject.[25] A Spartan ally presumably would not be allowed to make a bilat-

21. Xen. *Hell.* 6.2.33: καταστρεψάμενος δὲ τὰς ἐν τῇ Κεφαλληνίᾳ πόλεις; and sec. 38: πρῶτον μὲν εἰς Κεφαλληνίαν πλεύσας χρήματα ἐπράξατο, τὰ μὲν παρ' ἑκόντων, τὰ δὲ παρ' ἀκόντων.

22. *SV* 267; those inferring that this is a League membership alliance treaty include Beloch 3:1.160 n. 1 and 3:2.161f, and Accame 105. See also Schweigert, "Greek Inscriptions: 33. A New Fragment of the Treaty between Athens and Kephallenia," *Hesperia* 9 (1940) 321–324. The translated passage reads: [---βοηθεῖν Κεφα/λλ]ῆνας καθάπερ [οἱ ἄλλοι σύμμαχ/οι] (lines 7–9); the situation implied by the inscription would seem to resemble the situation of the cited passages of Xenophon, if editors have properly restored "[. . . so long as the wa]r goes on" ([---ἕως ἂν ὁ πόλεμ]/ος ἦι) in lines 19f, though other appropriate contexts could also perhaps be suggested.

23. Xen. *Hell.* 6.2.3 and 26.

24. *SV* 278 and comm.; Tod 134 comm.

25. *IG* II², 107; cf. the more regular order of, e.g., *IG* II², 1.

eral peace agreement with Athens when the two hegemones were at war, and would have no need to do so when they were at peace. For reasons suggested below, a Spartan ally should not have had to make a separate alliance treaty with the Athenian League in the period 369–362/1, and no such treaty is attested. I am inclined to believe that the inscription was an alliance (not a peace treaty), and that it was made before 368, probably in the late 370s. But I disagree with those who describe it as a League membership alliance,[26] again because of the absence of the name of Leukas on the League stele: the decree of Aristoteles specified that all League members were to be inscribed thereon. No real clues exist for determining whether the alliance with Leukas belongs among the alliances discussed in this chapter or among the bilateral alliances of chapter 5. I place it here only because of the type of state involved (a Greek πόλις) and the suggested date.

The peace of Athens of 371 deserves consideration here, because certain scholars persist in believing, with H. Swoboda (1894) that this agreement was not a restatement of the common peace, but the formation of a large alliance.[27] Athens is sometimes said to have attempted, successfully or unsuccessfully, to lure away the Peloponnesian states from their recently defeated hegemon, Sparta; some who believe this effort was successful think that the Peloponnesians at this time actually became members of Athens's League.[28] But such inferences unnecessarily create a great many problems for these scholars when they have to explain the Athenian-Spartan alliance of 369 (v. infra). Xenophon, moreover, makes it clear that the agreement of 371 was a peace with sanctions, not an alliance, and that Sparta must have been among the participants. A decisive refutation of several mistaken reconstructions is made by Marta Sordi, and her essential findings are repeated in concise English by Ryder.[29] Nothing about the peace treaty, of course, would

26. E.g., Marshall 83 and Tod 134 comm. The fact that Athens had to make an alliance with Leukas in the final years of its struggle with Philip (Dem. 18.237) puts no restrictions on the nature of this earlier agreement; many alliances by that time had been made and broken, and several were reestablished (chapter 10).

27. Swoboda, "Der hellenische Bund des Jahres 371 v. Chr.," *RhM* 49 (1894) 329–352.

28. See, e.g., Marshall 79 and Accame 162. Beloch, 3:1.173f and n. 2, though showing the weakness in Swoboda's argument, nonetheless asserts that Athens victimized Sparta at this peace conference; Sealey, "Callistratos of Aphidna and His Contemporaries," *Historia* 5 (1956) 193 refers to Athens's "abortive attempt" to absorb the members of the Peloponnesian League into its own.

29. Xen. *Hell.* 6.5.1–5, 10, and 33–37. Bengtson, *SV* 270 comm., calls the agreement a common peace and says that Sparta took part; Hammond, *HG²* 495 says that the states participating in the peace (not including Sparta) made a defensive alliance with the League, but did not join it; cf. the quibble of Larsen, *Rep. Govt.* 51. See especially Sordi, "La pace di Atene del 371/0," *RFIC* 29 (1951) 34–64; and Ryder, *KE* 131–133 (Appendix IV: "The Peace of 371 at Athens").

have prevented participants from making alliances with one another at the same time. For Athens, the struggle that loomed with Thebes was a positive incentive to make them, but no certain evidence connects any Athenian alliance with the peace of 371 (beyond the tentative suggestions made supra).

Athens actually refused to make an alliance with several Peloponnesian states against Sparta, when such an alliance was proposed in 370. In that same year, the Theban Epameinondas led the first of his four invasions of the Peloponnesos, in the process detaching several states from their allegiance to both Athens and Sparta. The harassed Spartans now themselves sought alliance with Athens. Those who accept some of the theories described in the preceding paragraph sometimes suggest that Sparta at this time followed its former allies in joining the Athenian League, entering the synedrion to cast its single vote along with the Aegean islets. In fact, however, Athens neither stole away Sparta's traditional allies in 371 nor made Sparta a member of its League in 369. In the latter year the Athenian League and the Peloponnesian League formed an alliance, with Athens and Sparta sharing the hegemony.[30] No doubt Athens was by now generally regarded as the senior partner,[31] but Sparta was not insulted by dwelling on this point.

Providing precise Attic dates, Apollodoros in the pseudo-Demosthenic oration *Against Polykles* (ca. 359 B.C.) lists several crises which occurred early in the archonship of Molon (362/1), including the fact that "the Prokonnesians, being allies, entreated you in the assembly to bring aid to them" against Kyzikos. On the basis of this passage, Marshall believes it is "very possible" that Prokonnesos was a League member, though its membership "is not by any means certain." Accame repeatedly describes Prokonnesos as a League member, but says it was recruited into that status by Timotheos in the period 364–362. This date itself would rule out League membership, however, and none of the other states taken by Timotheos during this period is called an "ally" by any extant source; perhaps even more interestingly, no source mentions Prokonnesos among these conquests—the connection is purely a modern inference. Prokonnesos could in fact have been a League member, but if so, it was recruited during the period (ending ca. 374) when all the others were, and its name would have been among those lost with the

---

30. Events in the Peloponnesos: Xen. *Hell.* 6.5.19, 22–32, and 49–52; Nep. *Ages.* 6; Diod. 15.62.3–66.1 and 67.1; Plut. *Ages.* 31f and *Pelop.* 24. On the refusal of the proferred alliance (Diod. 15.62.3), see Marshall 80f; Accame 163; and Ryder, *KE* 74. As to the sharing of the hegemony, Xen. *Hell.* 7.1.14 and Diod. 15.67.1 differ as to how it was worked out, but agree on the basic point; on the involvement of the Athenian League in the arrangement, see the conflicting opinions of Marshall 82; Beloch 3:1.179f; and Accame 165.

31. This seems to be the implication of Xen. *Poroi* 5.7 and Isok. 5.44 (the Loeb editor puts the latter passage in a context of 362 B.C., but it fits 370–369 more easily).

portion of the list broken away below the decree of Aristoteles. Nothing about the suggestion would be at all farfetched: nearby Byzantion was one of the earliest members of the League, Perinthos joined soon afterward, and Selymbria was added around 375 (chapter 2). But neither is there any support for Prokonnesos' League membership: the city is not described as an Athenian ally by any source earlier than the one cited (supra). Therefore, the most responsible interpretation of the available evidence is to take our clue from the dating of the only source we have, and to assign the alliance with Prokonnesos to the category of alliances attested for that general period, i.e., the type discussed in this chapter.[32]

In 362/1, probably after the battle of Mantineia, an Athenian decree proclaimed that "[since] the allies brought forth a dogma" on the subject, the Athenians would accept the Peloponnesian states of Arkadia, Achaia, Elis, and Phleious as "allies . . . [. . . for all] time of the Atheni[an demos and the allies . . .]." The Peloponnesians did not by this treaty enter the Athenian League, as is evident from the oaths exchanged: the signatories guaranteed to protect each other from forcible changes of constitution, an assurance that would have been unnecessary for allies guaranteed the protections of the decree of Aristoteles. Moreover, the agreement that each state would command when joint action was undertaken within its own territory would not have been made with League members, to whom Athens was always and everywhere hegemon.[33] One wonders how those who think that most of the Peloponnesian states joined the Athenian League in 371 would explain these states' need to become non-League member allies in 362/1. Conversely, the explanation is very simple and natural in the reconstruction adopted here, under which these states became allies of (not members of) the League in 369 in their capacity of Peloponnesian Leaguers under the leadership of Sparta. This interpretation is also consistent with the fact that when Korinth and certain other Peloponnesian states wished to make peace with Thebes in 366, they asked Sparta for permission to enter into negotiations, i.e., they still recognized Sparta as their hegemon.[34] If they and the Spartans were all simply equal members of Athens's League, they would have had to ask the permission of Athens. But by the time of the battle of Mantineia, Sparta had lost control over

32. [Dem.] 50.5: Προκοννήσιοι δὲ σύμμαχοι ὄντες ἱκέτευον ὑμᾶς ἐν τῷ δήμῳ βοηθῆσαι αὐτοῖς. Dem. 18.302 is too late and inexact to provide any help in categorizing Athens's relationship with Prokonnesos. See Marshall 99 n. 2 and 105; also Accame 101f, 135 n. 4, 180f, and 195.

33. SV 290, lines 12–19 (translated passage; see chapter 7 for the Greek), 25f and 29–32 (preservation of constitutions; cf. DA, lines 20f), and 34f (command provisions; cf. Diod. 15.28.4).

34. Xen. Hell. 7.4.6–9.

most of its Peloponnesian allies. When the Spartans refused to sign the common peace treaty drawn up subsequent to that battle (because it recognized the autonomy of Messene, separated from Spartan authority by Epameinondas in 369),[35] they effectively cancelled their alliance with Athens and the Athenian League. Peloponnesian states formerly connected with the Athenian League by virtue of their alliance with Sparta were cast adrift; to have the protection of Athens and its League, they had to make their own alliance with them.

Another treaty "for all time," between Athens and the Thessalian League (dated to 361/0 B.C.), includes the following provision: "And also let the al[li]es of (the) Athenians all b[e] al[l]ies of (the) Thessalian[s], and those of (the) [Th]essalians (the) A[the]nians'." Nothing is said about who shall command where, but provisions guaranteeing the defense of the contracting parties' forms of government resemble those of the treaty with the four Peloponnesian states. This alliance was apparently of the same general type.[36]

Certain refugees, probably expelled from their homeland by Philip of Macedon, are described in an extremely fragmentary Athenian inscription (no date extant) as seeking exemption from the tax on resident aliens. If very extensive but commonly accepted restorations may be trusted, they laid their case before both the Athenian demos and the allies, on the ground that they had themselves been allies of both. One of many uncertainties about this almost destroyed text is the identity of the state of those making the appeal. If, as some editors believe, the petitioners were Olynthians, their appeal was made by invoking their current or former League membership (under the rubric of the Chalkidians of Thrace; see chapter 2), and discussion of this inscription would have no place in the present chapter. Beloch, however, suggests that these allies of Athens and the League were not Olynthians but Methonaians, expelled by Philip from their city in (probably) 353/2 B.C. On this latter interpretation—and if Methone was not one of the names broken away from the right-hand column of names below the decree of Aristoteles —the Methonaians would have had the type of alliance with which this chapter deals. But the restoration of "Methonaians" is no stronger than the restoration of "Olynthians." Methone is listed among cities captured

---

35. Xen. *Hell.* 7.4.9; Polyb. 4.33.8f; Diod. 15.89.2; Plut. *Ages.* 35.3.

36. *SV* 293: date in line 2; permanence in line 4; translated provision in lines 12–14 (εἶ[ν]αι δὲ καὶ τοὺς Ἀθην/αίων συμμ[ά]χ[ο]ς ἅπαντας Θετταλῶ[ν] συμμ[ά]χος καὶ τὸς / [Θ]ετταλῶν Ἀ[θη]ναίων); guarantees of governmental forms in lines 18f and 28f. Tod 147 comm. and Bengtson, *SV* 293 comm., agree that this alliance included the members of Athens's League. It is impossible to know whether ἅπαντας (line 13) included Athens's other non-League allies as well (it is especially difficult to see what responsibilities bilateral Athenian allies would have had).

by Timotheos; neither it nor the other cities listed are called Athenian allies by any extant source.[37] Therefore, Methone probably was an Athenian possession, and the homeland of the refugees mentioned in the inscription must remain unknown. Their city was either a League member (its name extant, or among the few broken away from the stele of Aristoteles), or an ally of Athens and the League (either one of those attested by the sources here cited, or another of whose alliance we are ignorant). This is all that should be said on evidence that is so very shaky.

When the Athenians were negotiating terms with Philip for the Peace of Philokrates in 346 B.C., the synedrion of the Athenian League resolved, in effect, that the agreement should be a panhellenic common peace, but also accepted in advance whatever terms should be agreed upon by the Athenians and Philip's representatives. The synedrion's desire proved impossible to fulfill. Philip and his allies ultimately made peace only with the Athenians and "the allies"—a deliberately ambiguous phrase which in practice (i.e., as observed by Philip) meant exclusively the members of the League. The signatories of the peace also swore to an alliance, from which non-League Athenian allies were excluded. Many important historical and procedural issues are raised in the extensive and conflicting descriptions of these negotiations by Demosthenes and Aischines (chapter 7). But it remains an incontrovertible fact that in 346 Philip and his allies became allies of Athens and the League, without joining the League.[38]

The final two identifiable examples of alliances with Athens and the League are agreements made with former League members, whose withdrawal had been accepted. Good relations with the cities of Euboia had always constituted a major focus of Athenian foreign policy. After the publication of the decree of Aristoteles, the Euboians were the first new League members recruited; they had defected to the Boiotian alliance in ca. 370, but had been won back to League membership in 357; the Eubo-

37. *IG* II², 211; Tod 166 comm. discusses the various textual problems (WV intro. does not indicate that any exist). The [---'Ολύνθιοι---] restored in some texts in the first of two virtually complete unnumbered "lines" above the first extant line of the inscription has, of course, no basis at all—which probably is implied by the exclamation point following a quotation of the passage in Rhodes, *Boule* 73 n. 1. Beloch 3:1.496f, n. 4, suggests το[ῖς ἐκπεπτωκό/σι Μεθωναί]ων instead of the customary το[ῖς ἐκπεπτωκό/σιν 'Ολυνθί]ων in lines 7f, on the basis of the description of Philip's expulsion of the Methonaians in Diod. 16.34.4f (the date of 353/2 is Diodoros'). Dein. 1.14 and 3.17 says that Timotheos captured Samos, Methone, Pydna, Poteidaia, and twenty other (unnamed) cities. Methone was in use as an Athenian naval base in 360/59, according to Diod. 16.3.5f. Dem. 4.4 describes Methone, Pydna, and Poteidaia as cities εἴχομεν ποθ' ἡμεῖς. Less indicative of Methone's status are the statement (sec. 35) that Athenian expeditions arrived too late to help Methone, Pagasai, and Poteidaia, and the description (Dem. 1.9) of Methone, Pydna, Poteidaia, and Pagasai as cities (among unnamed others) besieged by Philip; still, the pattern of the groups of names in which Methone's appears is rather clear.

38. *SV* 329 devotes seven pages to quoting sources on this peace and alliance, categorized by topics. The agreement was inscribed, but its stele was later deliberately destroyed.

ians remained loyal throughout the Social War which immediately followed.[39] The Macedonians, however, soon replaced the Thebans as a threat to Athenian hegemony on the island. They apparently were involved in strife there in 348, which seems to have detached the Euboians from the Athenian League again.[40] Thus matters stood until, as Aischines tells it, Kallias of Chalkis persuaded the Athenians ca. 341 to agree to a different type of alliance with his city, under which Chalkis would be represented in, and pay contributions to, a new Euboian confederacy rather than the Athenian League.[41]

Aischines' sketchy description would apply equally well to an agreement involving only Athens and Chalkis, presumably one of a series of bilateral alliances with the different Euboian cities. But a fragment is extant of what appears to be a treaty with Eretria, probably signed about this time, in which the Eretrians accept obligations toward "the allies" as well as toward Athens. The oath associated with this treaty includes the following clauses:

> ἐμμενῶ τῆι συμμ[αχίαι καὶ συνθήκηι πρὸς τὸν δῆμ]-
> ον τὸν 'Αθηναίων [καὶ τοὺς συμμάχους δικαίως καὶ]
> ἀδόλως· καὶ ἐάν τ[ις ἴηι ἐπὶ τὴν χώραν τὴν 'Αθηναίω]-
> ν ἢ τοὺς συμμάχο[υς τοὺς 'Αθηναίων ἢ καταλύηι τὸν]
> 10   δῆμον τὸν 'Αθηναί[ων, βοηθήσω παντὶ σθένει κατὰ τ]-
> ὸ δυνατόν.

> I shall abide by the all[iance and agreement with the dem]os of (the) Athenians [and the allies justly and] guilelessly; and if an[yone comes against the territory of (the) Athenian]s or the allie[s of (the) Athenians, or overthrows the] demos of (the) Atheni[ans, I shall give aid in full strength so far as] possible.[42]

If this treaty is in fact placed and dated correctly, it and the treaties of the other Euboian cities (that of Chalkis, mentioned by Aischines, and

39. Euboian importance: Thuc. 8.95.2; Aristot. *Ath. Pol.* 33.1; Dem. 23.191; early League membership: chapters 2 and 3; defection to the Boiotians: Xen. *Hell.* 6.5.23 and *Ages.* 2.24; Diod. 15.85.2 and 6 and 15.87.3; reentry into Athenian League: *SV* 304; *IG* II², 125; Dem. 8.74 and 18.99; Ais. 3.85; Nep. *Timoth.* 3.1; Diod. 16.7.2. On Euboian affairs in the 350s, see Beloch 3:2.258–262; Schweigert, "Greek Inscriptions: 4. A Decree Concerning Elaious, 357/6 B.C.," *Hesperia* 8 (1939) 12–17; and Cawkwell, "Notes on the Social War," *C&M* 23 (1962) 34–49.

40. Macedonian involvement on Euboia: Ais. 2.12 and 120; 3.86–88; Dem. 4.17 and 37; 5.10; ?10.8f; 18.71, 79, 81, and 87; 19.22; Plut. *Phok.* 12–14. The soundest treatment of Euboian affairs in this period is P. A. Brunt, "Euboea in the Time of Philip II," *CQ* 19 (1969) 245–265, q.v., for further bibliography. Now add Cawkwell, "Euboea in the Late 340's," *Phoenix* 32 (1978) 42–67.

41. Ais. 3.89–105; Sch. Ais. 3.103 (quoted in Tod 153 comm.); see also *SV* 339 and 342.

42. *SV* 340, lines 6–11. Bengtson's text includes only fragment *a* of the inscription; for a text of fragment *b* (a list of ambassadors' names), see William Wallace, "The Demes of Eretria," *Hesperia* 16 (1947) 145.

others) probably were alliances with Athens and the League. Whether the Euboian confederacy, as an organization, made an alliance with Athens's League is problematic. No evidence exists except the negative implication of these testimonia for treaties signed independently by individual Euboian cities.[43]

In most of the cited cases, reasons can readily be seen why a sort of "in-between" alliance was more appropriate for these states than either joining the League or forming bilateral alliances with Athens. The Athenians' desire to avoid pointless antagonism of Sparta may explain the early examples. Sparta itself, the traditional hegemon of Greece, could not have been expected to share with its own Peloponnesian allies a position inferior to that of Athens. The defection of their hegemon also explains the four Peloponnesian states' need for a new alliance in 362/1. Philip, of course, was even less likely than Sparta to accept Athenian hegemony, whereas Athens had every incentive to protect as many of its own allies as possible by putting them into alliance with him in 346. The Euboian treaties were accommodations to necessity: Athens felt that Euboia was so vital to its interests that it granted former League members there exemptions from some of the responsibilities of League membership in order to regain their friendship. No such ready explanation is available in connection with the alliance made with the Thessalian League: perhaps it was of this type simply *because* during this period Athens normally made such alliances with Greek cities and confederations of cities. The clear examples having established the pattern, the pattern in turn may explain the less well attested examples. The alliances with Prokonnesos and with the unknown city of the refugees are only conjecturally placed among those discussed in this chapter; too little is known for any genuine certainty about their nature.

43. The inscription's fragmentary extant text would not exclude the idea that the agreement was Eretria's original League membership treaty of 377 B.C.; the only reason for preferring the later date is the script, which Kirchner, *IG* II², 230 comm. (echoing Koehler) says is appropriate to about the middle of the fourth century. Conversely, the only reason for dating an even more fragmentary agreement with Euboian Arethousa to 377, rather than grouping it with these later treaties, is the judgment of its editor, Meritt, that it is inscribed in "letters of the early fourth century" (chapter 2). Bengtson, *SV* 342 comm., seems to doubt that the Euboian confederacy had any separate existence, its members being connected to each other, in his opinion, only through their individual connections with Athens.

5

BILATERAL ALLIES OF ATHENS

When the Second Athenian League was organized, the Athenians clearly envisioned making only one type of alliance, i.e., the type which admitted the new ally to League membership. This general rule held for Greek city-states, regional confederacies, democratic factions, and tyrant-kings; examples of all appear in the lists of League members on the stele of the allies (chapter 2). But for various reasons the Athenians ceased to add members to their League in ca. 374 B.C. (chapter 3). They continued to make alliances nevertheless, in appropriate circumstances. Probably at around the same time the Athenians adopted the practice of allying "Athens and the League" with Greek city-states and confederacies (chapter 4), they also began making bilateral alliances (to which the League was not a party) with certain kings and tyrants. This third variety of alliance eventually became the norm for all types of states, and late examples of the second category of alliance (after ca. 360) are generally to be explained as products of particularly unusual circumstances.

Early examples of Athenian bilateral alliances during the period of the Second Athenian League are debatable as to category and uncertain as to date.[1] I suggest that one of the first such alliances was signed with Jason, tyrant of Pherai in Thessaly. Xenophon sets a visit to Sparta by Polydamas of Pharsalos, seeking aid against the expansionism of his neighbor Jason, between narratives of the battle of Alyzeia (375) and the signing of the peace of 375/4. Polydamas told the Spartans that the tyrant had described himself as the ally of the Boiotians and others fighting Sparta, but as unwilling to become an ally of Athens, also describing Alketas of Epeiros as one of his "subjects" (ὑπήκοοι). Jason had expressed interest in becoming lord (ταγός) of Thessaly and in challenging Athens for naval supremacy by controlling Macedon, Athens's source of ship timber; he was even contemplating the eventual conquest of Persia.[2] Yet

---

1. One should not be misled by Diodoros' statement that in 373 Πλαταιεῖς ἀντεχόμενοι τῆς Ἀθηναίων συμμαχίας μετεπέμποντο στρατιώτας (Diod. 15.46.4; this "alliance" is mentioned again in the following sentence). Plataia, though a traditional friend of Athens, had no alliance, or it would have been mentioned in contemporary sources—particularly in Isokrates' *Plataikos*, which is a plea to the Athenians to give Plataia assistance in precisely the situation described by Diodoros. But no Plataian alliance, of any kind, is mentioned by Isokrates or by Xen. *Hell.* 6.3.1 (or, for that matter, by Paus. 9.1.8), so Diodoros' phrasing is imprecise. The Plataians were simply Boiotians attempting to escape the dominance of Thebes by appealing to Athens.

2. Xen. *Hell.* 6.1.4–12; the critical passage is sec. 10:

in 373, according to Apollodoros, Jason and Alketas—allies of Athens —testified on Timotheos' behalf in his trial; both this incident and Jason's alliance seem to be confirmed by later sources.[3] In 371, however, Jason was a Theban ally, and apparently was contemplating naval action against Athens; this situation too is confirmed by a late source, which says that Athens was at war with Jason at some time later than the trial of Timotheos. Jason attained the position of tagos in 371 or 370, making further conquests and forming an alliance with Amyntas of Macedon, but he died by assassination in 370.[4] Thus the literary sources indicate that an Athenian alliance with Jason, of unspecified type, was made between 375 and 373, and had been terminated by some time in 371.

Beloch, however, redates the request of Polydamas for Spartan assistance to 371 and denies that Jason was ever an Athenian ally. Other scholars, accepting Fabricius' restoration of ['Ιάσω]ν in the erased line 111 of the stele of Aristoteles, have produced yet other reconstructions. Accame, e.g., suggests that Jason joined the Athenian League in 375 and was listed on the stele, but was expelled from the League shortly afterward, and his name was erased. The reason for this *damnatio memoriae* is to be found, Accame believes, in Jason's statement as reported by Polydamas in Xenophon (redated to Beloch's 371): he had dared to make his fellow League member Alketas his "subject."[5] In actuality, problems associated with the literary sources on Jason are quite minor, and no epigraphical sources are known to have mentioned Jason at all. The reconstruction of Jean Hatzfeld, according to which Jason became a non-League ally of Athens ca. 373 (shortly before the trial of Timotheos), is eminently sensible and should be accepted. Jason's desire for freedom of action vis-à-vis Sparta (he was a hereditary Spartan πρόξενος), suggested by Hatzfeld as his reason for not wishing to join the League, also makes sense. Bases for categorizing the alliance as bilateral, rather than as the type of alliance discussed in chapter 4, are more tenuous. I place the alliance with Jason among those of this chapter ultimately because certain alliances with other kings and tyrants clearly belong here. The supposition that Jason was a League member is in any case baseless. The

---

καὶ μὴν Βοιωτοί γε καὶ οἱ ἄλλοι πάντες ὅσοι Λακεδαιμονίοις πολεμοῦντες ὑπάρχουσί μοι σύμμαχοι. . . . καὶ ᾿Αθηναῖοι δὲ εὖ οἶδ᾽ ὅτι πάντα ποιήσαιεν ἂν ὥστε σύμμαχοι ἡμῖν γενέσθαι· ἀλλ᾽ ἐγὼ οὐκ ἄν μοι δοκῶ πρὸς αὐτοὺς φιλίαν ποιήσασθαι.

Jason's ambitions toward Persia are confirmed by Isok. 5.119f.

3. [Dem.] 49.10: ᾿Αλκέτου καὶ ᾿Ιάσονος, συμμάχων ὄντων ὑμῖν. See also Nep. *Timoth.* 4.2 and Polyain. 3.9.40.

4. Xen. *Hell.* 6.4.20–32; Diod. 15.54.5, 57.2, and 60.2–6; Isok. 5.20; Nep. *Timoth.* 4.3; Plut. *Mor.* 193B (cf. 583F).

5. Beloch 3:1.164–170; Accame 91–98. Accame's reconstruction is specifically denied by, e.g., Woodhead, "Jason" 369 n. 6.

known date of Jason's death insures that, if this was a bilateral alliance, it was among the earliest signed by Athens during the period of the League's existence.[6]

Only one other Athenian bilateral alliance, in fact, could have been made as early (or earlier), if it *was* a bilateral alliance: the one possibly sworn with Amyntas of Macedon, the father of Philip II. An inscribed fragment survives which mentions Amyntas and includes the following provision: "[And a]lso commend the ambassad[ors] sen[t fro]m the (Athenian) demos to M[ac]edonia concerning t[he a]l[l]iance." The date and the entire context of the agreement are lost, and different scholars have interpreted this alliance as belonging to each of the three types discussed in these chapters. The dates suggested for the treaty—most commonly 375 B.C., sometimes 373—are inferred from the supposed itineraries of voyages by Timotheos and Chabrias. But these voyages of recruitment of League members would in actuality put no restrictions on the date of a non-League membership alliance. Therefore the alliance with Amyntas, if of either non-League variety, could have been made at any time down to his death in 370/69—or at least until he became connected with Jason shortly before. Jason's statement, apparently made ca. 375, that Athens got its ship timber from Macedon implies that some form of friendly relations between Athens and Macedon already existed at that time, though this relationship need not have been an alliance.[7]

The evidence most frequently cited by those who believe that Amyntas became a member of the Athenian League is a statement made by

6. Hatzfeld, "Jason de Phères a-t-il été l'allié d'Athènes?", *REA* 36 (1934) 441–461. Hatzfeld does not discuss the particular type of non-League alliance Jason had with Athens; Woodhead, "Jason" 373, classifies him as what I have called an "ally of Athens and the League," but Woodhead does not seem to consider a bilateral alliance an available alternative. Sources which *may* imply that the alliance was bilateral are Polyain. 3.9.40, in that the ceremony depicted there seems to involve only representatives of Jason and of Athens, and Isok. *Lett.* 6.3 (v. infra), in that the implication that Athens had a bilateral alliance with Jason's heirs may tend to indicate that the same sort of alliance existed with their father.

7. The alliance treaty is *SV* 264: name in lines 2 ('Aμύ[ντο---]), 5f (entirely restored), 20 ([---'Aμύντα]ς 'Aρριδαίο), and 21 ([---'Aλέζανδ]ρος 'Aμύντο); translated passage in lines 8–10 (ἐπαινέσαι [δὲ κ]αὶ τοὺς πρέσβε[ις] / τοὺς πεμφθέντ[ας ὑπ]ὸ τοῦ δήμο εἰς M[ακ]/εδονίαν περὶ τ[ῆς συ]μ⟨μ⟩αχίας). Bengtson, *G&P* 224, says that Amyntas was a League member recruited either in 375 or 373; he gives the same two possibilities for the date in *SV* 264, but his comm. shows that he prefers 375; the same dating possibilities and preference are suggested by Tod 129 comm. and WV 29 intro.; WV say Amyntas "probably" was a League member; Ryder, *KE* 130, says "perhaps" he was; Woodhead, "Jason" 373, says Amyntas had the same type of alliance with Athens as Jason, i.e., an "alliance with Athens and the League"; Accame, 130 and 165f, classifies the alliance as bilateral, and dates it to ca. 370; Hatzfeld (supra n. 6), 452, dates the alliance to ca. 375, without discussing its type. Amyntas' death is dated to 370/69 by Diod. 15.60.3 and 16.2.4; *IG XII* (5), 444 = the *Marmor Parium* (*FGrH* 239), epoch 72, says 371/0. Accame, 130, concludes that the date was around 370—a conclusion important for the context he gives to Ais. 2.32 (v. infra).

Aischines in 343. He contends that Philip can have no just claim to Amphipolis:

συμμαχίας γὰρ Λακεδαιμονίων καὶ τῶν ἄλλων Ἑλλήνων συνελθούσης, εἷς ὧν τούτων
'Αμύντας ὁ Φιλίππου πατὴρ καὶ πέμπων σύνεδρον καὶ τῆς καθ' αὑτὸν ψήφου κύριος ὤν,
ἐψηφίσατο 'Αμφίπολιν τὴν 'Αθηναίων συνεξαιρεῖν μετὰ τῶν ἄλλων Ἑλλήνων
'Αθηναίοις.

For, when the alliance of the Lakedaimonians and of the other Greeks was meeting together, one of them being Amyntas the father of Philip, he also, sending a synedros and being in charge of his vote, resolved along with the other Greeks to help the Athenians in capturing Amphipolis (which was a possession) of the Athenians.

The fact that Amyntas' envoy to this meeting is called a "synedros" leads some to conclude that he was Amyntas' representative in the synedrion of the Athenian League. Accame, however, believes that the word is used here in a nontechnical sense, and the absence of Amyntas' name from the stele of Aristoteles makes me tend to accept his conclusion.[8] Otherwise, there would be no inherent unlikelihood that Amyntas, an Athenian ally possibly as early as 375, had joined the League—as, e.g., King Alketas had done.

Moreover, this possibility cannot absolutely be ruled out. The only place where Amyntas' name could have appeared on the stele is in the erased line 111, which has generally—but for no good reason (v. supra) —been reserved for Jason. The seven letters of 'Αμύντας, including the wide letter mu, would be a crowded restoration in an erasure which seems to cover about six letter spaces. But this list is nonstoichedon, and variations in spacing within its names do exist (chapter 2), so the suggestion—though bold—would not be epigraphically irresponsible. On historical considerations the restoration would make excellent sense. It seems incongruous that (on the conventional interpretation) Jason should have been deemed deserving of *damnatio memoriae*, while the name of the Thebans, whose secession severely damaged the League, remained on the stele, as did those of many others who defected. Some have in fact taken this apparent anomaly as indicating that the decree of Aristoteles was a "dead letter" no longer relevant to Athenian policy by

8. Ais. 2.32. Marshall, 73 and nn. 1 and 3, connects this passage with the peace conference at Sparta in 371; Bengtson quotes the passage among his sources for the peace of 375/4 (SV 265). Accame, 164–166, suggests, however, that the most reasonable context is the meeting at which the Athenian-Spartan alliance, signed in 369, was agreed upon. The phrasing of the first clause of the passage makes this interpretation, I think, virtually certain: the "alliance" which Aischines mentions belongs not only to the Lakedaimonians but also to "the other Greeks," and the Athenians and the members of their League were certainly not allies of the Spartans in either 375/4 or 371, whereas they obviously were involved in the vote Aischines describes. The sending of his representative to this meeting must have been one of Amyntas' last acts.

the time of Thebes' decisive defection in 371.[9] However, the most logical explanation of the *other* erasure within the inscription, i.e., that of the provision dealing directly with the maintenance of the King's Peace in lines 12–14, would set this development in a context of 367 or later (see chapters 2 and 10). Therefore the suggestion that the decree and its lists of names were irrelevant by 371 is extremely weak.

Some development regarded by the Athenians as momentous and irrevocable—not the mere misbehavior or defection of an ally whose loyalty might perhaps eventually be regained, as was that of others—probably led to the erasing of the name in line 111 (unless the mason was merely correcting his own error). A perfect occasion for the erasure from the stele of a name signifying "Macedon" is suggested by a fragment of Philochoros: in 340/39, on the motion of Demosthenes, the Athenians voted to pull down the stele on which were written the terms of the peace and alliance signed with Amyntas' son Philip in 346.[10] Philip had at this point been actively engaged in destroying the Athenian League for several years. Perhaps some earlier crisis in his relations with Athens would have served equally well as the occasion for the erasure. The germ of incontestable fact is that Amyntas had been some kind of Athenian ally. Since positive evidence that he joined the League is lacking, it is safer to assume that his alliance was of one of the two other types. As in the case of Jason, there is no real basis for deciding which, and I must again fall back on analogy with the more certain examples to be discussed.

Xenophon says that soon after the death of Jason, Alexander of Pherai "became a cruel tagos to the Thessalians and a cruel enemy to the Thebans and Athenians." The intensity of his conflict with Thebes, however, led him to make an alliance with Athens ca. 368 B.C. Marshall probably is correct in describing this alliance as bilateral.[11] The treaty was inscribed, but is not extant for a very good reason. Alexander later became Athens's enemy, and when in 361/0 the Athenians signed an alliance with the members of the Thessalian League (chapter 4), who were at war with him, one of the provisions of this agreement was: "And let the [treasurer]s of the goddess [de]st[ro]y [th]e st[e]l[e] wit[h] Al[exa]nd[e]r [con]cern[ing th]e [a]llianc[e]."[12]

9. See, e.g., Sealey, "Transf." 106f; cf. the slight variation on this theme in Burnett, "Expans." 14.

10. Philoch. *FGrH* 328 F 55a: . . . Δημοσθένους . . . παρακαλέσαντος αὐτὸν πρὸς τὸν πόλεμον καὶ ψήφισμα γράψαντος, ἐχειροτόνησε τὴν μὲν στήλην καθελεῖν τὴν περὶ τῆς πρὸς Φίλιππον εἰρήνης καὶ συμμαχίας σταθεῖσαν, κτλ (date from F 54).

11. Xen. *Hell.* 6.4.35: χαλεπὸς μὲν Θετταλοῖς ταγὸς ἐγένετο, χαλεπὸς δὲ Θηβαίοις καὶ 'Αθηναίοις πολέμιος. The alliance with Athens is attested by Dem. 23.120; Diod. 15.71.3; and Plut. *Pelop.* 31.4 and *Mor.* 193E. Marshall, 87, calls it bilateral; Accame omits it from his list of bilateral alliances (130f), but he also omits all substantive mention of it.

12. *SV* 293, lines 39f: [τὴ]ν δὲ στ[ή]λ[η]ν τὴ]ν πρὸ[ς] 'Αλ[έξα]νδ[ρ]ον [κα]θελ[εῖ]ν τὸς / [ταμία]ς τῆς θεõ [τὴν π]ερ[ὶ τῆ]ς [σ]υμμαχία[ς]. Sources for Athenian conflict with Alexander include [Dem.] 50.4; Polyain. 6.2.1f; and Diod. 15.95.1f (see chapter 10).

The first clear-cut example of an Athenian bilateral alliance during the period of the League is the alliance made with the tyrant Dionysios I of Syracuse. Dionysios was a Spartan ally, but his relations with Athens became cordial after Athens and Sparta themselves became allies in 369. In the following year, an Athenian decree honored the Sicilian tyrant and his sons for other reasons and "because [they] a[re] good [men to]ward the demos of (the) [Athenians and] the allies."[13] In 367, just before Dionysios' death, a treaty was signed which included the following clauses:

[---ἐπαινέσαι μὲν Δ]-
[ιονύσι]ο[ν] τὸν Σικελία[ς ἄρχοντα ὅτι ἐστὶ]-
[ν ἀνὴρ] ἀγαθὸς περὶ τὸν [δῆμον τὸν Ἀθηναίω]-
10   [ν καὶ τ]ὸς συμμάχους· εἶ[ναι δὲ συμμάχος αὐ]-
[τὸν κα]ὶ τοὺς ἐκγόνους [τοῦ δήμου τοῦ Ἀθην]-
[αίων ἐ]ς [τ]ὸν ἀεὶ χρόνον [ἐπὶ τοῖσδε·---]

Though Dionysios' friendly attitude toward "the allies" (line 10) was again cited among the reasons for commending him, the alliance itself was concluded only between Athens and Dionysios and his descendants (lines 10-12). Its terms, as well as the steps involved in ratifying the treaty (which together occupy the next twenty-eight lines), confirm this statement.[14] The references to Dionysios' goodwill toward the allies in both these inscriptions indicate that no change in *Athens's* attitude toward them was involved in the Athenian decision to make a bilateral agreement with Dionysios. This was simply a type of alliance which had come into use—or was just now coming into use (depending on whether the alliances already discussed were in fact bilateral)—in Athenian relations with a certain type of state.[15]

Around 359 B.C., Isokrates wrote to the children of Jason of Pherai,

13. *IG* II², 103, lines 21-23: ὅτι ε[ἰσὶν ἄνδρ/ες] ἀγαθοὶ [π]ερὶ τὸν δῆμον τὸν [Ἀθηναίων / καὶ] τοὺς συμμάχους (brackets as by Accame 157).

14. *SV* 280, lines 7-12; terms of the alliance in lines 12-30; ratification procedures in lines 30-40. The texts of recently published editions of this treaty are based on a combination of fragments of two stelai inscribed with apparently identical treaties; see Schweigert, "Epigraphic Notes: 2. A New Fragment of the Treaty between Athens and Dionysius, the Elder," *Hesperia* 7 (1938) 627. Accame, 130f, n. 7, argues that the copy is a renewed treaty (same terms) with Dionysios II, signed upon his father's death; this is possible, though unprovable.

15. Marshall, 86, concedes that the alliance treaty was bilateral "in form," but elsewhere (p. 30) expresses doubt that it could have been so in fact; Accame, 130, definitely classifies it as bilateral; Rhodes, *Boule* 80f, agrees that the alliance was bilateral, but argues (citing only these two inscriptions as sources) that the alliance took this form because the synedrion refused an Athenian request to participate in it. The synedrion was called upon, in fact, to address only Dionysios' written suggestions concerning the rebuilding of the Delphic temple and "the peace" (*IG* II², 103, lines 8-13), so I can see no basis for Rhodes' inference.

observing that alliances made by Athens were easily broken, and expressing concern "lest something of that sort should also happen in relation to you."[16] This phrasing seems to imply that Athens at the time had an alliance with Jason's heirs. Such "easily broken" alliances were probably bilateral.

Philip of Macedon, in the early years of consolidating his reign, engaged in complex diplomatic shifts as he endeavored to prevent potential enemies from combining for action against him. Athens, with allies and territorial possessions along the Thracian coast, shifting relations of its own with former League member Olynthos, and long-standing claims to Amphipolis, was very much involved in this process. In connection with a campaign which Diodoros, the only narrative source, places in 360/59 B.C., Demosthenes tells us that Philip released certain Athenians he had captured and let them go home, "sending a written message that he was ready to make an alliance and to renew his ancestral friendship. . . ." Diodoros says that "peace" was made between Athens and Philip in the following archon year.[17] In his *Second Olynthiac* (349 B.C.), Demosthenes tells the Athenian demos that Philip gained "the friendship of the Olynthians . . . by taking Poteidaia, which was yours, and wronging you, his former allies, to hand over to them . . ." (τὴν δ' Ὀλυνθίων φιλίαν . . . τῷ Ποτείδαιαν οὖσαν ὑμετέραν ἐξελεῖν καὶ τοὺς μὲν πρότερον συμμάχους ὑμᾶς ἀδικῆσαι, παραδοῦναι δ' ἐκείνοις . . .). Most editors and commentators have followed the lead of Blass in bracketing ὑμᾶς ("you") as an incorrect gloss. With this word removed, the reference of the phrase shifts from the Athenians to the Poteidaians, which would accord with the interpretation of one of the scholia on the passage. I can see no compelling reason to delete the word, however, and I agree with Schaefer and Beloch in accepting the veracity of the alliance.[18] If Philip and Athens, ca. 359 or 358, signed a short-lived alliance

16. Isok. *Lett.* 6.3: ὁρῶ γὰρ τὰς συμμαχίας τὰς πρὸς αὐτὴν (i.e., the city = Athens) γιγνομένας ταχέως διαλυομένας. εἰ δή τι συμβαίη καὶ πρὸς ὑμᾶς τοιοῦτον. . . .

17. Diod. 16.2.4–4.7 and 8.1–7 (16.4.1 mentions εἰρήνην); the translated passage is Dem. 23.121: πέμψας δὲ γράμματ' ἐπηγγέλλεθ' ἕτοιμος εἶναι συμμαχίαν ποιεῖσθαι καὶ τὴν πατρικὴν φιλίαν ἀνανεοῦσθαι . . . (sec. 111 calls the Athenians Philip's φίλοις . . . πατρικοῖς). See also Polyain. 4.2.17.

18. Dem. 2.7; the word is bracketed by OCT and *SV* 298; the Loeb text retains the word, but treats Blass's emendation sympathetically in a note *ad loc.* On problems associated with this passage (though dealing at greater length with the "secret agreement" of Dem. 2.6), see G.E.M. De Ste. Croix, "The Alleged Secret Pact Between Athens and Philip II Concerning Amphipolis and Pydna," *CQ* 13 (1963) 110–119. Some MSS have ἡμᾶς ("us") instead of ὑμᾶς, but in a speech by an Athenian before the Athenian demos both words would have the same meaning; De Ste. Croix (p. 111 n. 1) concludes that "there was surely no συμμαχία between Athens itself and Philip at any time before 346." See also J. R. Ellis and R. D. Milns, *The Spectre of Philip* (Sydney 1970) 45f, nn. 9–12. I infer Beloch's acceptance of ὑμᾶς from his assertion that there was an alliance (3:1.226; n. 1 cites Dem. 2.6f without hinting that any textual problem exists); De Ste. Croix quotes the opinion of Schaefer in the process of disagreeing with it.

treaty, that datum should be neither surprising nor disturbing. If there was such an alliance, it was surely bilateral.

An inscribed fragment that probably belongs to the agreement made by Chares with the Thracian kings Kersobleptes, Berisades, and Amadokos in 357 B.C. is sometimes called an "alliance." But the treaty's reference(s?) to "allies" apparently apply to cities associated with the respective contracting parties, not to the parties themselves in their relations with each other. Demosthenes' oration *Against Aristokrates* (ca. 352), whose detailed description of developments in the Thracian Chersonesos during this period provides the basis for identifying and dating the inscription, does not call the agreement an alliance.[19] Therefore, although Athens would soon make definite alliances with kings in this region (v. infra), and although this treaty is important in other contexts (Part IV), the inscription need not be discussed at this point.

An Athenian treaty dated to 356 B.C. is entitled "Alliance of (the) Athenians with Ketripor[is the Thracian and hi]s brothers, and with Lyppeios the [Paionian, and with Gra]bos the Illyrian." Ketriporis and his brothers were probably the sons of Berisades. This alliance was directed against Philip, and specifically toward preventing his acquiring the city of Krenides. But Athens, deeply involved in the Social War, apparently was unable to assist these northern kings—Diodoros' discussion of the alliance actually omits all mention of Athens's participation—and Philip defeated them all, taking Krenides and making it his own enlarged city of Philippoi. There is no reason to suggest that the members of the Athenian League were participants in this alliance. Though the "second party" consisted of three kings, the agreement from the Athenian standpoint was "bilateral."[20]

Kersobleptes of Thrace tried to maintain his own position through shifting relations with other northern kings and with Athens, his friend-

19. *SV* 303, called a "Bündnis" by Bengtson and an "alliance" in Tod 151; cf. the labels of Marshall 102 n. 5 ("agreement"), Beloch 3:1.223 ("Vertrag"); Accame 181 ("trattato"), and WV 51 ("settlement"). The treaty has a reference to οἱ σύμμα[χοι---] in line 2 and Bengtson accepts the restoration of [---συ/μμάχους---] in lines 16f. Dem. 23.170–173 repeatedly refers to συνθήκας and to things "sworn" at several stages in the negotiations, but never to any "alliance"; he summarizes later developments (sec. 10) by saying that Kersobleptes was guilty of "violating the oaths and the agreements which he made with you" (παραβὰς τοὺς ὅρκους καὶ τὰς συνθήκας ἃς μεθ' ὑμῶν ἐποιήσατο).

20. *SV* 309, lines 2–4 (title), 4f (date), 41–45 (direction against Philip), and 45 (mention of Κρηνίδ[α]ς). Dem. 23.10 does not identify Berisades' sons by name, but the identification is accepted as probable by, e.g., Beloch 3:1.231; Tod 157 comm.; Bengtson, *SV* 309 comm.; and WV 57 intro. The conquest of all three kings' lands is mentioned by Dem. 1.13 and Isok. 5.21; Illyria alone is mentioned by Plut. *Alex.* 3.5. *SV* 309 quotes Diod. 16.22.3 on the alliance. Accame, 130f, includes this alliance among those to which he says the League was not a party.

liness or unfriendliness toward the Athenians being determined largely by the number and quality of their military forces in his vicinity. Diodoros, in his account of events of 353/2 b.c., tells of Kersobleptes, "because of his hostility toward Philip and his friendship toward the Athenians, having handed over to the Athenians the cities in the Chersonesos except Kardia." Whatever the nature of his "friendship" with Athens, Kersobleptes was soon compelled to make some sort of arrangement with Philip.[21] He seems, however, to have at least attempted to switch sides again later on, since he is described as an "ally" of Athens in 346. No alliance treaty is extant, nor does any literary source mention negotiations connected with one. But since Demosthenes and Aischines, who contradict each other on almost everything else they say about Athens's relations with Kersobleptes in 346, agree on this one point, the existence of the alliance should probably be accepted.

What is absolutely certain is that Kersobleptes was not a member of the Second Athenian League: this very fact was used to exclude him from the peace and alliance Philip signed with Athens and the League in 346, despite his ambassador's desperate attempts to participate in the oath-taking ceremony at Athens. Philip was determined to complete his absorption of Kersobleptes' domains, whereas Athens, having taken over direct control of the Chersonesos (v. supra), had no critical need to risk further war with Philip on behalf of an ally of demonstrated inconstancy. The later attempts of Demosthenes and Aischines to blame each other for the "betrayal" of Kersobleptes reflect only their personal and political rivalry; allowing Philip to conquer Kersobleptes was a policy dictated by harsh necessity.[22] The Athenians seem always to have felt rather ill at ease in making alliances with tyrants. In denouncing a decree that he claimed would unreasonably benefit the mercenary commander Charidemos and, through him, Kersobleptes, Demosthenes asked what the consequences would be, if the Athenians were to pass such decrees for other dynasts: "And what good thing will we say, O men of Athens,

21. Dem. 23 describes Kersobleptes' maneuvers, *passim*. Translated passage is from Diod. 16.34.4: διά τε τὴν πρὸς Φίλιππον ἀλλοτριότητα καὶ τὴν πρὸς ᾿Αθηναίους φιλίαν ἐγχειρίσαντος τοῖς ᾿Αθηναίοις τὰς ἐν Χερρονήσῳ πόλεις πλὴν Καρδίας. *SV* 319 has sources for Kersobleptes' settlement with Philip, which Bengtson dates to 351. Beloch, 3:1.491 n. 4, 500 n. 2, and 506 n. 1, insists, however, that one of these sources (Sch. Ais. 2.81) refers to events of 347/6.

22. Kersobleptes is called an Athenian ally in Dem. 10.8 and in Ais. 2.9 and 3.61. Beloch, 3:1.505 n. 3, insists there was no alliance (despite the "Athen im Bündnis mit Kersebleptes" editorial title which is given to this part of his narrative on pp. x and 489); Accame, 130f, does not list Athens's connection with Kersobleptes among his bilateral alliances, nor call the relationship an alliance at any point. Kersobleptes' representative excluded from oath-taking ceremony: Ais. 2.85f and 3.74. Mutual accusations of betraying Kersobleptes: Dem. 19.174 and 181; Ais. 2.82–90 and 3.64f and 73f.

if, maintaining we are leaders of the Greeks in the cause of freedom, we appear as spear-bearers for those employing troops for their own advantage against the populace?"[23]

Several Athenian agreements with tyrants, kings, and dynasts during the period of the League's existence should not be classified as alliances. Straton, king of Sidon in Phoenicia, was honored in an Athenian inscription of ca. 367 B.C. The well preserved text mentions "commercial agreements" (σύμβολα), but no alliance.[24] Menelaos of Pelagon, king of the Lynkestians, actually gave Timotheos military assistance in the Thracian area, for which an Athenian decree of 362 praises and rewards him, but it says nothing to indicate the existence of a formal alliance.[25] Leukon, ruler of Bosphoros in the Crimea, and his family had a long and friendly relationship with Athens but, again, apparently no actual alliance.[26] A fragmentary treaty (part of which has been lost since its first publication) between Athens and Orontes, satrap of Mysia, may just possibly refer to an alliance, but probably was a commercial treaty.[27] Kleomis, tyrant of Methymna, was honored in an Athenian decree of ca. 345, but no ancient source indicates that Methymna was not still a member of the League, despite its change of government; thus no new alliance with the tyrant should have been necessary.[28] Alketas the Molossian had been a League member, but his family fell on troubled times after his death. His eldest son, Neoptolemos (listed with his father on the League stele), died by 357, and a younger son, Arybbas, emerged as ruler. He was expelled ca. 343 or 342 by Philip of Macedon, who had married his niece Olympias (daughter of Neoptolemos). Around 342,

---

23. Dem. 23.124: καὶ τί φήσομεν, ὦ ἄνδρες Ἀθηναῖοι, καλόν, εἰ τῶν Ἑλλήνων ἐπ' ἐλευθερίᾳ προεστάναι φάσκοντες τοὺς ἰδίᾳ δυνάμεις ἐπὶ τοῖς πλήθεσι κεκτημένους δορυφοροῦντες φανούμεθα;

24. IG II², 141, line 19; for current areas of discussion, see Robert A. Moysey, "The Date of the Strato of Sidon Decree (IG II² 141)," AJAH 1 (1976) 182–189.

25. IG II², 110, lines 6–9; apparently later Menelaos was made an Athenian citizen (Syll.³ 188, lines 1f) and aided the Athenians against Philip (Dem. 4.27).

26. IG II², 212 (= Syll.³ 206); Syll.³ 209–219; SV 306; Dem. 20.29–41. S. M. Burstein, "I.G. II² 653, Demosthenes and Athenian Relations with Bosporus in the Fourth Century B.C.," Historia 27 (1978) 428–436 offers a plausible argument for the signing of a defensive alliance with this dynasty in the early 320s, however.

27. SV 324 provides a text for the lost fragment a and the extant bcd; the indications of alliance come from lines a14 (---μμαχ---) and bcd4 (---φίλοι καὶ σ---); Bengtson concludes that it was a commercial treaty. Michael J. Osborne, "Athens and Orontes," ABSA 66 (1971) 297–321 provides facsimiles of very different copies of a, and concludes that it may not even have come from the same stele as bcd. Dates assigned to the treaty, all mere guesses, include 361/0 (Osborne), 351/0 (Marshall 118), and 349/8 (Bengtson—with a question mark—and Rhodes, Boule 105 n. 5 and 260). See also Osborne, "Orontes," Historia 22 (1973) 515–551.

28. IG II², 284; Isok. Lett. 7.8f praises this tyrant's benevolent rule; DA, lines 20f, pledges Athenian noninvolvement in League members' governments.

Athens passed a decree in honor of the exiled Arybbas that included a clause calling for the Athenian generals to assist him in recovering his realm, but the decree nowhere referred to him as an ally.[29]

Most Athenian alliances with Greek city-states and federations, after the closing off of additions to the League and before the rise of Philip as Athens's primary enemy, were alliances in which the League participated (chapter 4). The earliest datable case of an Athenian alliance with such states that did not involve the League members is Athens's treaty with the Arkadian confederacy of 366 B.C. There was something anomalous in this agreement, which was essentially designed to protect the Arkadians from Spartan attack, at a time when Athens was an ally of Sparta. Some Athenians objected to making the alliance on this basis. The treaty was approved on argument that without it the Arkadians would be compelled to seek protection from Sparta through alliance with Thebes. So the Athenians agreed to provide cavalry support to the Arkadians if their territory should be invaded, but not to attack Lakonia under any circumstances. This alliance, which represented part of Athens's delicate, balanced policy in the Peloponnesos (as described some years later by Demosthenes in his oration *For the Megalopolitans*) clearly did not commit the members of the Athenian League: both Xenophon and Diodorus describe Athenian assistance to the Arkadians in conflict with Elis a couple of years later, without mentioning any participation of the Athenian allies.[30] No doubt the Athenians saw no purpose in involving their maritime allies—who, under the agreement of 369, were themselves also Sparta's allies—in an agreement calling for cavalry they were not likely to be able to supply.

Other known examples of Athenian alliances with Greek states and confederacies that apparently were bilateral all date from the 350s and later, and most of them were products of a single situation, the growing fear of Philip among the Greeks.[31] Athens's alliances with Phokis (356 B.C.) and Opuntian Lokris (356/5?) date from the period of struggle with Thebes, but extend into the time of conflict with Philip. The fate of Phokis was in fact bracketed with that of Kersobleptes in controversies at the time of and after the signing of the peace of Philokrates.[32]

29. *IG* II², 226, lines 40–45; sources for the summary presented here are to be found in Tod 173 comm.

30. Xen. *Hell.* 7.4.2f and 6 (see *SV* 284); the scene in Plut. *Mor.* 193CD and 810F, and in Nep. *Epam.* 6.1–3, appears to be set at an earlier dramatic date (ca. 370—this interpretation disagrees with Beloch 3:1.191 n. 1), and the incident probably is not very factual (cf. Dem. 16.12; Xen. *Hell.* 6.5.49; Diod. 15.62.3). Athenian assistance to the Arkadians: Xen. *Hell.* 7.4.29; Diod. 15.77.3.

31. See the summaries of, e.g., Diod. 16.54.1 and Plut. *Dem.* 17f.

32. See *SV* 329f for sources on Phokis' defeat.

After the Chalkidian confederacy had seceded from the Athenian League and had become fragmented, its chief city, Olynthos, made an apparently bilateral alliance[33] with Athens (349). Other late allies include Megara (343); Achaia, certain Arkadians including Mantineia, Argos, Megalopolis, and Messene (342); Korinth, former allies Leukas and Korkyra, former League members Akarnania and Byzantion (by 340); and finally the chastened and fearful Thebans (339). Demosthenes managed to combine different types of Athenian allies into what is often called a Hellenic League, organized in 340 and crowned with the recruitment of Thebes in 339; its forces went down to defeat against Philip and Alexander at Chaironeia in 338.[34]

Just as not all Athenian agreements with kings and tyrants should be described as alliances, one should not assume that documented treaty relations with Greek states necessarily indicate the existence of alliances between these states and Athens. An inscribed Athenian resolution of complaint against the Aitolian League (367 B.C.) seemingly admits the absence of any treaty relations, in that it can only accuse the Aitolians of having acted "contrary to the [comm]on laws of the Greeks."[35] Woodhead calls a group of undated, fragmentary Athenian inscriptions "*symbolai*-documents." That such agreements reveal the existence of no particular relationship between Athens and the other states involved is apparent from the states with whom these particular agreements were made: (a) Troizen and some Kretan city (Kydonia?), which are not known to have been Athenian allies of any kind; (b) Stymphalos, presumably a non-League ally by virtue of its participation in the Arkadian confederacy (v. supra); and (c) Siphnos, a listed member of the Second Athenian League.[36] An agreement between Athens and Naxos, also undated, shows that Naxos must have had some sort of close relationship with Athens, but does not reveal what the specific relationship was.[37]

33. Marshall, 119, suggests that Olynthos possibly rejoined the League, but he does not insist on the point.

34. This summary paragraph accepts Bengtson's dates for these alliances; the states named here are those mentioned in the sources of SV 310f, 323, 332, 337, 343, and 345 —omitting names appropriate to chapter 4 and of states that were continuous members of the League.

35. Text published in Schweigert, "Greek Inscriptions: 3. A Decree Concerning the Aetolian League, 367/6 B.C.," *Hesperia* 8 (1939) 7, lines 13f: παρὰ τοὺς νόμους τ/[οὺς κοιν]οὺς τῶν Ἑλλήνων.

36. Woodhead, "Inscs.," *passim*; see texts of these fragments in SV 235, 279, 294, and 296. Some of the dates Woodhead suggests are debatable, particularly that of SV 235; cf. D. M. Lewis, "Athens and Troizen," *Hesperia* 28 (1959) 250, who would prefer to place the inscription well prior to the establishment of the Second Athenian League; Bengtson tends to agree with Lewis.

37. SV 321 (one of three extant fragments); dates suggested include ca. 350 (Bengtson) and before 353/2 (*IG* II², 179 comm.). The Siphnos and Naxos inscriptions (SV 294 and 321) are discussed at greater length in chapter 8.

An Athenian inscription of 355 B.C. may very well refer to Neapolis as πόλ[εως] συμμα[χίδος?---], but this phrase should not have convinced Bengtson that the inscription is itself Athens's alliance treaty with Neapolis. The city was a League member, and is not known to have become disaffected; it was being used as a base for the Athenian fleet about a year after the date of this inscription, though soon afterward it fell to Philip.[38] One would be similarly mistaken in considering the alliance treaty between Athens and Mytilene of 346 B.C. a new agreement, comparable to some of those mentioned in this and the preceding chapter. The treaty was simply a renewal of Mytilene's League membership after a period during which it was removed from the League by the tyrant Kammys.[39]

At this point, every state identified by any ancient source—correctly or incorrectly—as an "ally" of Athens during the period of the existence of the Second Athenian League (378–338 B.C.) has been discussed, and an attempt has been made to place each such alliance (sometimes admittedly very tenuously) in the appropriate one of three categories. Both these steps are crucial for understanding the history and functioning of the League, and for evaluating the actions and the attitudes of the Athenians during its forty years of existence. No fair analysis of Athens's leadership of, or relations with, its "allies" is likely to be produced by commentators who lump enemy or conquered states with the allies. "Love your friends and hate your enemies" may not be very profound personal ethics, but it has always been an accepted maxim of diplomacy, and the Athenians are entitled to be judged on this basis, not measured against abstractions such as "panhellenism."

Just as truly, no fair evaluation of Athens's behavior as leader of its League is to be expected from those who insist on treating allies of less favored status as members of the League. Of course, one may legitimately point out certain Athenian acts in relations with non-League allies that appear discreditable—usually errors of omission, such as lukewarm or nonexistent support in some crisis. Insofar as these actions (or non-actions) are seen to have affected the League members' confidence

38. *SV* 312, line 15 (the question mark is Bengtson's); title and comm. there refer to the treaty as an alliance; cf. the noncommittal titles of Tod 159 and WV 59. Rhodes, *Boule* 249, cites the inscription using the correct date (which is extant) and calls it an "alliance?", but on p. 80 he removes the question mark and misdates the treaty to 357/6. Athenian fleet's presence: Polyain. 4.2.22.

39. This is an uncontroversial position, as is indicated by the titles given this text in *SV* 328, Tod 168, WV 66, and Rhodes, *Boule* 76 and 260. Bengtson, *SV* 328 comm., believes Dem. 15.19 proves that the oligarchical government which preceded the rise of Kammys already had taken the city out of the League; but this inference is weakened by Isokrates' reference, in his letter to the Mytilenaian oligarchs, to ὑμῶν καὶ τῶν ἄλλων συμμάχων (Isok. *Lett.* 8.7). Kammys definitely was an Athenian ἐχθρός ([Dem.] 40.37). Dittenberger, *Syll.*[3] 263 n. 2, explains the confused reference to tyrant(s) on Lesbos in Athenaios 10.442f.

in their hegemon, they are in fact strictly relevant to an evaluation of Athens's relations with the League—but only insofar as there was such an effect. Its existence should not be assumed *a priori*. The members of the League obviously were aware that Athens had its own interests to pursue, its own fears, and its own limitations; they were similarly aware that they occupied a special, privileged position of closeness with the great democracy. Like the Athenians, they were primarily concerned for themselves: whether Athens helped protect them, whether the Athenians mistreated them, whether membership in the Athenian League was more to their advantage than association with some rival great power, or perhaps whether they felt strong enough to have independent ambitions of their own.

The definitional stage represented by the three chapters of Part II is a necessary preliminary too often either overlooked or handled arbitrarily. The remaining chapters are concerned exclusively with Athens and the members of its League.

Part III

THE ORGANIZATION OF
THE LEAGUE

6

JOINING THE LEAGUE

The decree of Aristoteles (chapter 2) is careful and specific in describing its promises to prospective members of the Second Athenian League, and in outlining safeguards to make those promises believable (see chapters 8 and 9). But the document assumes an already functioning League, and therefore it says little about the League's methods of operation. Similarly, little is said about the mechanics of joining the League, beyond the method of inscribing new members' names—which is a procedure that apparently begins with the publication of the decree. The only other possibly substantive provisions concerning the process of joining appear in the very poorly preserved rider at the bottom of the stele:

> Ἀριστοτέλης εἶπε· [-------------------------------------ἐπει]–
> δ⟨ὰ⟩ν πρώτο[ν ---]
> ἑκόντες π[ρο]σχωρῶσι [----------------------------ἐψη]–
> φισμένα τῶι δ⟨ή⟩μωι καὶ τ[-------------------------------------]
> 95 ν⟨ή⟩σων εἰς τὴν συμμ[αχίαν----------------------------]
> τοῖς τῶν ἐψ⟨η⟩φι[σμένων----------------------------------]
> ----------------------

The extant phrase of line 93 appears to refer to states voluntarily joining the League, or voluntarily seeking admission to it. This could be part of an assertion (true or false) that all member states join the League voluntarily, or it may merely single out voluntary joiners as contrasted (perhaps implicitly) with involuntary ones, for special praise or encouragement. The implication of line 95 is that some islanders have come, or are invited to come, into the alliance. Line 94 cites certain resolutions, possibly connected with these states' entry into the League, passed by the Athenian demos and perhaps (if we should accept a reasonable restoration) by τ[οῖς συμμάχοις---], i.e., by the synedrion. Given the fragmentary state of lines 91–96, however, the only thing we can learn with certainty about the process of joining the League from the decree of Aristoteles is that the names of all members were to be listed on the stele (lines 69–72).

Ironically, one of the most useful sources for this investigation is an inscribed agreement that apparently was partially abortive: the treaty Athens made in 375 B.C. with Korkyra, Akarnania, and Kephallenia. Another document that will prove helpful is a treaty which, I have argued, is *not* a League membership treaty: the undated Athens-Korkyra alliance. Treaties which record renewals or reformulations of member states' relations with Athens may give us clues about the provisions of these states' original (usually lost) alliance treaties. Athenian decrees that are not treaties, e.g., resolutions in honor of states or individuals, may also provide indirect clues. Where the sources are so sketchy, and often tangential to our purpose, a good bit of inference is necessary, and little certainty is possible.

The first stage in joining the League was either recruitment or application, i.e., either someone sought out and encouraged (or coerced) a state to join, or a state by its own decision petitioned for membership. The sources indicate that both processes were at work. It is of course impossible always to tell whether an application is the product of a prior effort at recruitment, or whether some instances of recruitment were or were not coercive. Presumably the first few League members joined voluntarily; Athens possessed little coercive power at the time these alliances were made. The change in the status of Methymna from bilateral Athenian ally to member of the League appears to have been made at the Methymnaians' request, since the resolution embodying the change was introduced by the phrase περὶ / ὧν οἱ Μηθυμναῖοι λέγοσιν.[1] The Chalkis alliance of 377 includes a similar phrase, and the additional statement "th[at th]e boule res[olves] to accept the allianc[e] f[rom the] Chalkid[ia]ns, for good fortune, as [t]he Chalkidians req[ues]t."[2] Thus the tone of early League membership treaties seems consistent with that of the summary statement of Diodoros: "The Athenians sent out the most worthy among themselves as ambassadors to the states dominated by the Lakedaimonians, calling on (them) to hold on to the common freedom." While it is true that Diodoros records the dispatch of an Athenian military force under Chabrias to Euboia in 377, he places this event *after* most of the cities of the island had joined the League, and apparently is correct in saying that the troops were sent by the Athenians for "the protecting of their allies and the subduing of their opponents."[3] There is no reason to doubt that voluntary adherents were received throughout the period in which League members were being added. Allies whose names appear in lists of the stele of Aristoteles in sequences not reasonably connected with known recruitment voyages of Athenian generals (v. infra) probably sent presbeis to Athens and requested admission to the League on their own initiative; a reasonable example is Perinthos (line 84).

At a very early date, however, members began to be added in direct

1. SV 258, lines 3f.

2. SV 259, lines 7f (περὶ ὧν λ/[έγοσιν] οἱ Χαλκιδῆς) and 10–13 (ὅ[τι] δο/[κεῖ τῆ]ι βολῆι δέχεσθαι τὴν συμμαχία[ν] π/[αρὰ τῶν]Χαλκιδ[έω]ν τύχηι ἀγαθῆι, καθὰ ἐπ/αγγ[έλλον]τα[ι ο]ἱ Χαλκιδῆς).

3. Diod. 15.28.2 (chapter 3) and 15.30.3: δύναμιν ἐξέπεμψαν εἰς τὴν Εὔβοιαν τὴν παραφυλάξουσαν μὲν τοὺς συμμάχους, καταπολεμήσουσαν δὲ τοὺς ἐναντίους.

consequence of visits by Athenian naval squadrons. Chabrias gave the Euboians the aid mentioned in the preceding paragraph; then "he, sailing to the Cyclades islands, won over Peparethos and Skiathos and some others controlled by the Lakedaimonians." One can only speculate whether a coercive action is concealed by the verb translated "won over" (προσηγάγετο).[4] Defending the inherited privileges of Chabrias' son in his oration *Against Leptines* (355 B.C.), Demosthenes says that one consequence of Chabrias' victory at Naxos in 376 was that he "captured most of those islands and handed them over to you, and converted to friendship those formerly feeling enmity." The orator then has a clerk read out a list of ships and cities and treasures which Chabrias "took," and follows with his own summary statement that "he captured seventeen cities." But the same source comments on the refusal of the Chians, against whom Chabrias fought and died during the Social War, to abrogate the honors they had paid to him, because "they have considered his former kindnesses greater than his more recent offenses." The imperialistic tone of some of Demosthenes' other phrases may therefore be deceptive. The coerciveness of Chabrias' recruitment of League allies ultimately remains in doubt.[5] Timotheos won allies for Athens in 375 because of the mildness of his treatment of the conquered state of Korkyra (chapter 4). Korkyra itself was obviously offered the opportunity to join the League, but its magistrates (v. infra) apparently felt free to break off the process at an advanced stage; if the state suffered at Athens's hands for this, the sources certainly do not say so, and soon Korkyra became an ally of Athens and the League. Timotheos recruited more allies for the confederacy in the region of Thrace at some time shortly before or after his western voyage.[6] Iphikrates' recruiting plans, which were definitely coercively oriented,[7] were cancelled because of the signing of the peace of Sparta of 371.

The tendency to view Athens's recruitment of League members as originally voluntary and noncoercive, then becoming increasingly forcible and imperialistic, is rooted in false presuppositions about which

4. Diod. 15.30.5: αὐτὸς δὲ ταῖς Κυκλάσι νήσοις ἐπιπλέων προσηγάγετο Πεπάρηθον καὶ Σκίαθον καί τινας ἄλλας τεταγμένας ὑπὸ Λακεδαιμονίοις. A homiletic episode in another late source (Plut. *Phok.* 7.1) seems to attribute some harshness toward the allies to Chabrias (see chapter 10); the passage does not deal with recruitment, in any case.

5. Dem. 20.77 (εἷλε δὲ τῶν νήσων τούτων τὰς πολλὰς καὶ παρέδωκεν ὑμῖν καὶ φιλίας ἐποίησεν ἐχθρῶς ἐχούσας πρότερον), 78 (ἔλαβεν), 80 (ἑπτακαίδεκα μὲν πόλεις εἷλεν) and 81 (τὰς πάλαι χάριτας μείζους τῶν καινῶν ἐγκλημάτων πεποίηνται). One of the crowns dedicated to Chabrias on the base of his statue in the Athenian agora came from the citizens of another allied state, i.e., Mytilene (see B&E 80). The reference in *IG* II², 404 to Chabrias' dealings with the cities of Keos is neutral in tone.

6. Diod. 15.47.2f; see chapter 3 for dating problems. See also Ais. 2.70, which has its own problems (chapter 2).

7. Xen. *Hell.* 6.2.38 (quoted in chapter 3).

states became members of the League (chapters 4 and 5). Recruitment of League members was in fact an activity lasting only a few years, terminating around 374 (chapter 3). The safest interpretation of the meager evidence is that Athens employed both carrot and stick all along, in recruitment as in other areas. Incentives to join the League probably were coupled—explicitly or implicitly—with warnings of the consequences for those who refused. The alternative was not, however, the doom that had faced the Melians in the fifth century. The leaders of the fourth-century League lacked the power, and apparently also the arrogance, that is reflected in Thucydides' Melian Dialogue. A state refusing to join the League might simply be left to the doubtful mercy of the Spartans, and it might later be granted an Athenian alliance on less favorable terms. The Athenians, of course, organized their League primarily for their own advantage, as a means of regaining their lost status of leadership in Hellas; neither they nor their allies would have questioned the propriety of this motive. But small states gained advantages in joining the League, even if their adherence might be somewhat reluctant: for them it was a case of choosing the lesser of available evils. The fifth-century Empire was not reincarnated in the recruiting practices of the Second Athenian League.

Let us turn now to the stages beyond recruitment. When the Thebans joined the new League in 378, Diodoros says, *the Athenians* admitted them into equal membership (chapter 3). The treaty with Chalkis (377), although it appears to have referred to "the dogmat[a of the allies]" and in general to have recognized the existence of the League, seems to have been executed between Chalkis and Athens alone. Its oaths are said to have been sworn by "t[h]e ci[ty]" (i.e., Athens) and the Chalkidians, and the agreement is labeled "[Allian]ce of (the) Chal[kid]ians on Eu[b]oia [and (the) Athenia]ns."[8] The League membership treaty of Methymna, however, which seems to have been signed somewhat earlier, had involved the participation of the synedrion in the exchanging of its oaths, both in Athens and at Methymna:

ὀμόσαι δὲ τὴν πρ-
εσβείαν τῶν Μηθυμναίων τὸν αὐτὸν
ὅρκον, ὅμπερ καὶ οἱ ἄλλοι σύμμαχοι
ὤμοσαν, τοῖς τε συνέδροις τῶν συμμ-
15   άχων καὶ τοῖς στρατηγοῖς καὶ τοῖς
ἱππάρχοις. ὀμόσαι δὲ τοῖς Μηθυμνα-
ίοις τός τε συνέδρος τῶν συμμάχω[ν]
καὶ τὸς στρατηγὸς καὶ τὸς ἱππάρχο-
ς κατὰ ταὐτά. ἐπιμεληθῆναι δὲ Ἀί[σι]-

8. SV 259, lines 25f (τὰ δόγματ[α τῶ/ν συμμάχων---]), 13–15 (ὀμόσαι δὲ τ[ὴ]ν / πό[λιν Χα]λκι[δεῦ]σ[ι]ν καὶ τὸς Χαλκιδέα[ς 'Α]/θη[ναίοι]ς), and 20f ([συμμαχ]ία Χαλ[κιδ]έων τῶν ἐν Εὐ[β]οίαι [καὶ / 'Αθηναί]ων).

20   μον καὶ τὸς συνέδρος τὸς ἐπὶ τῶν [νε]-
    ῶν ὅπως ἂν ὀμόσωσιν αἱ ἀρχαὶ αἱ Μ[ηθ]-
    υμναίων καθάπερ οἱ ἄλλοι σύμμαχο[ι].

The embassy of the Methymnaians is to
swear the same oath, just as also the other
allies swore, to the synedroi of the allies
and to the generals and to the hipparchs.
And to the Methymnaians, the synedroi of
the allie[s] and the generals and the hipparchs are to swear in the same way. And
Ai[si]mon and the synedroi on the [sh]ips
are to see to it that the magistrates of (the)
M[eth]ymnaians swear just like the other
allie[s].[9]

Probably the definitive admission procedure was being worked out
piecemeal in these early treaties. Methymna was converting a bilateral
alliance into membership in the League, and the connection with the
other League members was the essential new element, so naturally their
representatives would be involved in the process. Chalkis, on the other
hand, was just coming into relationship with Athens, at a time when the
only alliances Athens was making were League membership alliances, so
perhaps the participation of the synedrion (or the mention of it in the
text of the treaty) may have seemed less necessary; or perhaps this Athenian resolution to make the alliance preceded a similar resolution of the
synedrion.

In any case, the involvement of the synedrion in the admission of
states to the League became standardized at an early date. Although the
treaty of 375 with Korkyra, Akarnania, and Kephallenia records an
agreement that was never fully carried out, there is no reason to believe
that the process it envisioned had not become the regular and normal
admission procedure. After the dating formula, the inscribed treaty
reads as follows:

    ἔδοξ[εν τῆι βολῆι καὶ τῶι δήμω]ι· Κρ[ιτ]-
5   [ί]ος εἶπε· περὶ ὧν λέγ[ουσιν ἐν τῆι βουλῆ]ι οἱ πρέσβ[ε]-
    [ς] τῶν Κερκυραίων καὶ τ[ῶν Ἀκαρνάνων κα]ὶ τῶν Κεφα[λ]-
    λήνων, ἐπαινέσαι μὲν τ[οὺς πρέσβες Κερκ]υραίων κα-
    ὶ Ἀκαρνάνων καὶ Κεφαλ[λήνων ὅτι εἰσὶ ἄ]νδρες ἀγαθ-
    οὶ περὶ τὸν δῆμον τὸν [Ἀθηναίων καὶ τὸς] συμμάχος [κ]-
10   αὶ νῦν καὶ ἐν τῶι πρόσθ[εν χρόνωι· ὅπως δ'] ἂν πραχθε[ι]
    ῶν δέονται, προσαγαγε[ῖν αὐτὸς ἐς τὸν δ]ῆμον, γν[ώ]μ[η]-
    ν δὲ ξυμβάλλεσθαι τῆς β[ουλῆς, ὅτι δοκεῖ] τῆι βουλῆ-
    ι ἀναγράψαι τῶν πόλεων τ[ῶν ἡκουσῶν τὰ ὀ]νόματα [ἐ]ς
    τὴν στήλην τὴν κοινὴν τῶ[ν συμμάχων τὸν] γραμμα[τ]έ-

9. SV 258, lines 11–22.

15   α τῆς βουλῆς καὶ ἀποδôνα[ι τὸς ὅρκους τα]ῖς πόλε[σι]
τοῖς ἥκόσαις τὴν βουλὴν [καὶ τὸς στρατηγὸς καὶ το]-
ὺς ἱππέας· καὶ τὸς συμμά[χος ὀμόσαι ὡσαύτως τὸν ὅρ]-
κον· πραχθέντων δὲ τούτ[ων ἑλέσθαι τὸν δῆμον καθ' ὅ]-
τι ἂν δόξει τῶι κοινῶι [τῶν συμμάχων ἄνδρας τὸς ἀπ]-
20   οληψομένος τὸς ὅρκος [παρὰ τῶν πόλεων τὸς καὶ ἀνα]-
γραφη[σομέν]ος εἰς τὴν στή[λην τὴν κοινὴν οὗ οἱ σύμ]-
μαχοι ἐ[γγ]εγραμ⟨μ⟩ένοι εἰσίν. π[έμψαι δὲ καὶ συνέδρο]-
ς τῶν πό[λ]εων ἑκάστην ἐς τὸ συν[έδριον τῶν συμμάχω]-
[ν] κατὰ τὰ δόγματα τῶς συμμάχω[ν καὶ τὸ δῆμο τὸ 'Αθην]-
25   [α]ίων.

4–10   Resol[ved by the boule and the demo]s. Kr[iti]os moved:
Concerning the things which the presb[eis] of the Korkyraians and t[he Akarnaians an]d the Kepha[l]lenians sa[id
in the boule], commend t[he presbeis of (the) Kork]yraians
and Akarnanians and Kephal[lenians because they are] good
[m]en toward the demos of (the) [Athenians and the] allies,
[b]oth now and in the form[er time].

10–15   [And so that] the things which they require may be ac-
complishe[d], brin[g them] forward [into the d]emos, and
send along a re[s]olu[t]ion of the b[oule, to the effect that]
the boule [resolves (that) the] secre[t]ary of the boule is to
inscribe [the n]ames of the states w[hich have come o]n the
common stele of th[e allies].

15–18   And the boule [and the generals and th]e knights are to
giv[e their oaths] to [t]he stat[es] which have come; and the
alli[es are to swear in like manner the oa]th.

18–22   The[se] things having been accomplished, [the demos is to
choose, just] as the League [of the allies] resolves, [men for
re]ceiving the oaths [from the states and for in]scri[bing
them] on the [common] ste[le, where the al]lies are l[i]sted.

22–25   Each of the st[a]tes [is also to] s[end synedro]i to the
syn[edrion of the allies] according to the dogmata of the allie[s and the demos of (the) Athen]ians.[10]

The presbeis of the would-be allies have addressed the Athenian boule
(lines 5–7), and the boule has recommended to the demos that their
cities' names be added to the list of League members (lines 12–14). In the
carrying out of this recommendation, the Athenians and the synedrion
share joint authority: allied and Athenian officials are to swear the oaths
at Athens (lines 15–18), and a committee for receiving the oaths of the
new members is to be chosen by the demos according to the synedrion's
recommendation (lines 18–20). Apparently the same committee (if not,

10. SV 262, lines 4–25 (all that remains is a fragmentary reference to some provision
concerning the Akarnanians; its content is impossible to determine).

another chosen in the identical manner) is to take care of the actual listing of the new member states' names (lines 20–22). The resolutions of the synedrion and the Athenians are to govern the sending of the new members' synedroi (lines 22–25). The process is entirely cooperative; there is no hint of Athenian dictation. Even the implication that the presbeis have addressed only the Athenian boule is doubtful; probably the synedrion was also approached. This contention is supported by the phrasing of a document that appears to be Thebes' League membership treaty of 378. The main text is lost, but Stephanos' amendment begins as follows: περὶ ὧν / [λέγοσιν οἱ ἐς τὸς συμμά]χος πρεσβεύσαντες / [τὰ μὲν ἄλλα καθάπερ τῆι] βολῆι. . . .[11] It seems clear that in this instance, the visiting presbeis have had some dealings with both the boule and the synedrion prior to the agreement on the alliance; one would certainly expect the same sort of procedure some three years later, when the synedrion was far larger and more firmly established. A resolution of the boule and demos simply need not make reference to concurrent action by the allies.

Both Marshall and Accame, however, believe that the admission of new allies to the League was an exclusive power of the Athenians. Marshall suggests that the synedrion could originally nullify the procedure by refusing to join in the oaths, but eventually lost this safeguard (he does not explain how), and Athens forced the synedrion to accept unwanted members, thus increasing allied dissatisfaction and contributing to the destruction of the League. He denies that the phrase κατὰ τὰ δόγματα τῶς συμμάχω[ν καὶ τὸ δήμο τὸ 'Αθην/α]ίων in lines 24f of the treaty quoted (supra) refers to any actual resolutions passed in connection with the new members' admission, arguing that it is instead a mere general admonition that synedroi are to be sent "according to the foundation principles of the Confederacy." Accame agrees with Marshall both in denying the synedrion's participation in the admission of League members and in asserting that it did have joint authority with Athens in making certain alliances *not* involving additions to the League. The acceptance of the latter proposition (which is true; see chapter 4) seems incongruous with the denial of the former. I see no reason to accept a strained interpretation ultimately based on the false presupposition (shared by both scholars) that Athens compelled the reluctant League allies to accept the admittance of most of Sparta's Peloponnesian allies to their synedrion. The clear import of the inscription quoted seems otherwise. In the particular phrase of lines 24f, after all, the reference to the dogmata of the allies is extant, whereas the participation of the Athenian demos must be restored.[12]

11. *SV* 255, lines 4–6.

12. Marshall 26–28, 79, and 103; Accame 126–129 and 160–162; cf. Rhodes, *Boule* 60 n. 5 (though I differ with some aspects of his discussion; see chapter 7).

Based on the treaty with Korkyra, Akarnania, and Kephallenia, further clarified by phrases within other inscribed treaties, the steps involved in a state's joining the Second Athenian League may be outlined with some certainty. The would-be member's ambassadors appeared before the Athenian boule[13] requesting the alliance; upon the approval of the boule, the presbeis were presented to the demos,[14] accompanied by the boule's favorable resolution.[15] The demos, which was the final authority in all the public acts of the Athenian democracy, then voted to make the alliance.[16] A resolution of the synedrion was also passed, in conjunction with any of the stages mentioned heretofore (before the state's ambassadors addressed the boule, between their visits to the boule and demos, or after the action of the demos). The acceptance of the alliance by the demos would have either envisioned its future acceptance or acknowledged its prior acceptance by the synedrion. An attractive, though unprovable, explanation of the inclusion of "the allies" in the title of some alliance treaties and their omission in the title of others is that the Athenian resolution included the phrase when the synedrion had already voted to accept the alliance and omitted it when the vote of the synedrion had not yet been taken.[17] In any event, the presbeis of the applicant state then swore the appropriate oaths to designated Athenian and League officials, and received these same persons' oaths in response.[18]

Certain alliance treaties appear to call for the inscribing of the new member state's name on the list of allies at this point, or even earlier.[19] Certainly no time was wasted in inscribing the individual state's alliance treaty,[20] and praise and hospitality for the visiting presbeis[21] must also have been awarded directly. But the actual listing of new League

13. Ais. 2.58 attests that this was standard diplomatic procedure. SV 262, line 5, and SV 259, lines 7–10, are clear as to this stage; SV 258 is surprising in its general omission of the participation of the boule (perhaps the inscription's general terseness accounts for it, or perhaps the mere conversion of an existing alliance into League membership was handled without referring the matter to the boule).

14. SV 259, lines 8f; SV 262, line 11.

15. SV 259, lines 9–11; SV 262, lines 11f.

16. SV 256, lines 3–6; SV 259, line 4; SV 262, line 4.

17. Allies included in "title": SV 256, lines 4–6; SV 258, lines 6–8. Allies omitted in "title": SV 259, lines 20f. There is no "title" in SV 262. The kind of verbal deference to the equal authority of the synedrion suggested here would probably have been appreciated by the allies, and could have done the Athenians no conceivable harm. It is equally—or more—believable, however, that only the customary Greek willingness to vary formulae is at work; see Rhodes, Boule 74: " . . . Athenian documents seem to have been so carelessly drafted that arguments from lack of logical cohesion can have little force. . . . "

18. SV 256, lines 8–10; SV 258, lines 11–19; SV 259, lines 13–15; SV 262, lines 15–18.

19. SV 258, lines 8–11; SV 262, lines 12–15.

20. SV 259, lines 15–18; SV 262, an inscribed treaty that was nevertheless partially aborted, is a particularly strong example.

21. SV 256, lines 12–15; SV 258, lines 23–25; SV 262, lines 7–10.

members on the stele of Aristoteles seems to have taken place only after the exchange of a further set of oaths: a committee was sent to receive the oaths of the applicant state's magistrates at home.[22] Only after these oaths had been received would the previously resolved listing of the state's name take place. This is the only interpretation that can reasonably account for the fact that an alliance made with Korkyra, the Akarnanian confederacy, and (apparently) all four of the cities of Kephallenia led to the listing of only the Akarnanians and one Kephallenian city (Pronnoi) on the stele of the allies. A minor consequence of this procedure is that the order of names on the lists should logically reflect the sequence in which notification reached Athens that member states' magistrates had taken the required oaths—not (as Accame contends) the order in which states' ambassadors came to Athens to make their treaties of alliance.[23]

The synedroi of individual states were presumably not allowed to take their seats until their states' officials had given their oaths and their states' names had been listed among the members of the League. Some time might elapse between the archival listing and the actual inscribing of a state's name,[24] but this would have caused no problems: surely a state would have been granted the privileges of the League from the time of the former. Its active membership would have begun with the seating of its representative(s) in the synedrion. The ancient evidence does not encourage any separation between League membership and the sending of synedroi, nor should the latter be seen as any sort of separate stage in, or degree of, League membership. When the same treaty (quoted supra) calls for the swearing of oaths, the listing of states' names, and the sending of synedroi, common sense infers that all were aspects of the same process: joining the League. The unlisted or unrepresented League member is purely a creation of modern scholarship.

Much has already been said about oaths and oath-takers, but little about the precise identity of the latter or the exact phraseology of the

22. *SV* 258, lines 19–22; *SV* 262, lines 18–22. There was a similar clause in the Athens-Chios alliance, signed prior to the organization of the League (*SV* 248, lines 32–35). Philip's strategy for excluding certain states from the protection of the peace of Philokrates in 346 (chapter 4) reflects his exploitation of this same principle of treaty ratification.

23. Accame 74 and 90.

24. The Methymna treaty presumably was signed before the passage of the decree of Aristoteles, since Methymna's name appears within the group of allies at the time of the decree. Thus there was no stele of Aristoteles when the treaty provided: ἀναγρ/άψαι αὐτὸς τὸν γραμματέα τῆς βολῆ/ς, ὥσπερ καὶ οἱ ἄλλοι σύμμαχοι ἀναγ/εγραμμένοι εἰσίν (*SV* 258, lines 8–11). This phrase, accordingly, must refer to an archival list. The apparent simultaneity of the inscribing of all the names of lines 99–130 on the stele of Aristoteles tends further to indicate that an archival record was kept prior to inscription. The convoluted geographical order of these names, moreover, supports the contention of the preceding paragraph, which thus applies to the preliminary list as well as to the stele. In connection with this note in general, see chapter 2.

former. Only one extant inscription (the Methymna treaty) specifically says that the ally's presbeis in Athens were to swear an oath, but the phrase τὸν αὐτὸν / ὅρκον, ὅμπερ καὶ οἱ ἄλλοι σύμμαχοι / ὤμοσαν indicates that their swearing was standard procedure.[25] The same treaty also shows that the taking of oaths from the allied state's magistrates was standard procedure: the magistrates of Methymna are to swear καθάπερ οἱ ἄλλοι σύμμαχο[ι].[26] As to which specific local magistrates are meant, the vagueness of phrases used[27] would appear to allow whatever magistrates the member state designated as appropriate to take its oaths, most probably its boule and military leaders.

Certainly there was variation in the identity of the oath-takers on the other side, i.e., that of the Athenians and League officials. The variation among extant treaties may reveal a natural development in procedure. Before the League was established, when Athens made a defensive alliance with Chios, the Athenians taking the oath were the boule, generals, and taxiarchs.[28] Byzantion joined an existing coalition, but one which apparently did not yet have a representative body, so the persons who swore oaths to the Byzantines were still all Athenians: boule, generals, and hipparchs.[29] Methymna became a member of a functioning League: the Athenian generals and hipparchs swore, but instead of the boule, the synedroi of the allies gave their oaths.[30] If Buckler's conjecture that the seventeen Theban representatives of *IG* II[2], 40 correspond to seventeen Athenian/allied oath-takers is sound, then his suggestion that these were the ten generals, the two hipparchs, and five synedroi of the five states admitted to the League prior to Thebes also would make excellent sense.[31] The Chalkis alliance is not very illuminating, saying only that "the city," i.e., Athens, swore alliance with Chalkis, whose representatives are likewise unspecified.[32] All bases are covered in the agreement with Korkyra, Akarnania, and Kephallenia: oaths were sworn by the boule, generals, knights, and "the allies."[33] Thus it had become standard

25. *SV* 258, lines 11–14. Note also the various types of references to presbeis in *SV* 248, lines 30–32 and 36–43; *SV* 255, lines 2f and 13(?); *SV* 256, lines 12–15 and 17–25; *SV* 259, lines 8 and 13; *SEG* XXI, 230, lines 3–6; and *SV* 262, lines 5–10 and 15f.

26. *SV* 258, lines 19–22.

27. *SV* 248, lines 32f; ἐγ Χί[ω]ι δὲ [τὴμ βολὴν / καὶ τὰς ἄλλ]ας ἀρχάς; *SV* 258, lines 21f: αἱ ἀρχαὶ αἱ Μ[ηθ]/υμναίων.

28. *SV* 248, lines 31f.

29. *SV* 256, lines 8–10; the lacuna which immediately follows could have held a reference to the synedroi, a fact that would destroy the neat developmental sequence suggested here, but would not affect any general conclusions.

30. *SV* 258, lines 17–19.

31. Buckler, "Theban Treaty Obligations in *IG* II[2] 40: A Postscript," *Historia* 20 (1971) 507f.

32. *SV* 259, lines 13–15; the treaty with Arethousa (*SEG* XXI, 230) is too fragmentary to add any information on this point.

33. *SV* 262, lines 15–18. The inclusion of the entire class of ἱππεῖς, rather than only their

procedure for oaths to be taken by certain Athenian officials (variable) and by the synedroi, whenever a new member was to be admitted to the League.

None of the treaties thus far cited provides the texts of the oaths themselves. Of extant Athenian treaties from the period of the Second Athenian League, only five include the wording of the oaths associated with them. Four of these are dated to years well after the cessation of additions to the League, and none of the four tells us much. A reformulated (non-League) alliance with the Euboian city of Eretria (341) is appropriately general in form, but it is the latest and briefest of the four. The settlement with rebellious cities of Keos (362), the alliance of Athens and its League with the Thessalian League (361/0), and the "bilateral" Athenian alliance with three northern kings (356) are all tailored to very specific situations, and their oaths may therefore be atypical.[34] However, the statement within the Thessalian treaty that "the same oath" is to be taken by the ally's presbeis at Athens and its magistrates at home probably does reflect general diplomatic practice, and would therefore also hold true for the double set of oaths required of states joining the League.

The only other Athenian treaty from this period that includes the wording of the oaths exchanged, and the only one of the five that dates from the early years of the League (i.e., during or shortly after the period in which oaths were exchanged with representatives of states joining the League) is the Athens-Korkyra alliance. I have argued (chapter 4) that this undated inscription, generally thought of as a League membership alliance of 375, is in fact a non-League membership alliance of 374–371. Accordingly, I cannot wholeheartedly accept Marshall's judgment that "The treaty of alliance with Korkyra preserves the form of oath taken by the Athenians on the one hand and the new ally on the other. There can be little doubt that here we have a formula going back to the very foundation of the Confederacy. . . ."[35] Since, however, the treaty *is* apparently early and since oaths are generally traditional and formulaic, it is a source which—with caution—we may employ. Its oaths read as follows:

15   ὅρκος· *vacat*
βοηθήσω Κορκυραίων τῶι δήμωι παντὶ σθένει κατὰ τὸ δυνατόν, ἐάν τις ἴηι ἐπὶ πολέμωι ἢ κατὰ γῆν ἢ κατὰ θάλατταν ἐπὶ τὴν χ-
ώραν τὴν Κορκυραίων καθ' [ὅ]τι ἂν ἐπαγγέλ-

---

leaders (the ἵππαρχοι), should have no significance: Rhodes, *Boule* 44, points out that such variation was typical fourth-century practice.

34. Eretria: SV 340, lines 6–11 (quoted in chapter 4); Keos: SV 289, lines 58–85; Thessaly: SV 293, lines 16–20 and 26–31; Northern kings: SV 309, lines 38–47.

35. Marshall 31.

20   λωσι Κορκυραῖοι, καὶ περὶ πολέμου καὶ ε-
ἰρήνης πράξω, καθότι ἂν τῶι πλήθει τῶν σ-
υμμάχων δοκῆι, καὶ τἆλλα ποιήσω κατὰ [τ]ὰ
[δ]όγματα τῶν συμμάχων. ἀληθῆ ταῦτα νὴ τὸ-
[ν] Δία καὶ τὸν Ἀπόλλω καὶ τὴν Δήμητρα· [ε]ὐο-
25   [ρ]κόντι μέμ μοι εἴη πολ[λ]ὰ καὶ ἀγαθά, εἰ δὲ
[μή], τἀναντία.   *vacat*
[βοηθήσω Ἀθ]ηναίων τῶι [δ]ήμωι παντὶ σθέν-
[ει κατὰ τὸ δυν]ατόν, αἴ κά τις ἐ[πίηι ἐπὶ πο]-
[λέμωι ἢ κατὰ γ]ῆν ἢ κατὰ θάλασσαν ἐ[πὶ τὴν]
30   [χώραν τὴν Ἀθην]αίων, καθ' ὅτι κ' ἐπαγ[γέ]λλω-
[ντι Ἀθηναῖ]οι, καὶ περὶ πολέμ[ο]υ κ[αὶ εἰρ]ή-
[νης πράξω, καθ' ὅ τ]ι κ[α] Ἀ[θ]ηναίο[ι]ς κ[α]ὶ [τῶι] π-
[λήθει τῶν συμμάχ]ων δ[ο]κῆι, κ[αὶ τἆ]λλα ποι-
[ήσω κατὰ τὰ δόγματα] τὰ Ἀθηνα[ί]ων κα[ὶ τῶ]ν
35   [συμμάχων. ἀληθῆ δὲ ταῦ]τα να[ὶ τ]ὸν Δία [κα]ὶ
[τὸν Ἀπόλλωνα καὶ τὰν Δά]ματ[ρα]. εὐορκ[έο]ν-
[τι μέμ μοι εἴη πολλὰ καὶ ἀγαθ]ά, εἰ δὲ μή, [τὰ]-
[ναντία].

Oath:

16–26   (Athenians:) I will give aid to the demos of (the) Korkyraians in full strength so far as possible, if anyone comes for war either by land or by sea against the territory of (the) Korkyraians, according to [w]hat (the) Korkyraians request; and concerning war and peace I will act according to what is resolved by the majority of the allies, and I will do other things according to [t]he [d]ogmata of the allies. (I swear) these things truly by Zeus and Apollo and Demeter. May ma[n]y good things befall me if I s[w]ear [t]ruly, but if [not], the opposite.

27–38   (Korkyraians:) [I will give aid] to the [d]emos of (the) [Ath]enians in full streng[th so far as poss]ible, if anyone c[omes for war either by l]and or by sea a[gainst the territory] of (the) [Athen]ians, according to what (the) [Athenian]s re[qu]es[t]; and concerning wa[r] a[nd pe]a[ce I will act according to wha]t is res[o]lved by (the) A[th]enia[n]s a[n]d [by the] m[ajority of the alli]es, a[nd I will do ot]her things [according to the dogmata] of (the) Athen[i]ans an[d th]e [allies. (I swear) the]se things [truly] b[y] Zeus [an]d [Apollo and De]met[er. May many goo]d things [befall me if I] swe[ar] truly, but if not, [the opposite].[36]

Both the Athenian oath (lines 16–26), in Attic dialect, and the oath of the Korkyraians (lines 27–38), in a mixture of Attic and Doric, have

36. SV 263, lines 15–38.

essentially three parts: (1) a pledge to defend the other party, if attacked; (2) an agreement to be bound by the general policies of (Athens and) the League, and (3) the invocation of the traditional deities, with blessings and curses for compliance or noncompliance with the oath. The mutual pledges to render aid to the other party, if attacked, were standard for any defensive alliance; surely the oaths of states joining the League would have included a similar provision. It may be significant that whereas the body of the treaty (quoted in chapter 4) pledges mutual defense also of the signatories' democratic constititions, the oaths themselves pledge only defense of their territories. This slight difference might indicate that the oath formula was more standardized and traditional than the terms of the individual treaty itself.[37] If so, the "tradition" invoked is likely to have been the phrasing of the oaths connected with League membership alliances in the years just prior to the signing of this treaty. The promises to allow Athens and the allies to determine questions of war and peace and τἆλλα seem (as I have argued in chapter 4) a bit too broad in their implications to have been standard inclusions in oaths of League members in years prior to the peace of 375/4; these pledges are in fact the primary reason I would prefer to date the treaty possibly as late as 371. But surely some general undertaking to act in accord with the hegemon and the majority of the synedrion had always been included, though probably phrased with more delicacy. Divine blessings and sanctions also were standard parts of many oaths, presumably including the oaths taken by states joining the Athenian League. If this alliance had committed Korkyra to membership in the League (as I contend it did not), one additional element should logically have been included: a pledge to defend the territory of any League member, if attacked. The precise wording of the oath taken by the synedroi probably would not have been inscribed; it could not have differed greatly from those of the Athenians and the individual state joining the League. All in all, it is a reasonable inference that the oaths exchanged when allies were added to the confederacy were quite similar to the oaths of the Athens-Korkyra alliance.

Joining the League involved application or recruitment, an exchange of oaths in Athens, the reception of further oaths from the new allied state's magistrates at home, the listing of the new member's name on the stele of the decree of Aristoteles, and the sending and seating of its representative(s) to the synedrion. Who were the synedroi, who chose them, and how many were there?

Accame thinks that probably the presbeis of the original five League members were themselves made the first synedroi.[38] This theory may

---

37. Certain fourth-century Athenian alliance treaties, in fact, simply direct their signatories to swear "the customary oath" (τὸν νόμιμον ὅρκον), e.g., SV 229, lines 8f; SV 280, lines 37f; SV 293, lines 19f.

38. Accame 36.

well be sound—at least *some* of them may have become synedroi. The developed practice probably was different, however. A treaty readmitting Euboian cities to League membership in 357 included the following provision: "Commend [the demos of (the) Kar]ystians and [the pr]esb[ei]s of the Karystians [and the syn]edros and invit[e t]hem f[o]r hospitality to the pry[taneion] on the morrow."[39] Here a city's plural presbeis are clearly differentiated from its single synedros, and all are in Athens at once. While no reason appears to exist for excluding the ambassadors who sign League membership alliances from being chosen as synedroi for their states, there is no demonstrable connection between the holding of the two posts.

At the founding of the confederacy, says Diodoros, the Athenian demos established a synedrion of all the allies, καὶ συνέδρους ἐπέδειξαν ἑκάστης πόλεως. The only available subject for the third-person plural verb ἐπέδειξαν ("appointed") is ὁ δῆμος, a usage which Greek grammar permits.[40] Accordingly, Diodoros is saying that (at least originally) *the Athenians* chose the allies' synedroi. It is very likely that Diodoros is simply employing careless language, but if not, developed usage apparently differed in this area. The treaty signed with Korkyra, Akarnania, and Kephallenia in 375 (v. supra) included a provision (lines 22–25) that each of the states was to send synedroi "according to the dogmata of the allie[s and the demos of (the) Athen]ians." This phrasing implies that either the synedrion and the Athenian demos cooperated in choosing new members' synedroi, or more likely that they cooperated in establishing guidelines whereby new members might choose their own. In either case, there was little likelihood that any synedros strongly inimical to Athens would have been appointed. No serious conflict between the demos and the synedrion is to be discovered in the sources[41]—assuming that we may discount the rhetorical accusations of Aischines in connection with the negotiation of the peace of Philokrates of 346 (chapter 4). It is to be noted that when a representative of the synedrion was desired to accompany the Athenian embassy sent to Philip in that year, he was chosen by the Athenians, though Accame may be correct in inferring that there was a preceding allied decree.[42]

39. *SV* 304, lines 7–10: ἐπαινέσαι δὲ [τὸν δῆμ/ον τὸν Καρ]υστίων καὶ [τοὺς πρ]έσβ[ει]ς τῶν Καρυστίων [καὶ τ/ὸν σύν]εδρον καὶ καλέσ[αι α]ὐτὸς ἐ[π]ὶ ξένια εἰς τὸ πρυ[τανε/ῖον] εἰς αὔριον.

40. Diod. 15.28.3 (fuller quotation in chapter 3). H.W. Smyth, *Greek Grammar*[2] (Cambridge, Mass. 1956) 263, no. 950, states the rule, providing an excellent contemporary example in Xen. *Hell.* 3.3.4.

41. Rejecting (chapter 5) Rhodes's interpretation of the action of the synedrion in negotiations with Dionysios of Syracuse. Cf. the constant wrangling within the Peloponnesian League: see R. E. Smith, "The Opposition to Agesilaus' Foreign Policy, 394–371 B.C.," *Historia* 2 (1954) 282.

42. Ais. 2.20, addressing the demos, refers to Ἀγλαοκρέοντα τὸν Τενέδιον, ὃν ἐκ τῶν συμμάχων εἵλεσθε; Accame 202.

No one doubts, nor is there any reason to doubt, the assertion of Diodoros that each state, regardless of its size, had one vote in the synedrion. Busolt and Accame infer that each state therefore had only one synedros.[43] This was certainly true for the Euboian city of Karystos in 357 (v. supra). The provision that "synedroi" are to be sent by "each" of the states of Korkyra, Akarnania, and Kephallenia (also v. supra) represents only a difference between Greek and English syntax: the phrasing neither requires nor excludes singular or plural representatives for any of the three individual states. An Athenian decree of 340/39 commends Aratos of Tenedos, who is known from another inscription to have been a Tenedian synedros, a fact which tends to justify the long restoration ἐπαι/[νέσαι δὲ τὸν σύνεδρον τῶν Τενεδίω]/ν Ἄρα[τ]ον. A line further along, some editors wish to make a somewhat more adventurous restoration: ἐπ[αι]νέ[σαι δὲ καί . . . .[16]. . . . . . .τοὺς σ]/υνέ[δρ]ο[υς τῶν Τενεδίων---].[44] The restoration of the plural form [σ]υνέ[δρ]ο[υς] cannot absolutely be ruled out, but it is certainly too shaky a basis for any generalizations. The repetition of the verb does indeed make it unlikely that the phrase refers again to Aratos as the single synedros. It still remains possible, however, that a representative of some other state is being praised along with Aratos the Tenedian.[45] Another possibility would be that Aratos is praised as outgoing or incoming synedros, and that the second commendation applies to his successor or predecessor. Thus this inscription too is unhelpful in determining whether or not states might have more than one synedros.[46]

One inscribed text, however, seems decisive. An Athenian decree of 368/7 includes the following invitations to hospitality:

καλέσαι δὲ καὶ τοὺς συνέδρο[υ]-
[ς τοὺς] Μυτιληναίων ἐπὶ ξένια εἰς τὸ πρυταν[ε]ῖο[ν] εἰς αὔ[ρι]-
[ον. κ]αλέσαι δὲ καὶ τοὺς συνέδρους τῶμ Μηθυμναίων
[καὶ Ἀ]ντισσαίων καὶ Ἐρεσίων καὶ Πυρραίων ἐπὶ ξ[ένια]
30   [εἰς τ]ὸ πρυτανεῖον εἰς αὔριον.[47]

The plural article of line 26 makes the restoration of the plural συνέδρο[υς] of Mytilene certain, though the usual sort of uncertainty exists for the number of representatives the other cities (lines 28f) have. Accame, defending his thesis that each League member had only one synedros, is

43. Diod. 15.28.4 (quoted in chapter 3); Busolt 689; Accame 37 and 109f.

44. *IG* II², 233, lines 27f and 29f (the line numbers of Tod 175 differ); Aratos is identified as a Tenedian synedros in *IG* II², 232, lines 6f.

45. Cf. the praise for Antimachos the Chian and someone from Mytilene in what appears to be a Theban alliance treaty (*SV* 255, lines 10f; text in chapter 3).

46. The mention of plural Byzantine synedroi in *IG* VII, 2418, line 11, is irrelevant: Byzantion at this time (ca. 355–351) was disaffected from the Athenian League, and these synedroi were apparently representatives to the Boiotian alliance.

47. *IG* II², 107, lines 26–30, brackets as by Accame 109.

forced to explain away this clear reference in a primary source to the plural representatives of Mytilene, and he formulates the following ingenious theory. The mason intended, says Accame, to inscribe an all-inclusive invitation to hospitality, directed toward the synedroi (one each) of all these cities of Lesbos, so he began by cutting the phrase "And invite also the synedroi of (the) Mytilenaians . . . ," intending simply to add "and of (the) Methymnaians, etc." But, perhaps because the majority of the inscription had dealt with the Mytilenaians alone, he absentmindedly forgot to complete his list, and cut instead the end of the formula: ". . . for hospitality to the prytaneion on the morrow." Only at this point, says Accame, did the stonecutter notice his omission, so he corrected it as best he could by repeating the invitation for the representatives of Methymna, Antissa, Eresos, and Pyrrha.[48]

I see no reason to accept this adventurous reconstruction, and I agree instead with scholars who have been willing simply to accept what the inscription says. J. A. O. Larsen offers a sensible argument for believing that some states had more than one representative in the synedrion:

In the Second Athenian League it must have often been impossible to get instructions from home. For that reason the states which could afford it may well have found it desirable to have more than a single representative on hand. This may indirectly have made it possible to send *synedroi* along on embassies and other executive missions without interfering with the efficiency of the *synedrion*.[49]

Since each League member cast a single vote in the synedrion, it was probably quite immaterial to the Athenians whether an ally sent one representative or several (just so all who were sent were "acceptable"? v. supra). Beyond the apparent facts that Karystos at some point had one synedros and Mytilene at another point had more than one, we know absolutely nothing about the size of the various states' delegations. No basis exists for suggesting any sort of "proportionality" in states' size or importance, such as was reflected in representation—and voting—in some other confederacies.

A state became a participant in the Second Athenian League after the prerequisites heretofore discussed, when it began to be represented in the synedrion. Beyond its participation in this very process of adding new members, we must still attempt to determine the main business of the synedrion.

48. Accame 109f.
49. Larsen, *Rep. Govt.* 59. Others accepting the implication of this text include Marshall, 22 and 52f, and Burnett, "Expans." 9 n. 9, who sees in "the synedroi on the ships" of SV 258, lines 20f (v. supra) an example of the sort of mission on which extra synedroi might be employed. If Aglaokreon was one of plural Tenedian representatives, his going with the Athenian embassy to Macedon would not have deprived his city of its vote in the synedrion during his absence.

7

THE SYNEDRION AND ITS POWERS

The synedrion of the Second Athenian League sat at Athens. Its precise meeting place is unknown. The stele of the allies, by one of its own provisions, was to be set up "beside the (statue of) Zeus Eleutherios," which apparently was located in front of the Stoa of Zeus, near the northwest corner of the agora. It might be reasonable to suspect that the meeting place of the allies was somewhere close by. The only place concretely associated with any action of the synedrion, however, is the Strategion (generals' headquarters), near the southwest corner of the agora; it is the place where the ambassadors of Philip received the oaths of the synedroi in connection with the peace and alliance of 346 B.C. Showing how irregularly, yet how frequently, the synedrion was called upon, Marshall and Accame argue convincingly that the synedroi resided at Athens, and that the synedrion apparently did not have regularly scheduled meetings, but met as needed.[1]

Although no ancient source explicitly says that Athens was *not* represented in the synedrion, it is clear from the phrasing of several sources —especially the Athens-Korkyra alliance treaty—that the Athenians did not have a vote therein.[2] Nor does it appear that any Athenian(s)—even without a vote—presided over the deliberations of the synedrion. The only extant inscribed decree of the allies (dated 372) is introduced by the following formula: "_____ (the) [Th]eban having called for the [vot]e, resolved by t[h]e [a]llies. . . ." Thebes had no special legal status among the allies (relations between Athens and Thebes were in fact rather strained at this time), so presumably a presiding officer of the synedrion could have been a representative of any member state. We do not know his title, nor whether he presided alone or was only one member of a presiding committee.[3] Accame believes that the prytaneis of the

---

1. Accame, 107 nn. 1 and 3, cites sources showing that the synedrion sat at Athens, including *IG* II², 103, lines 14f; Isok. 14.21 and 8.29; Ais. 3.91; and Diod. 15.28.4. Location of stele: DA, lines 65f. Oaths at Strategion: Ais. 2.85. Locations of Stoa of Zeus and Strategion: John Travlos, *Pictorial Dictionary of Classical Athens* (London 1971) p. 25, fig. 34, nos. 37 and 40. Continuous presence and irregular meetings: Marshall 22f, esp. n. 7; Accame 107-109. Larsen, *Rep. Govt.* 54, agrees.

2. Accame 112-114; see also Marshall 22f; Larsen, *Rep. Govt.* 58; and Ryder, *KE* 56f.

3. *SV* 268 (text of Accame 230), lines 15f: ἐ[πιψηφί]ζοντος / . υ ... [Θ]ηβαίο, ἔδοξεν τ[οῖ]ς [συ]μμάχοις. Larsen, *Rep. Govt.* 60f, argues from the institutions of later confederacies that the Theban who called for the vote was one of a group of officers of the synedrion called πρόεδροι. While the *Athenian* proedroi seem to have been organized at about the time of the establishment of the League, the inference that the title was also used in the synedrion is unwarranted.

Athenian boule held the authority to call the synedrion into session,[4] but there is no evidence. It seems equally possible that the synedrion's own presiding officer(s) convoked its meetings.

A handful of inscriptional and literary passages throw light on what we may call, for want of a better term, the "legislative" relationship between the synedrion and the institutions of the Athenian government. In 368, the boule resolved:

περὶ μὲν τῶν γρα[μ]μά[των ὧ]-
[ν ἔπε]νψεν Διονύσιος [τῆς] ο[ἰκ]οδομ[ίας τ]-
[οῦ νε]ὼ καὶ τῆς εἰρή[ν]ης τὸς συ[μ]μά[χους δ]-
[όγμ]α ἐξενενκε[ῖν εἰς] τὸν δῆμον, [ὅτι ἂν α]-
[ὐτο]ῖς βουλευ[ο]μ[έ]νοι[ς δοκ]ῆι ἀρί[στον ε]-
[ἶνα]ι.

10

Concerning the wr[i]ti[ngs which] Dionysios [se]nt (about) [the] (re)b[ui]ldi[ng of the (Delphic) temp]le and the pea[c]e, the a[l]li[es] ar[e to] bring in [a dogm]a [into] the demos, [whatever] to [them], h[a]vin[g] conside[r]ed, [see]ms [to b]e be[st].[5]

In 362/1, the Athenians decreed:

[ἐπει]-
[δὴ δ]ὲ οἱ σύμμαχοι δόγμα εἰσήνεγκαν εἰς τ[ὴν βουλ]-
[ήν, δ]έχεσθαι τὴν συμμαχίαν καθὰ ἐπαγγέλ[λονται ο]-
[ἱ Ἀρ]κάδες καὶ Ἀχαιοὶ καὶ Ἠλεῖοι καὶ Φλε[ιάσιοι, κα]-
[ὶ ἡ βο]υλὴ προβούλευσεν κατὰ ταὐτά, δεδό[χθαι τῶι δ]-
[ήμωι εἶ]ναι συμμάχους τύχηι ἀγαθ[ῆι τοῦ δήμου εἰς]
[τὸν ἀεὶ] χρόνον Ἀθηναί[ων τὸν δῆμον καὶ τοὺς συμμά]-
[χος καὶ Ἀ]ρκάδ[ας, κτλ].

15

[Since] the allies brought forth a dogma into t[he boule] to [a]ccept the alliance on terms [the Ar]kadians and Achaians and Eleans and Phle[iasians] requ[est, and the bo]ule offered a probouleuma to the same effect, [it] has [been] reso[lved by the demos that], to the goo[d] fortune [of the demos], allies [for all] time are to [b]e [the demos of] (the) Atheni[ans and their allies and (the) A]rkad[ians, etc.].[6]

In 343, Aischines claimed to be quoting what was "expressly" (διαρρήδην) said in a decree of the allies three years earlier:

ἐπειδὴ βουλεύεται ὁ δῆμος ὁ Ἀθηναίων ὑπὲρ εἰρήνης πρὸς Φίλιππον, οἱ δὲ πρέσβεις οὔπω πάρεισιν, οὓς ἐξέπεμψεν ὁ δῆμος εἰς τὴν Ἑλλάδα παρακαλῶν τὰς πόλεις ὑπὲρ τῆς

4. Accame 118; cf. Larsen, *Rep. Govt.* 211 n. 23.
5. *IG* II², 103, lines 8–13, brackets as by Accame 115.
6. *SV* 290, lines 12–20.

ἐλευθερίας τῶν Ἑλλήνων, δεδόχθαι τοῖς συμμάχοις, ἐπειδὰν ἐπιδημήσωσιν οἱ πρέσβεις καὶ τὰς πρεσβείας ἀπαγγείλωσιν Ἀθηναίοις καὶ τοῖς συμμάχοις, προγράψαι τοὺς πρυτάνεις ἐκκλησίας δύο κατὰ τὸν νόμον, ἐν δὲ ταύταις βουλεύσασθαι περὶ τῆς εἰρήνης Ἀθηναίους· ὅ τι δ' ἂν βουλεύσηται ὁ δῆμος, τοῦτ' εἶναι κοινὸν δόγμα τῶν συμμάχων.

Since the demos of the Athenians is deliberating concerning peace with Philip, but the presbeis are not yet present, whom the demos sent out into Greece encouraging the states on behalf of the freedom of the Greeks, it has been resolved by the allies that, when the presbeis shall have returned home and shall have reported their business to the Athenians and the allies, the prytaneis are to call two meetings according to the law, and in these the Athenians are to deliberate concerning the peace; and that whatever the demos shall decide, this shall be the common dogma of the allies.[7]

In 330, Aischines apparently referred again to this resolution, amended by the synedroi to the effect that any Greek state might add its name to those of the signatories over a three-month period. Aischines and Demosthenes accuse each other of sabotaging the allies' intent by inducing the demos to support instead a resolution sponsored by the traitor Philokrates.[8] The kernel of truth buried within their mutual invective is that the peace made with Philip was on terms different from those desired by the synedroi, and that an alliance, which the synedrion had not sought, was coupled with the peace.

From the quoted passages it is clear that all of the following procedures were operative:

1. The boule could direct the synedrion to prepare a dogma on a subject prior to the consideration of it by the demos;

2. The synedrion could produce a dogma prior to the consideration of its subject by either the boule or demos;

3. The synedrion could pass a resolution on a topic currently under discussion by the demos; and

4. The synedrion could direct the Athenian prytaneis to convene the demos for discussion of a specified topic.

A reasonable inference from the combination of these passages is that an item of League business might be taken up initially by either the Athenians or the allies, and that the other partner might begin its consideration of the subject simultaneously with any stage in the deliberations of the partner who took up the issue first.

If there was no prescribed chronological order in which the allies and the Athenians could begin dealing with a subject, it would logically follow that neither should there be an invariable order in which the partners would complete the process, i.e., would pass their respective resolutions. It happens that in two of the three cases documented by the

7. Ais. 2.60.
8. Ais. 2.61–68 and 3.69–75; Dem. 19.15 and 144; 18.7–24.

quoted passages the synedrion definitely passed its resolution earlier than the demos, and that in the third case (the negotiations with Dionysios) it was called upon by the boule to do so, and probably complied. We must bear in mind, however, that our sources are overwhelmingly Athenian. An allied dogma passed later than an Athenian resolution on the same subject would probably mention the Athenian resolution, just as the two quoted Athenian inscriptions mention past and immediately prospective allied dogmata prior to action by the demos. But resolutions of either the synedrion or the demos, if passed before the other body has considered the topic, might very well not make reference to the body that has not yet passed its resolution. The safe inference from the omission of reference to allied participation in an Athenian decree, when that decree deals with some subject known from other sources sometimes to have involved the synedrion's participation, is that the allies had not *yet* acted. This is far different from the inference that in the particular case the synedrion would not or need not act.

Scholars differ widely in their views on Athenian-allied "legislative" relations. P. J. Rhodes, citing the same sources I have quoted, concludes: "For matters requiring action from Athens as well as her allies, the Athenian ecclesia seems to have been the sovereign body, with the Athenian boule and the allied συνέδριον as parallel probouleutic bodies. . . ." Cf. the viewpoint of Hammond: "If on a specific matter the resolution of the Athenian State and the resolution of the Council of the Allies were at odds, no action was taken by the Alliance as a whole; for the two bodies were equal in power, and a dead-lock between them could not be broken. If the resolutions were in agreement, the matter was thereby decided for the Alliance as a whole."[9] I strongly prefer Hammond's statement of the legal situation, as do many scholars, though some of the same persons suggest that Athenian assertiveness eventually led to increasing Athenian domination of the partnership.[10] The position of Rhodes implies a legal inferiority of the synedrion to the Athenian demos. But, whereas it is obviously true that the synedrion could not make League policy without the concurrence of the demos, the import of the dogma quoted by Aischines is that the same situation prevailed in the other direction. A probouleutic body would not have to inform the sovereign assembly that the resolution it should adopt was approved in advance; only a body having concurrent authority would serve notice that in a particular case it was waiving that authority.

9. Rhodes, *Boule* 60f; Hammond, *HG²* 486f.

10. See, e.g., Marshall 43; Larsen, *Rep. Govt.* 58; Meiggs, *AE* 403; N. N. Grebensky, "Elements of Parliamentarism in the Second Maritime Confederacy," *VDI* 122 (1972) 118 (English summary); F. E. Adcock and D. J. Mosley, *Diplomacy in Ancient Greece* (London 1975) 76f; and Sealey, *City-Sts.* 410.

Nor did the Athenians abuse their allies' generosity, as the mutual incriminations of Aischines and Demosthenes might lead one to suppose. The synedrion of course wanted a better arrangement with Philip than it got, but its resolution amounted to a virtual "blank check" to the Athenians to make whatever arrangement was possible in the circumstances. Neither of the rival orators suggests that any of the synedroi were disinclined to swear to the ultimate agreement, which was essentially dictated by Philip's ambassadors. Athens and the League members had a common interest in these negotiations, but Philip had the power to extort concessions from both. There is very little evidence for an increasing Athenian usurpation of power at the expense of the synedrion. This widespread belief is largely a consequence of the supposition that the Athenians were somehow carried away by "idealism" in the early days of the League, and granted their allies an equality they later came to regret. The sources seem rather to indicate that the letter of "legislative equality" between Athens and its allies was, from first to last, observed by the power everyone recognized as in reality the stronger, i.e., Athens. Let us now turn to a discussion of the various areas in which the synedrion's formally equal powers were exercised.

Since a resolution of the synedrion was necessary for the admission of a new member to the League (chapter 6), one would expect that the formation of *any* alliance involving the League would require the passage of an allied dogma. Clearly such resolutions were passed in connection with the alliance requested by the four Peloponnesian states in 362/1 and prior to the alliance signed with Philip in 346, as passages quoted (supra) show. Testimonia associated with other alliance treaties are less clear-cut. Xenophon's account of the making of the alliance between the Athenian and Spartan confederacies[11] in 369 appears, *prima facie*, to indicate that the Athenians accepted the alliance without any consultation of the synedrion. But Xenophon, who nowhere shows any interest in the Athenian League, apparently simply omits to describe the doubtless very brief and perfunctory discussion of the alliance within the synedrion, which probably took place after the debate before the Athenian demos which he describes. Otherwise, we would have to suppose that Athens allowed the allies of Sparta to participate in the formation of the general alliance while not allowing its own to do so, for Prokles the Phleiasian addressed the demos in the debate.[12] The alliance treaty

11. It is impossible to deny that the members of the Athenian League were bound by the alliance (chapter 4): they are clearly most, if not all, of the "allies" who are said to have preferred the Athenians as leaders at sea, and some of them may have been included among the "allies" who proceeded to Korinth after the treaty was signed (Xen. *Hell.* 7.1.5 and 15).

12. Xen. *Hell.* 7.1.1–15; the terse account of Diod. 15.67.1 does not mention the allies of either hegemon; see *SV* 274.

signed by the Athenians and the Thessalian League in 361/0 had a provision that the respective allies of each should be included, yet its text mentioned no participation of the synedroi in the oath-taking or at any other stage of making the agreement.[13] In this case also, I believe it is safer to be ruled by the above-mentioned clear examples of the synedrion's participation, which are dated both before and after the signing of this treaty, than to see in the omissions within its formulae an exception to general practice. Principles I have already invoked—from mere terseness to conscious Athenian deference to the synedrion's not yet having voted—can explain such omissions more easily than any theory yet suggested can explain some apparent chronological pattern of "alternation" of the synedrion's involvement and noninvolvement in making alliances to which the League was a party.

The Athens-Korkyra alliance, which I contend (chapter 4) was one such alliance despite its deceptive "title," includes what may be regarded as the governing principle. The Athenian representatives were to swear: περὶ πολέμου καὶ ε/ἰρήνης πράξω, καθότι ἂν τῶι πλήθει τῶν σ/υμμάχων δοκῆι.[14] An "alliance" (συμμαχία) was in essence a pledge, in certain circumstances, to make war in common (συμμαχεῖν), and to maintain peace between the parties to the pledge. Thus the making of alliances to which the League was a party must always have been a process in which the League members' representatives were involved; otherwise, their "autonomy" as free allies was meaningless from the very beginning, even legally speaking.

In the same Korkyra treaty, Athens swore not only to follow the allied majority on questions of war and peace, but promised in addition: καὶ τἆλλα ποιήσω κατὰ [τ]ὰ / [δ]όγματα τῶν συμμάχων. The expression τἆλλα appears broad enough to Wickersham and Verbrugghe to warrant the translation "all other matters."[15] Their interpretation seems excessive; the Greek lacks any word signifying "all." But this provision within the oath undoubtedly recognized wide areas of authority shared by the Athenians with their League allies as represented by the synedrion. A passage in the Athenian decree honoring Dionysios of Syracuse (quoted supra) shows that the synedrion was involved with "peace" (which is hardly surprising) and with the rebuilding of the Delphic temple, which had been severely damaged by fire or earthquake in the winter of 373–2.[16]

The synedrion participated in the readmission of rebellious allies to

13. SV 293 (see chapter 4).
14. SV 263, lines 20–22.
15. SV 263, lines 22f; WV 26—translating similarly in the body of the treaty (line 14) and the oath of the Korkyraians (line 33).
16. Inscriptions recording contributions to rebuild the temple are collected in Fouilles de Delphes (Paris 1932) III (5), 1–13; see summary in Tod 140 comm.

the League. A fragmentary inscription includes the following provision of an Athenian resolution:

> ἀναγρ[ά]ψαι δὲ τὸ [ψ]ήφισμα καὶ τὰς διαλ–
> λαγὰς [ἃ]ς ἐπ[οιήσ]αντο οἱ σύμμαχοι τοῖ–
> [ς] Παρίο[ι]ς, κτλ.
>
> (Someone) is to inscr[i]be the (Athenian) [r]esolution and the agreements [whi]ch the allies m[ad]e with th[e] Paria[n]s . . . .

The stone in fact bore the text of both. The quoted passage (at the end of the Athenian resolution, most of which is lost) was followed by the only extant inscribed decree of the synedrion, put to the vote by a Theban presiding officer (supra). The provisions of the dogma, though poorly preserved, make the subject matter of the entire inscription clear: Paros had rebelled and was being taken back into the League, with both reassurances and warnings.[17] The oaths of a treaty of 363/2 readmitting rebellious Keans to the League (chapter 6) were sworn by "the allies" in addition to Athenian officials, and the rebels also swore their oath to them. Moreover, any Kean who no longer wished to live in his native island was given permission "to live wherever he wishes among th[e allied sta]tes."[18] It would be very difficult to believe that the synedrion was not consulted in connection with this promise. Once again, such clear examples of allied participation outweigh the negative impression which might arise from the omission of reference to allied involvement in other readmission treaties, e.g., those of Karystos (357) and Mytilene (346).[19]

Certain "judicial" powers (to use another admitted anachronism) of the synedrion were outlined in the decree of Aristoteles itself. One such passage directed that if any magistrate or private person should bring forth a proposal contravening any part of the decree,

let (this) [s]uffice for him to be without civic rights, and let [hi]s [g]oo[ds] be public (property), and [t]he ti[th]e (be the property) of the go[ddess], and let (him) be judged among (the) Athen[ian]s and t[he] allies as destroying the allianc[e], and let them [p]unish him by death or exile from wh[erever] (the) Athenians and the allies contro[l].[20]

The key phrase, κρινέσθω ἐν Ἀθην[αί/ο]ις καὶ τ[οῖς] συμμάχοις, has led several scholars to argue that offenders were to be judged—to employ Marshall's words—"in (a joint court of) the Athenians and their allies."

17. SV 268 (text of Accame 230); quoted passage in lines 7–9.
18. SV 289, lines 58 (allies swear), 70 (Keans swear to allies), and 64–66 (passage partially translated: εἰ δέ τις / [μὴ βούλεται οἰ]κεῖν ἐγ Κέωι, ἐάσω αὐτὸν ὅπο ἂν βόληται τῶ/[ν συμμαχίδων πόλ]εων οἰκόντα τὰ ἑαυτὸ καρπὸσθαι).
19. SV 304 and 328. Accame, 130, draws the same conclusion from the same two clear examples.
20. DA, lines 54–61.

Accame goes so far as to suggest that this "joint court" was perhaps made up of equal numbers of Athenian and allied representatives. But this widely held interpretation rests ultimately on nothing more substantial than the mere absence of a second preposition ἐν before τ[οῖς] συμμάχοις. I strongly prefer the viewpoint of those, e.g., Larsen, who contend that the phrase refers to two separate trials—one before an Athenian court and one before "the allies," i.e., in the synedrion. This interpretation is consistent with the general pattern of authority within the confederacy that has been emerging throughout this chapter: each of the two formally equal partners—Athens and the allies—acted separately, and decisions of the League as a whole required the agreement of both.[21] An Athenian decree of ca. 357–6 prescribed punishment similar to that threatened in the passage just quoted, for anyone—Athenian or allied citizen—who should invade Attica or any allied state: he is to be condemned to death, his property is to be confiscated (the tithe to the goddess), and his goods are to be recoverable from any allied state, which shall owe them to the League if it refuses to surrender them.[22] I infer that this decree—so much in the League members' interests—was paralleled by a similar dogma of the synedrion. The inscription does not specify the method of determining the offender's guilt, but it would make sense to suggest the same sort of double trial prescribed by Aristoteles for persons "destroying the alliance" by contravening provisions of his decree. No record exists of anyone ever having actually been brought to trial for either offense.

The decree of Aristoteles included another "judicial" provision. After its statement of prohibition of Athenian ownership of real property in allied territories comes an outline of enforcement procedure:

And if [an]yone buys or acquires or takes on mortgage (such properties) by any such method, it shall be permitted to anyone of the allies who wishes to give evidence to the synedroi of the allies. Let the synedroi, auc[t]ioning (the offender's

21. Marshall 35–37 (citing earlier authors who took his position); Accame 138–140; Hammond, *HG*² 487; Tod 123 comm. (with slight misgivings). Cf. Larsen, *Rep. Govt.* 63, whose position is explicitly accepted by D. M. Lewis, "Entrenchment-Clauses in Attic Decrees," in D. W. Bradeen and M. F. McGregor (eds.), ΦΟΡΟΣ: *Tribute to Benjamin Dean Meritt* (Locust Valley, N.Y. 1974) 88f and n. 39.

22. *IG* II², 125, lines 9–17 (underdotting as in Tod 154):

[---ἐὰν]
10   δέ τις τοῦ λοιποῦ χρόνου ἐπιστρατ[εύσηι ἐπὶ Ἐρέ]-
      τριαν ἢ ἐπ' ἄλλην τινὰ τῶν συμμαχί[δων πόλεων, Ἀθη]-
      ναίων ἢ τῶν συμμάχων τῶν Ἀθηνα[ίων, θάνατον αὐτοῦ]
      κατεγνῶσθαι καὶ τὰ χρήματα δ[ημόσια εἶναι καὶ τ]-
      ῆς θεοῦ τὸ ἐπιδέκατον· καὶ εἶν[αι τὰ χρήματα αὐτοῦ]
15   ἀγώγιμα ἐξ ἁπασῶν τῶν πόλεω[ν τῶν συμμαχίδων· ἐὰν]
      δέ τις ἀφέληται πόλις, ὀφείλ[ειν τῶι κοινῶι τῶι τ]-
      ῶν συμμάχων.

property), give [the one h]alf to th[e] informer, and let the r[est b]e [com]mon (property) of the al[l]ies.[23]

Here again (more clearly) the synedrion itself is to act as a court on behalf of the allies. The money from the sale of the confiscated property (beyond the informer's reward) is to go to the League treasury, as in the case of the decree concerning persons who attack Attica or League members' territories (supra). But this particular provision has something new and perhaps surprising about it: *no joint jurisdiction of the Athenians is suggested.* In this carefully phrased Athenian decree, such an omission was probably not accidental. The decree of Aristoteles here seems to be granting an exclusive power to the allied synedrion, a power involving the property of Athenian citizens.

It is easy to see the reason for this particular exception to the general pattern of equally shared authority. Ownership of property in allied territories by Athenians (chapter 9) was one of the most hated aspects of the fifth-century Athenian Empire. Guarantees against the recurrence of the practice had to be ironclad to be at all reassuring to potential allies —and probably also to convince certain Athenians of the impossibility of recovering properties they had once held in the "good old days" of Athenian oppression. Therefore, in this particular area, the allies were conceded absolute and final authority. It should be noted, however, that no Athenian's life, civic rights, or property in Attica or anywhere outside the territory of League members was affected. Nor did the prohibition apply to all forms of economic activity. Nothing indicates that Athenians could not freely trade in allied markets; they simply were not allowed to own "real" property—just as resident aliens were not allowed to own it in Attica. Further, the provision may not have taken effect until the end of the current archon year, so that Athenian property holders perhaps had a few months during which to dispose of their holdings.[24] Enlightened pragmatism, once again, seems to be a more reasonable description of the Athenians' attitude than some sort of doomed "idealism." Both the apparent method of trying persons and the League's right to dispose of the property of offenders may reasonably be viewed as consistent throughout the history of the League. The paucity of evidence

23. DA, lines 41–46.
24. The prohibition for which the quoted passage is the enforcement provision begins ⟨ἀ⟩πὸ δὲ Ν/αυσινίκο ἄρχον[τ]ος (DA, lines 35f). There is an admittedly problematic relationship between this provision and the straightforward statement of lines 25–30, which could prescribe the immediate abandonment of all current Athenian holdings in allied territories. However, it is also possible that both passages—and the intervening provision about stelai unfavorable to allied states (possibly treaties granting Athenians γῆς ἔγκτησις, the right to hold landed property, in these states' territories)—comprise one connected guarantee, with its enforcement provisions and effective date (see chapters 8 and 9).

must of course be admitted, but nothing indicates any growth of the Athenians' "judicial" role at the expense of that of the synedrion.[25]

The decree of Aristoteles says nothing at all about financial matters, beyond the simple promise that no League member will pay "tribute" (φόρος). But of course the League had a navy to support, and some funds were necessary. A member was therefore expected to make a "contribution" (σύνταξις) to the League treasury, and the sum of these συντάξεις helped operate the navy and meet other necessary expenses. Athens did not itself pay a syntaxis, but did provide certain funds for the League's military operations and supply many ships and troops, as well as the commanders of the League forces. Opinions differ on both the nature of the syntaxeis and on who determined their amounts. Cynicism about them is not lacking in ancient sources. The Alexandrian lexicographer Harpokration, citing a fourth-century author, says:

ἔλεγον δὲ καὶ τοὺς φόρους συντάξεις, ἐπειδὴ χαλεπῶς ἔφερον οἱ Ἕλληνες τὸ τῶν φόρ-
ων ὄνομα, Καλλιστράτου οὕτω καλέσαντος, ὥς φησι Θεόπομπος ἐν ῑ Φιλιππικῶν.

They even called the tributes syntaxeis, since the Greeks ill bore the name of phoroi, Kallistratos having named (them) thus, as Theopompos says in *Philippika X*.

Plutarch, in his *Life of Solon*, offers the generalization that the Athenians covered up unpleasant things with auspicious names; among other euphemisms, he says they called τοὺς δὲ φόρους συντάξεις.[26]

Busolt, citing these passages, infers that the syntaxeis of the Second Athenian League, like the phoroi of the Athenian Empire, were unilaterally imposed by the hegemon on the League members. Marshall inclines to share this viewpoint. Tod, citing Marshall, comments: ". . . The 'contributions' (συντάξεις) required for the operations of the Confederacy differed little, save in name, from the old φόρος. . . ." At the other extreme of scholarly opinion is the assertion of Beloch that the synedrion set member states' syntaxeis without Athenian participation, a position which is cited approvingly by Victor Ehrenberg. However, both Beloch and Ehrenberg conclude that the originally very differently assessed syntaxeis metamorphosed over time into something very like the fifth-century phoroi. Other scholars, e.g., Accame and Hammond, hold that the synedrion set the syntaxeis, but that its dogmata were confirmed by Athenian resolutions. The known anti-Athenian bias of Theopompos makes his pronouncement, though contemporary, less than decisive, and Plutarch is of course very late.[27] I share Ehrenberg's inability to believe that prospective allies, at least originally, could have been

25. Athenian "judicial" relations with individual allied states are discussed in chapter 8.
26. DA, line 23, states the prohibition; Theopomp. *FGrH* 115 F 98; Plut. *Sol.* 15.2f.
27. Busolt 703 and 713; Marshall 40 and 130; Tod 123 comm.; Beloch 3:1.150 n. 2 and 3:2.165; Ehrenberg, "Zum zweiten attischen Bund," *Hermes* 64 (1929) 337f (p. 338 n. 1 cites a later work of Beloch for his change of position); Accame 132 and 134; Hammond, *HG²* 487 (Marshall attributes positions like those of Accame and Hammond to E. Meyer and P.

content with a mere change of name. There must initially have been allied participation in establishing the various League members' syntaxeis. The questions worthy of serious consideration are: (1) whether the synedrion's jurisdiction in this area was exclusive or was shared with the Athenians, and (2) whether the Athenians (initially involved or not) eventually emerged as the party determining the syntaxeis. These are the questions to bear in mind as we examine direct, contemporary references to the syntaxeis of the Second Athenian League.

Beloch's suggestion that establishing allied states' contributions was an exclusive power of the synedrion is not necessarily farfetched. I have argued (supra) that such an exclusive power was granted in preventing Athenian property ownership in allied territories, because lingering suspicions of Athenian imperial inclinations could not otherwise have been overcome. The fifth-century tribute was hated just as much as Athenian property ownership, and the promise not to reinstitute it might have seemed hollow without the granting of some similarly exclusive allied power over the area of League finances. As late as 356, an Athenian decree referred to the disbursement of certain funds ἐκ τῶν συντάξεων κ[α]τ[ὰ τ]ὰ δόγ[μα/τ]α τ[ῶ]ν συμμάχων.[28] But the omission in this provision of any reference to the participation of the Athenians is not decisive. This usage is paralleled by a clause in the League membership alliance of Chalkis (377), which promises the Chalkidians they shall not receive an Athenian garrison or pay phoros or accept a governor παρὰ τὰ δόγματ[α τῶ/ν συμμάχων].[29] Though the phrasing omits mention of the fact, these promises were of course also made by the Athenians: they are a close paraphrase of lines 21–23 of the decree of Aristoteles. While the evidence is indirect, in that disbursement of syntaxeis funds or collection of syntaxeis are not the same thing as establishing what particular contributions League members are to pay, the safest inference seems to be that—at least originally—both the Athenians and the synedrion were involved in the process.

The pseudo-Demosthenic oration *Against Theokrines* (ca. 341 or 340) seems to imply that the Athenians in later years determined an allied state's syntaxis. In describing troubled relations with League member Ainos, the speaker refers to τὸ ψήφισμα . . . τοῦτο τὸ περὶ τῆς συντάξεως, and argues that, before the machinations of the defendant threw matters into confusion, "the demos was willing that the Ainians should pay the syntaxis which they agreed on with Chares the general . . . ."[30] A similarly late document, an Athenian decree honoring and rewarding League

---

Panske). A kinder view of Theopompos is taken by Gordon Shrimpton, "Theopompus' Treatment of Philip in the *Philippica*," *Phoenix* 31 (1977) 123–144.

28. *IG* II², 123, lines 11f (underdotting as in Tod 156).

29. *SV* 259, lines 23–26.

30. DA, line 103: Αἴνιοι; [Dem.] 58.37f, translated passage: ... τὸν μὲν δῆμον συγχωροῦντα τὴν σύνταξιν διδόναι τοὺς Αἰνίους ὅσην Χάρητι τῷ στρατηγῷ συνεχώρησαν....

member Tenedos in 339, exempts the Tenedians from all types of monetary collections for a period of time (chapter 10). Its heavily restored text directs that collections are not to be made by a general, nor anyone else, "nor by the s[ynedroi is there to be] a levy made during t[his] time."[31] Underlying my version of this clause is the translation "to make a levy" for the aorist infinitive κατατάξαι (from κατατάσσω, Attic -τάττω). My translation could apply, as I believe the Greek word could apply, either to the designating of the amount of payment owed or to the collecting of it, or perhaps to the entire process. This ambiguity eliminates certainty, but leaves open the definite possibility that the synedrion was involved in establishing the level of contribution owed by the Tenedians at this very late date. As is so often the case, the data will fit opposite presuppositions. The synedrion clearly must have been involved in the determination of League members' syntaxeis in the confederacy's early years, and these sources do not *exclude* its involvement in later years (e.g., that Chares should make an agreement and the demos pass a resolution on the syntaxis of Ainos should not exclude a concurring allied dogma), whereas one of them at least hints that the synedrion *was* involved. It is therefore reasonable to assume that practice was consistent throughout the history of the League. The only real reason scholars doubt this is, as usual, the widely shared belief that Athens's power and assertiveness steadily grew at the expense of the allies.

One development sometimes seen as evidence of this trend is the admitted fact that the syntaxeis—which originally[32] were probably special, irregular contributions in varying amounts appropriate to the scope of individual crises—at some point became regular annual payments of standardized amounts. Aischines in 343 recalled that in recent years Chares and his officers "were collecting sixty talents syntaxis each year"; in 330 he stated that the combined syntaxeis for Oreos and Eretria had been ten talents at some point in the late 340s. Demosthenes remarked that in the final struggle with Philip Athens could draw on a total syntaxis of only forty-five talents.[33] Beyond these statements—all applying to quite late dates, by which time many allies had been lost to the League —nothing is known about the amount of annual syntaxis of any allied

31. *IG* II², 233, lines 12–18, translated phrase (lines 15f): μηδὲ τοῖς σ[υνέδροις εἶναι] / κατατά{το}ξαι ἐν τῶι χρόνωι το[ύτωι---] (line numbers of Tod 175 differ).

32. Marshall, 38, argues that syntaxeis were collected from the very establishment of the League, because the quotation from Harpokration links them with Kallistratos, whose activity in connection with the League came in its early years. Cawkwell, "Peace" 91–93, contends that they were not introduced until ca. 373, and that up to that time each state simply paid the troops of its own contingent within the League's forces. The chronology of Plut. *Phok.* 7.1 is too vague to provide support for Marshall's position. I offer no opinion on this issue.

33. Ais. 2.71 (καθ' ἕκαστον ἐνιαυτὸν ἑξήκοντα τάλαντα εἰσέπραττον σύνταξιν) and 3.94 (Oreos and Eretria); Dem. 18.234.

state, or of the League as a whole.[34] It seems apparent from the quoted passages concerning Ainos and Tenedos that alterations in a League member's rate of contribution could always be made in special circumstances, even after regular annual payments had become the rule. In any case, regularization of syntaxeis should not necessarily be taken as implying any development contrary to the interest of the allies, or diminishing the synedrion's powers. Any organization which operates over a long period of time (e.g., the forty years of the Second Athenian League) quite naturally feels its way from experimental, *ad hoc* procedures to regular and consistent procedures which have been shown to be reasonable.

The citation (supra) showing the synedrion's involvement in the disbursement of syntaxis funds in 356 is sufficient basis for the generalization that it held a concurrent power, with the Athenian demos, of determining the projects on which these funds might be spent. No evidence exists of their being employed for any exclusively Athenian purpose, such as Perikles' gigantic fifth-century building project financed by the tribute of the Athenian Empire.[35] We need not suppose that no abuses existed in connection with the syntaxeis. But the documented cases of conflict (some of which may be questionable), as well as the counterexamples which tend to show Athenian efforts to avoid giving offense, are generally associated with the process of *collection*, not establishment or disbursement, of League members' contributions. This power, so far as we can tell, was always held by the hegemon, and was not shared in any degree by the synedrion. Even in this area, however, one may well invoke the suggestion of Sealey, who points out that the very infrequency of mention of the syntaxeis in the sources may itself indicate that they were the source of little conflict; the hated fifth-century phoroi are, conversely, well documented.[36]

In sumary, the synedrion was a body permanently resident in Athens in which each of the League allies had one vote. The Athenians

34. The computations by Beloch, 3:2.167f, of syntaxeis paid by the League's full membership (cited by Accame 135f) are unreliable both because they are highly inferential and because they include figures for many states that were not in fact League members. It is nevertheless possible to agree with Beloch and Accame that the syntaxeis were lower than the fifth-century phoroi, both in the total amount (since the Second Athenian League had far fewer members) and in the amounts paid by individual members. Comparing Athens's fourth-century income with its far greater fifth-century resources based largely on tribute, Meiggs, *AE* 260, concludes that fourth-century Athens "could never sustain an aggressive policy for long. . . ."

35. Note the arrogance of Plut. *Per.* 12.3f.

36. Sealey, *City-Sts.* 433. In my discussion of syntaxeis, I have intentionally refrained from citing *SV* 303, line 16, in which some editors print a wholly restored σύνταξιν; this has no more epigraphical basis than the equally common restoration of Athenian φόρους in line 8—though the latter (which is totally without fourth-century parallel) is far less excusable.

were neither represented in the synedrion nor presided over its deliberations, though in several ways it was subject to Athenian influence. The preponderance of the ambiguous and sometimes confusing evidence indicates a formal equality between the allied synedrion and the Athenian demos: each could veto the League policies suggested by the other, and neither could override the other's veto. The Athenians seem generally to have paid deference to their legal position of equality and to allied sensitivities. The synedrion's areas of authority were theoretically as wide as those of the Athenian demos, save only that the Athenians held the ἡγεμονία, i.e., essentially the command of the League's military and naval forces—which carried with it the (sometimes unpleasant) duty of collecting and spending money, theoretically in accord with the instructions of both ruling bodies. The only known exclusive power of the synedrion was its authority to confiscate the illegal holdings of Athenians in allied territories.

The organization of the Second Athenian League, which seems to have remained unchanged throughout the history of the confederacy, represented a recognition of the pragmatic value of both fairness to the weak (the island allies) and sensible deference to the greater power and responsibility of the strong (Athens). The League's structure avoided the Athenian Empire's cynical and transparent pretense of absolute equality,[37] and also the Peloponnesian League's explicit investiture of almost all power in the hegemon. The organization of the confederacy gave its two component parties what each wanted and needed: (1) to the Athenians leadership and consequent panhellenic influence, with reasonable limitations, and (2) to the allies protection, with believable guarantees.

Let us now turn to examine how this League, admirably conceived in theory, functioned in actual practice. What protections did the allies have, and were they in fact effective—especially against the most hated abuses of the Athenian Empire? What factors led to the League's losses of members and its eventual defeat?

---

37. I accept the conventional interpretation of the voting structure of the Delian League, recently defended by Phyllis Culham, "The Delian League: Bicameral or Unicameral?", *AJAH* 3 (1978) 27–31; cf. N. G. L. Hammond, "The Origins and Nature of the Athenian Alliance of 478/7 B.C.," *JHS* 87 (1967) 41–61, and G. E. M. De Ste. Croix, *The Origins of the Peloponnesian War* (London 1972) 303–307.

Part IV

ATHENIAN TREATMENT

OF THE LEAGUE ALLIES

8

GUARANTEES AND PROTECTIONS

In the decree of Aristoteles (chapter 2), the Athenians offered detailed guarantees and protections to current and potential members in their League. This public, extant set of principles provides an appropriate yardstick against which the Athenians' treatment of their League allies can legitimately be measured.[1] Three separate issues must, however, be addressed:

1. To whom did the Athenians offer the guarantees and protections?
2. What did the Athenian promises actually mean?
3. To what extent did the Athenians keep their promises?

The first question is answerable, in principle, with absolute certainty. The decree repeatedly addresses its assurances to "those making the alliance,"[2] i.e., to states joining the League—and therefore by obvious implication to no other states. This point is so elementary that it should hardly require stating, yet scholars have frequently treated at least some of the promises of the decree as if they had been made to the world at large. The identification of members and nonmembers of the League among Athens's allies is treated at length in Part II. The general conclusion advanced there is that only those states listed, as the decree (lines 69–72) directs, on its stele, were League members—the great majority whose names are extant, and a handful whose names have been lost from the stone (some of whom can be fairly certainly identified, others more doubtfully). No examination of the second and third issues which ignores this initial question should be relied upon. This chapter and the following chapter are devoted to these latter issues, each chapter dealing with both issues as they apply to separate groups of the decree's guarantees and protections.

The most basic guarantee of the decree is its promise of "freedom" and "autonomy." The King's Peace of 386 B.C. had directed, beyond specified exceptions, "that the other Greek states, both small and great, should be left autonomous." The Athenians in 384 made the Chians their allies "on the basis of fre[e]dom and autonom[y]." Only this standard rhetoric of Greek diplomacy[3] is being employed—no actual promise is

---

1. Passages of DA are quoted here (and in chapter 9) exclusively in translation; see chapter 2 for the Greek text of each. Note the comment of F. E. Adcock and D. J. Mosley, *Diplomacy in Ancient Greece* (London 1975) 76: "The virtually unprecedented attention to detail in drawing up the document shows that care had been lavished upon the proposals."

2. DA, lines 18f, 25f, 29f, 32f, 38, 47f, and 70–72.

3. King's Peace: Xen. *Hell.* 5.1.31 (full quotation in chapter 1); Chios alliance: *SV* 248,

being made—when Aristoteles begins his resolution with a pointed invocation of the "autonomy" clause of the King's Peace, and of the Spartans' self-serving method of "enforcing" it, saying: "So that (the) Laked[aimo]nians shall leave the Greeks fr[e]e [an]d autonomous . . ." (lines 9f). When the guarantee is offered, a few lines farther along, the passage does not apply to "the Greeks" in general: only those (Greeks or barbarians) "whoe[ver do not] belong to (the) [Ki]ng" are invited to join the League, "being [fre]e and autonomous" (lines 15–20). What did the Athenians mean, and their allies understand, by this phrase, [ἐλευθέρ]ωι ὄντι καὶ αὐτονόμωι?

As a political catchword, ἐλευθερία was older than αὐτονομία. Greek propaganda had made the Persian Wars a struggle for ἐλευθερία, and the setting up of the stele of Aristoteles near the statue of Zeus Eleutherios (lines 65f) was undoubtedly designed to associate the new League with the principles of this glorious struggle. The term αὐτονομία had also been long in use as political propaganda, but states might be called "autonomous" which were subject to considerable restraint. A clause of the peace of Nikias (421 B.C.), quoted by Thucydides, prescribed, for instance, that:

τὰς δὲ πόλεις φερούσας τὸν φόρον τὸν ἐπ' Ἀριστείδου αὐτονόμους εἶναι.

The states paying the tribute as established by Aristeides are to be autonomous.[4]

In 395, according to Xenophon, the Persian King announced that

τὰς δ' ἐν τῇ Ἀσίᾳ πόλεις αὐτονόμους οὔσας τὸν ἀρχαῖον δασμὸν αὐτῷ ἀποφέρειν.

The states in Asia, being autonomous, are to render to him the ancient tribute.[5]

As we have seen, however, in the rescript imposing the King's Peace itself, the King contrasted the Asian Greek states that were "his" with Greek states that were to be "autonomous." Some scholars appear to believe that the phrases following the promise of freedom and autonomy in the decree of Aristoteles—those specifying self-government and the nonimposition of garrisons, governors, and tribute (lines 20–23)—were meant to be clarifications of the basic promise.[6]

My own inclination, however, is to treat these phrases as separate and more specific guarantees. "Autonomy" was certainly still a rather elastic

---

lines 20f (ἐπ' ἐλευθ[ε]ρίαι καὶ αὐτον/ομί[α]ι); see also similar phrasing (in 369/8) in IG II², 107, lines 41–45 (quoted infra).

4. Thuc. 5.18.5.

5. Xen. Hell. 3.4.25.

6. I believe this implication is present, e.g., in Bengtson's observation (SV 257 comm.) that states joining the League "werden Freiheit und Autonomie, dazu Freiheit von Besatzung und Tribut zugesichert." I must thank Prof. E. Badian, whose 1976 Sather Lectures led me to some of the sources and ideas of this paragraph, though some of my conclusions differ from those he then expressed.

concept in 371, when the Spartans took the oaths of a peace treaty on behalf of their "autonomous" Peloponnesian allies.[7] More striking still is an inscription of ca. 357, in which Bengtson's text restores the following passage:

[---τὰς δὲ πόλει]ς τὰς Ἑλληνίδας τὰς ἐ[ν Χερρονήσω]-
[ι ὑποτελούσας Β]ηρισάδει καὶ Ἀμαδόκ[ωι καὶ Κερσ]-
15   [εβλέπτηι τὸμ φό]ρον τὸμ πάτριον καὶ Ἀ[θηναίοις τ]-
[ὴν σύνταξιν, ἐλε]υθέρας εἶναι καὶ αὐτονό[μους συ]-
[μμάχους οὔσας Ἀ]θηναίοις. . . .[8]

Since only one state of the Chersonesos is listed among the extant names on the stele of Aristoteles (Elaious, line 123), the restoration of "syntaxis," the contribution paid by League members, in line 16 of this inscription is doubtful, and the states which it says "are to be [f]ree and autono[mous, being allies] to [(the) A]thenians" (lines 16f) are apparently non-League allies.[9] Whoever they are, they seem to be described as both free and autonomous *and* subject to a traditional tribute to the three kings mentioned by the inscription (lines 14f). Accordingly, even at this late date, tributary status could be treated as compatible with freedom and autonomy—though Athenian League members were, of course, specifically exempted from tributary status vis-à-vis Athens (infra).

I therefore prefer the interpretation of the word αὐτόνομους offered by Sealey:

Study of the usage of this word . . . shows that it is systematically ambiguous; at each occurrence it derives its meaning from the context and especially from the condition with which "autonomy" is contrasted . . . . Accordingly, when the word "autonomous" was used without any implied or explicit contrast, it had hardly any factual content. It retained the overtones of enthusiasm which commonly adhere to words expressing freedom, but it became exceedingly vague.[10]

Something similar could presumably also be said of ἐλεύθερος. The Athenians thus were offering only a general reassurance in promising that a state might join their League [ἐλευθέρ]ωι ὄντι καὶ αὐτονόμωι. They were saying, essentially, that their allies would not be dominated and treated as subjects, as they had been under the Athenian Empire—and in addition offering certain specific guarantees and protections. Modern scholars, however, have often treated "freedom" and "autonomy" as very precise and exact concepts, and have suggested several instances of

7. Xen. *Hell.* 6.3.19.

8. *SV* 303, lines 13–17; the restoration of [φό]ρον in line 15 is strengthened by an extant φόρους in line 6 (see chapter 7 n. 36 for more problems with this inscription).

9. Cf. Accame 181.

10. Sealey, *City-Sts.* 397.

Athenian infringement of League members' freedom and autonomy. This evidence requires reexamination.

An Athenian decree of ca. 357–6, passed in response to military attacks upon Eretria, condemns to death any Athenian or allied citizen who makes any such future attack upon Eretria or any other allied state, further proclaiming that the offender's property shall be confiscated, and shall be recoverable from any allied state. Marshall condemns the measure as "the pronouncement, by Athenian ψήφισμα alone, of outlawry throughout the entire territory of the Confederacy," and cites the decree as evidence in arguing: "It was only too plain that Athens was very ready to seize upon any excuse for infringing the autonomy of the allies." Rhodes's description of this decree as "regulations imposed on . . . Eretria" seems also somewhat condemnatory.[11] In fact, it is quite obvious that this Athenian decree—even if there had been no allied dogma to the same effect, which there might well have been—was simply designed to guarantee protection to Eretria and all League members against armed attack. Using such a document as evidence for Athenian usurpation is equivalent to finding an imperialistic intent in lines 51–63 of the decree of Aristoteles, where persons who attempt to abrogate the decree are banned from allied territory as well as from Attica.[12]

Another Athenian inscription (often conjecturally dated to the Social War period) includes the following provision:

πολιτεύεσθαι Κ[είου]ς κατὰ πόλεις κατ[ὰ τοὺς ὅρ]-
15 [κους καὶ τὰ]ς συνθήκας καὶ τὰ ψηφ[ίσμα]τα τοῦ δήμου τοῦ ᾿Α[θηναίων].

(The) K[ean]s are to govern (themselves) by cities accordin[g to the oaths and th]e agreements and the dec[re]es of the demos of (the) A[thenians].

D. M. Lewis appears to see in the specification that the Keans are to govern themselves "by cities" (line 14) an Athenian encroachment on their autonomy, in that the Keans are apparently prohibited from operating under their traditional federal constitution. This particular requirement, however, need not be viewed as a matter of Athenian dictation. In the early days of their League, the Athenians adhered rather carefully to the provisions of the King's Peace, which were widely seen as prohibiting the existence of such federal unions (thus all the names on the front face of the stele of Aristoteles are those of individual πόλεις—notably "Thebes" as contrasted with "Boiotia"). Assuming that the inscription

11. *IG* II² 125, lines 9–17 (Greek quoted in chapter 7 n. 22); Marshall 106 (both passages—see also pp. 47–49); Rhodes, *Boule* 81 (cf. "Regulations for Eretria," p. 260).

12. Marshall, 47–49, treats as similarly indicative of "how Athens came to disregard the autonomy of the allies" (p. 47) a proposal of 352 B.C., attacked by Demosthenes (Dem. 23.35 and 91). Here the only aspect of "autonomy" at issue would be whether an allied state had the right to harbor the murderer of an Athenian general—a claim which, of course, would never have been made.

under discussion is not itself the Keans' original League membership treaty of ca. 375 (the actual date is unknown), it may nonetheless have incorporated certain phrases from that treaty, including the passage quoted. The deference to the decrees of the Athenian demos is also formulaic: citations of the authority of Athenian decrees and allied dogmata—either or both—are found in other alliance treaties from the early days of the League (chapter 7). The intervening reference to oaths and agreements shows that the authority of the decrees of the Athenian demos is limited and defined by treaty, i.e., presumably the Keans' League membership alliances.[13] Other passages within this inscription are discussed in different contexts (infra).

Two fragmentary inscriptions discovered at the Kean city of Ioulis appear to record treaties of isopolity between (1) Keos and Eretria(?), and (2) Keos and Hestiaia. No sort of dating formula is extant in either treaty. Arguments adduced in connection with these documents are more or less the converse of those associated with the inscription discussed in the preceding paragraph. Editors generally date these two inscriptions to periods either before the Keans joined the Athenian League,

---

13. *IG* II², 404 (text and line numbers of F. G. Maier, *SEG* XIX, 50), lines 14f. Discussion of the inscription's date centers on the restored phrase [---]ῶνος ἐ[ν]άτ[ηι---] (the ninth day of some Attic month) in line 2. Koehler dated the treaty to 338/7 or later because no such dating formula was attested for any earlier Athenian inscription. Schweigert, "Greek Inscriptions: 4. A Decree Concerning Elaious, 357/6 B.C.," *Hesperia* 8 (1939) 14 n. 1, restores a formula of related type in *IG* II², 122, line 5: [---ἕκτει ἱσταμέ]νου [---] (the sixth of the waxing moon of some month). He dates this latter inscription to the Social War period and uses its date as support for a similar date for the Keos inscription. Lewis, "The Federal Constitution of Keos," *ABSA* 57 (1962) 1–4 cites Schweigert's argument and describes (p. 4) his approximate dating of the inscription as "unquestionably" correct; the translation of WV 56 is dated "ca. 356 B.C." But in reality there is no basis for Schweigert's Social War date for *IG* II², 122—a tiny fragment (twenty-eight extant letters in five lines) of unknown subject matter, broken away on all sides, to which he assigns a completely arbitrary line length (a process which forces him, e.g., to argue that although the number of the day was inscribed, the name of the month was not). This being the case, his date for *IG* II², 404 has no more support than Koehler's. Rhodes, *Boule* 73 n. 1 and 261, nicely symbolizes the ultimate uncertainty of scholarship: his two citations employ the two different dates. An internal clue for the date appears to exist in lines 12–14, where reference is made to agreements struck with the Keans by the Athenian general Chabrias, who is known to have negotiated a settlement of 362 after an attempted secession from the League (*SV* 289, lines 17–19; this inscription is discussed in some detail, infra). But Chabrias was also active in recruiting League members among the Aegean islands in 376 and 375 (chapter 6), during which period the Keans joined the League. Thus the agreements to which the inscription refers could have been the Kean cities' original League membership alliance treaties; passages referring to the process of joining the League (lines 8–11) strengthen this possibility. The provision (line 16) that coastal cities of Keos are to repair their walls adds nothing either way: such a measure would be equally appropriate at any time of war or danger. One other phrase (line 7) commonly interpreted as implying a Social War date is discussed in chapter 9, in connection with similar phrasing elsewhere.

or while Keos was in revolt in the late 360s, or after the League was dissolved—primarily because both inscriptions appear to employ "Keans" as a political term, which implies to the commentators the existence of an island-wide confederation, which they believe the hegemon would not have tolerated. It is also generally assumed that Athens would not have permitted its League allies to make treaties of isopolity among themselves.[14] The inferences are unwarranted, however. While it is true (as said supra) that the Athenians for a while paid deference to the King's Peace and its hostility toward confederacies, it is equally true that they soon came to accept certain confederacies as members of their own League (chapter 3). The ambiguous way the Keans themselves were listed on the League stele (lines 119–122) makes it unclear whether they became members individually or jointly: under the rubric "Of Keans" appear the names of the three cities of Ioulis, Karthaia, and Koresos (the separate listing of Poiessa in line 82 is another problem; see chapter 3). Once the League was firmly established, it was undoubtedly a matter of very little consequence to Athens whether the Kean cities operated separately or as a unit. There is no reason, in fact, why the Kean poleis might not function separately for some purposes (e.g., League membership—which would be to their advantage, since it meant more votes in the synedrion) and in unity for others (e.g., the making of nonmilitary agreements, such as these two isopolity treaties). Lewis shows that a dated Athenian inscription of 362 (on which more, infra) refers repeatedly to the "Keans" and to individual Kean cities in ways that reveal no consistent pattern.[15] In sum, the two isopolity treaties—which may or may not date to periods when the Keans were Athenian League members—tell us nothing at all about any Athenian limitations on the Keans' autonomy. An inferred restriction leads some editors to doubly-inferred dating, but the entire process lacks any basis in the sources.

The most frequently cited sort of evidence for Athenian abridgement of League members' autonomy is the presence of provisions for the appeal of certain types of cases to Athens in several inscribed agreements

14. The stoichedon Keos-Eretria(?) treaty (SV 232), discovered in 1947, was published in Christiane Dunant and Jean Thomopoulos, "Inscriptions de Céos: Ioulis I. Traité d'isopolitie," BCH 78 (1954) 316–322. The nonstoichedon Keos-Hestiaia treaty (SV 287) was published in 1898. The two inscriptions are filled with similar formulae—each is, in fact, the main source for restorations within the other's text. Dunant and Thomopoulos argue from these similarities of content that the two treaties should be dated close together (both prior to 377, they say), with the Hestiaia treaty being slightly the later on the basis of script differences. As their own survey of scholarship shows, however, dates as early as the 390s for the Eretria(?) treaty and as late as the third or second century for the Hestiaia treaty have been suggested. It may or may not be significant that the clearest parallel to the two treaties is IG XII (5), 526f, a Kean isopolity agreement with Naupaktos of the Aitolian league, whose date is definitely in the late third century or afterward.

15. Lewis (supra n. 13) 3f, referring to SV 289, passim.

with League allies. An undated treaty with Siphnos (DA, line 126) is generally restored to the effect that the Siphnians are not to execute or prosecute any Athenian without the participation of the Athenian demos, or to put an Athenian to death without trial. Another undated (and fragmentary) inscription, concerning Athenian relations with Naxos, possibly but not certainly a League member (chapter 2), mentions law courts on Naxos and in Athens and refers to an unnamed "appellate (city)," apparently Athens. Woodhead sees both of these treaties as evidence of the conversion of the Second Athenian League into an ἀρχή, and Marshall cites the Naxos inscription as evidence that rebels restored to the League "were liable to have their judicial independence impaired." In reality, these documents tell us so little that they should probably be left out of the argument. All the key passages of the Siphnian treaty[16] are uncertain restorations. The very fragmentary Naxian treaty[17] tells us neither the identity of the criminals, their crimes, nor the penalties applied—and Naxos may well not have been a League member.

The Kean treaty already discussed (supra) in connection with the implication of government "by cities" also includes an appeal provision:

[εἰ δέ τι]
[ἐγκαλοῦσιν αὐτοῖς τ]ῆς πεντηκοστῆς τῆς [ὀφειλ]ομένης ἕνεκ[α ᾽Αθηναῖοι,]
[περὶ τούτων δί]κας εἶναι Κείοις ἐ[ν τῆι ἐ]κκλήτωι ᾽Αθή[νησιν . 4. .]
[. . . . .13. . . . .]ς κατὰ τοὺς ὅρκου[ς καὶ τὰς] συνθήκα[ς καὶ τὰ ψηφί]-
20 [σματα τοῦ δήμου τ]οῦ ᾽Αθηναίων καὶ [. . . . .12. . . . .]Ν[. . . .11. . . . . . .]

[And if (the) Athenians charge them (with) anything] on account o[f t]he 1/50th (import tax at Peiraieus) being [owe]d, [concerning these things] (the) Keans are to have a [su]it i[n the a]ppellate (city) Athe[ns----------] according to the oath[s and the] agreement[s and the decrees of the demos] of (the) Athenians and [--------------------].

Editors who comment on other appeal provisions are oddly silent on this one.[18]

16. SV 294, lines 9–13 (restored by Woodhead):

[. .5. .]τ[. .᾽Αθηναῖον δὲ τὸν δῆμον]
10 [τ]ὸ[ν] Σιφνίων [μὴ κτένεν ἄνευ τὸ]
δήμο τὸ ᾽Αθηναίων [μηδὲ διώκεν·]
ὡς δ' ἂμ μηδὲς ἀποθ[άνηι ᾽Αθηναί]-
[ω]ν ἄκριτος, ἀντισσ[. . . .12. . . . . . .]

See Bengtson's comm.; cf. Woodhead, "Inscs." 232f.

17. SV 321, lines 9 ([δικασ]τήριον τὸ ἐν Νάξωι), 12 (τὸ δικαστήριον τὸ ᾽Αθήνησι), and 14 (ἐν δὲ τῆι ἐκκλήτωι παρέχειν Ναξί[ους---]). IG II², 179 also includes two other fragments of this inscription, not printed by SV. See Woodhead, "Inscs." 225 n. 7 and 233; Marshall 46f; and Accame 184.

18. IG II², 404, lines 16–20 (Maier: see n. 13 supra). Neither Marshall nor Accame cites this inscription at all; it does not appear in Bengtson's selection. The customary restoration

The Keans are involved in another undated inscription, found at Athens, which includes reasonably well preserved resolutions of Koresos and Ioulis, and (above them) remnants of a resolution of Karthaia. It is generally accepted that an Athenian decree was originally inscribed above the three Kean cities' resolutions (and possibly also an intervening decree of Poiessa). Though an early editor suggested a third-century date for this nonstoichedon inscription, most commentators have preferred a date sometime before 350.[19] The subject matter of the two legible resolutions, and presumably also of those wholly or partially lost, is the granting of an Athenian monopoly on the export from Keos of μίλτος (ruddle or red ocher), a mineral valuable for coloration. Extensive enforcement powers for the protection of this monopoly are also granted. Both extant decrees recognize the validity, in advance, of any subsequent Athenian decrees on the subject of this protection. The Koresians resolve: [ἐὰν δέ τι ἄλλο ψηφίζωντα]/ι 'Αθηναῖοι περὶ φυλακῆς τῆς μίλτου, κύρια εἶναι κατακομι[σθέντα(?) τὰ ἐψηφισμένα], and the Ioulietans decree: [ἐὰν δέ τι ἀλ]/λο ψηφίζωνται 'Αθηναῖοι περὶ φυλακῆς τῆς μίλ[του ---κύρια εἶ]/ναι ἃ ἂν 'Αθηναῖοι ψηφίζωνται. The Koresian resolution (which apparently renews concessions previously granted) also grants any informer or complainant against violators of the Athenian monopoly appeal to Athens: [εἶν]/αι [δὲ] καὶ ἔφεσιν[20] 'Αθήναζε καὶ τῶι φήναντι καὶ τῶι ἐνδεί[ξαντι]. Marshall cites this inscription as another datum showing Athenian impairment of the allies' "judicial independence"; Accame uses it in arguing that after their revolution in the 360s the Kean cities were left judicial authority over only secondary matters.[21]

The final inscription to be discussed in this context is also the best preserved and the only one with an extant date. This Athenian treaty with

___

of [καὶ ἐ/ν τοῖς συμμάχοι]ς in lines 18f creates more problems than it solves. If correct, it adds another category of cases to those apparently subject to trial by both the Athenians and the allied synedrion (chapter 7). In the absence of supporting evidence, it is probably better to refrain from making the restoration; a restoration of [τῶν συμμάχων] after καί in line 20 would be equally or more defensible, but this temptation too should be resisted. WV 56 intro., incidentally, provides the erroneous information that Chabrias died at Keos (he was actually killed at Chios, as many sources testify; see chapter 10); this inscription is also mis-cited as no. 52 in the cross-reference of WV 44 intro.

19. SV 320, lines 1–8 (fragmentary Karthaian resolution), 9–24 (Koresian resolution), and 25–40 (Ioulietan resolution). Tod 142 comm. argues for inclusion of a Poiessian resolution; Lewis (supra n. 13) 2 says that most scholars now doubt that there was one; IG II, 546 comm. says Boeckhius vero nescio qua causa permotus saeculo tertio adscripsit.

20. I cannot tell whether this word has in the present context a meaning different from ἔκκλησις, the process associated with the form ἔκκλητος in inscriptions discussed supra. Eberhard Ruschenbusch, "ΕΦΕΣΙΣ. Ein Beitrag zur griechischen Rechtsterminologie," ZRG 78 (1961) 386–390 discusses theories of the word's meaning(s) in detail. The Koresian agreement is described as καθάπερ πρότερον in lines 10f and 16.

21. Quoted passages from lines 21f, 31–33, and 20f, respectively; Marshall 46; Accame 141 (see also p. 184).

the Kean city of Ioulis (362 B.C.) includes two appeal provisions. The first, which refers to persons listed by the generals of Ioulis as rebels subject to exile, says:

45   ἐὰν δέ [τινες τῶν] ἀπογραφέντων ἀμφισβητ-
ῶσι μὴ εἶναι τούτων τῶ[ν ἀνδρῶ]ν, ἐξεῖναι αὐτοῖς ἐνγυη-
τὰς καταστήσασι πρὸς [τ]ὸ[ς] σ[τρ]ατηγὸς τὸς Ἰολιητῶν τριάκοντα ἡμερῶν δίκα[ς] ὑ[π]ο[σχ]ὲν [κα]τὰ τ[ὸ]ς ὅρκος καὶ τὰς
συνθήκας ἐν Κέωι καὶ [ἐν τῆι ἐκκ]λήτωι [π]όλει Ἀθήνησι.

If [any of those] listed argue that they are not of those [me]n, it shall be permitted to them to deposit securities with [t]h[e] g[en]erals of (the) Ioulietans within thirty days to u[n]de[rt]ake a sui[t, acco]rding to t[h]e oaths and the agreements, in Keos and [in the app]ellate [c]ity Athens.

Marshall is of somewhat divided mind on the import of this provision: "In ordinary circumstances such an appeal would have been a distinct infringement of Kean αὐτονομία. In this case, however, circumstances perhaps justified it, since it might be impossible to secure a fair trial in Keos, where party feeling would run high." The second passage, in the Keans' oath, says:

          τὰς δὲ δίκας καὶ τ-
[ὰς γραφὰς τὰς κατ' Ἀθηναίων ποιήσομαι] πάσας ἐκκλήτος κ-
75 [ατὰ τὰς συνθήκας, ὁπόσαι ἂν ὦσιν ὑπὲρ ἑ]κατὸν δραχμάς.

The suits and t[he indictments against Athenians, which-ever are over a h]undred drachmas [I shall make] all appealable ac[cording to the agreements].

Marshall is more decisive here, saying that this provision "shows that the independence of Keos in judicial matters had received a decided limitation." Accame treats the two provisions as equally indicative of Athenian violation of Kean freedom and autonomy.[22]

  The Ioulis treaty of 362—with its date, its completeness (ca. 65 of its more than 80 lines are quite well preserved), and its absolutely clear content (it describes arrangements made after an abortive Kean revolt) —provides a standard for determining the implications for League members' autonomy of the appeal procedures of all these treaties. Seen within the context of the entire inscription, the appeal provisions of the Ioulis treaty are mere details. The fundamental nature of the settlement is shown in the oaths sworn to the Keans by the Athenians and the allies, which include promises to bear no malice for past events, to punish no one by death and to limit the number punished by exile, and to allow Keans who wish to emigrate to take up residence anywhere within

22. SV 289: date in line 2; quotations from lines 45–49 and 73–75, respectively; Marshall 46 (both comments); Accame 184.

League territory without loss of property. Perhaps most significant in its implications is the promise that εἰς δὲ τὴν συμμαχίαν εἰσά/[ξω καθάπ]ερ τὸς ἄλλος συμμάχος, meaning "[I shall] adm[it] (them) to the alliance [just li]ke the other allies." The status of the rebel Keans is thus explicitly said to be the same as that of free and autonomous League members who have never attempted to secede. It necessarily follows that none of the provisions of the treaty (including the appeal provisions) could have been understood as abridging the Keans' autonomy. The viewpoint of Tod, who calls the agreement a settlement "of a surprisingly moderate character," seems consistent with the content of the inscription as a whole.[23]

But if granting a right of appeal to accused Kean rebels and reviewing lawsuits (of substantial amounts) involving Athenians were not seen as abridgements of the Ioulietans' autonomy, then neither should we see Athenian usurpation in the protection of Athenian citizens' lives in the Siphnos treaty, the vague appeal provisions of the Naxos treaty, or the appeal granted to informers and complainants in the miltos inscription. The appeal granted to the Keans in connection with the two percent Peiraieus import tax actually constitutes an appeal against Athenian law, in Attica, granted to citizens of another state—no wonder scholars have omitted this particular appeal provision from their schemata of Athenian oppression! But any autonomous state, like the Athenians, could grant such privileges, and all the texts discussed (supra) are inscribed treaties wherein such concessions are granted. Possibly some degree of unofficial coercion of the weaker by the stronger *was* exerted in gaining these concessions; no student of diplomacy would find such a thing surprising in any century. But it is not demonstrable that the Greeks of the fourth century B.C. saw these appeal provisions as incompatible with the autonomy of the states granting them. Modern scholarship has created this problem in Athenian-allied relations, drawing upon an anachronistic understanding of "autonomy" and—frequently—an *a priori* assumption that the Second Athenian League developed into a second Empire.

Such attitudes can allow scholars to overlook other data which could even indicate positive Athenian encouragement of allied autonomy. An inscription recently published by R. S. Stroud may attest this sort of encouragement. The document, dated to 375/4 B.C., records a law regulating the flow of silver coinage in Athens and Peiraieus. It chiefly concerns procedures for determining which coins are good and which counterfeit, and enforces the acceptance of all the former as legal tender. The identification of one category of acceptable coins is particularly intriguing. Stroud restores and translates the relevant passage as follows (his brackets):

23. Oaths in lines 57–66 (quoted passage from lines 61f); Tod 142 comm.

ἐὰν δέ τις προσενέγκηι ξ[ε]ν[ικὸν ἀργύριον]
ἔχον τὸν αὐτὸγ χαρακτῆρα τῶι ᾿Αττι[κῶ]ι, ἐ[ὰν καλόν,]
10   ἀποδιδότω τῶι προσενεγκόντι.

If anyone brings forward [foreign silver currency] which has the same device as the Attic, [if it is good,] let the Tester give it back to the one who brought it forward.

In other words, such coins may then be used in trade (other provisions deal with the treatment of counterfeit coins). Stroud's interpretation is that coins minted outside Attica, if of the proper metal and weight and stamped with Athenian numismatic devices, must be treated by Athenian merchants just as if they were coins of the Athenian mint itself.[24] If this plausible interpretation is correct, we have here a picture of Athens, in the early days of its Second League, following a policy at the opposite extreme from that of the Athenian Empire, with its notorious Coinage Decree. Whereas fifth-century Athens compelled its subject allies to adopt Athenian coinage (and weights and measures) in their own commerce, fourth-century Athens is forcing its own businessmen to accept Attic-style coins, regardless of their source. The implication is that the practice is already so well established that counterfeiting has become widespread, and the Athenian merchants have become suspicious. Though no evidence exists for asserting that this liberal monetary policy was connected with the establishment of the League, the policy probably would have been attractive to allies and potential allies, as encouraging their trade.

Whether or not we accept this inscription as evidence for Athenian encouragement of allied autonomy, it remains true that arguments for Athenian encroachment on League members' autonomy are tenuous and suspect. If we are to discover Athenian abuses, we must find them in connection with more specific guarantees. The brief remainder of this chapter is devoted to a summary treatment of comparatively uncontroversial promises, reserving discussion of three more widely debated promises for chapter 9.

The decree of Aristoteles guarantees that anyone joining the Second Athenian League may do so "gov[ernin]g (himself according to the)

24. Stroud, "An Athenian Law on Silver Coinage," *Hesperia* 48 (1974) 157–188, esp. 157–159 and 168f; date in lines 1f, quotation from lines 8–10. Adalberto Giovannini, "Athenian Currency in the Late Fifth and Early Fourth Century B.C.," *GRBS* 16 (1975) 185–195 rejects Stroud's restoration and interpretation; each remains unmoved after an exchange of communications ("Addendum," p. 195). F. Sokolowski, "The Athenian Law Concerning Silver Currency (375/4 B.C.)," *BCH* 100 (1976) 511–515 alters Stroud's restoration but accepts his interpretation. J. and L. Robert, "Bulletin Épigraphique," *REG* 90 (1977) 337f review the controversy, saying (p. 337): "Nous ne pouvons suivre l'interprétation de Giovannini et nous croyons très exacte celle de Stroud." Philippe Gauthier, "Sur une clause pénale de la loi Athénienne relative a la monnaie d'argent," *RPh* 52 (1978) 32–35 differs with Stroud on an issue unrelated to this argument.

constitution which he prefers" (lines 20f). The fifth-century Empire's support of democratic factions and even, at times, forcible imposition of pro-Athenian democratic governments on its subject allies would have been remembered with suspicion. It is clear that this consideration—plus the desire to offer a contrast with Sparta's recent imposition of oligarchic regimes on unwilling allies (e.g., Thebes, until its liberation)—led the Athenians to make this promise. In effect, it means that a member state may be a democracy, an oligarchy, a state led by a king or tyrant, or one which none of these labels fits. Probably it is also implicit in the guarantee that a state joining the League under one form of government could alter its own constitution without Athenian interference or loss of League membership—though of course certain states under new governments would themselves attempt to secede from the League, and this might well bring on Athenian intervention.

Athenian involvement in factional politics on Zakynthos and Thera(?) in the early days of the League (chapter 3)—a policy which led to war and was quickly abandoned—is not directly connected with this guarantee. Zakynthos was a Spartan ally when the Athenian meddling took place (we have no data on the other example, but it was presumably analogous), and the acceptance of its democratic faction as a League member involved the participation of the synedrion (chapter 7). Support for democracy remained a staple of Athenian rhetoric,[25] but no example of any Athenian attempt to alter the government of a League member is known. Even in the case of states brought back into the League after rebellion (see discussion of the Kean documents, supra), the Athenians might have restored exiles and protected their own partisans, but they do not seem to have dictated the establishment of any particular type of constitution—and the synedrion was involved in the readmission process also.

Apparent evidence for Athenian toleration of changes within League members' constitutions exists for two cities of Lesbos. Mytilene joined the League as a democracy—at least the demos of the Mytilenaians was praised in Athenian decrees of 369/8 and 368/7. But after an oligarchical takeover there, Isokrates addressed the city's new rulers as if Athens and Mytilene remained allies (the tyrant Kammys did finally bring about the city's secession, and it had to be readmitted to the League after his demise). At Methymna, even the establishment of the tyranny of Kleomis seems not to have affected the alliance with Athens. In sum, so far as the meager evidence allows us to judge, the Athenians kept their pledge that League members might choose their own form of government.[26]

25. See, e.g., Isok. 4.16 and 104–106; [Dem.] 13.8; and Dem. 15.4, 17–21, and 33.

26. *IG* II², 107 includes both decrees regarding Mytilene (in reverse chronological order); the demos is praised in lines 15 and 37f (and mentioned again in an unclear context

"Paying tribute" is among the things which, according to the decree of Aristoteles, League members will not be required to do (line 23). This item has received sufficient attention in my discussion of the nature of the League's σύνταξις (chapter 7). In brief, no fourth-century source indicates that any League member ever paid φόρος to Athens.[27]

The assurance that prospective members will join "on t[h]e same (terms), just like (the) Chians and Thebans an[d] the other allies" (lines 23–25) indicates that there will be no special privileged—or unprivileged—classes of League members. There is no evidence of such subdivisions within the League having developed. The principle of equality of League allies was invoked in the phrasing of treaties, early and late.[28] The League membership as a whole constituted a privileged class within the Athenian system of alliances (Part II), but that is a different matter.

"[. . . If there h]appe[n] to be stelai at Athens unfavorabl[e] to the states [making] the alliance with (the) Athen[ians, t]he boule sitting at the time shall [b]e empowered to destroy (them)," says another provision of the decree of Aristoteles (lines 31–35). If this pledge constitutes a separate promise within the decree, it is only an uncontroversial statement that the current alliances supersede earlier alliances or agreements whose terms differ. We have no documentation either for this promise having been acted upon or for its having been neglected, in Athenian relations with members of the League. Testimony does exist, however, for the destruction of certain fourth-century non-League alliance treaties, when new alliances or new conditions rendered them outmoded.[29] The stelai to which the passage refers may have been, specifically, agreements granting Athens γῆς ἔγκτησις (the right to own landed property) in allied states.[30] If so, the passage should not be treated as a separate

---

in lines 51f). SV 328 is Mytilene's readmission treaty; IG II², 284 shows friendly Athenian relations with the tyrant of Methymna; see also Dem. 15.19; Isok. Lett. 7.8f and 8.7; and chapter 5 n. 39. The provision that the Keans are to govern themselves "by cities" in IG II², 404, lines 14f, is irrelevant (see argument, supra). Since Korkyra was not a League member (chapters 2 and 4), Xen. Hell. 5.4.64 cannot be cited as positive evidence for Athenian non-interference in League members' governments—though we would hardly expect Athens to treat its most favored allies any less well. Equally irrelevant (because also applying to Korkyra) is the misbehavior of Chares described in Diod. 15.95.3 (see chapter 10).

27. On the irresponsible restoration of Athenian φόρους in SV 303, line 8, see chapter 7 n. 36; the states involved were in any case apparently not League members (supra).

28. SV 256, lines 6f (restored); SV 258, lines 10f, 13f, and 21f; SV 267, lines 7–9 (mostly restored); SV 289, lines 61f; IG II², 125, lines 10f and 14f; SV 328, lines 9–13. The loose phrasing of Dem. 15.15 provides no basis, however, for statements such as that of Marshall 17 n. 1: "The allies were to be exactly on an equal footing with Athens." They were to be equal to each other, not to their common hegemon.

29. SV 293, lines 39f; Philoch. FGrH 328 F 55a (both quoted in chapter 5).

30. This is the opinion, e.g., of P.A. Brunt, "Athenian Settlements Abroad in the Fifth Century B.C.," in E. Badian (ed.), Ancient Society and Institutions: Studies Presented to Victor Ehrenberg on His 75th Birthday (New York 1967) 86f; Marshall, 17, appears to take a similar position.

pledge, but as part of a long and detailed provision (lines 25–46) guaranteeing prospective League members that Athenians would not be permitted to own real property in their territories (chapter 9).

The final provision to be treated in this chapter is both specific and clear: "If anyone co[mes] for war against t[ho]se making the alliance either by l[an]d or by sea, (the) Athenians and the allies shall give aid to them both by land and by sea, in full strength so far as possible" (lines 46–51). Any defensive alliance, of course, would include such phrasing, and the meaning is unambiguous; we have only to evaluate the Athenians' performance. Athenian relief missions are attested on behalf of the Euboians (377/6), Thebes (376), Zakynthos (374), Akarnania (373/2), Peparethos (361/0), Euboia again (357), and Neapolis (355–4), among states which were League members at the time such expeditions were sent.[31] Citing many of these campaigns, Hammond concludes: "Athens . . . made a supreme effort which justified her position as hegemon." He shows, further, that the Athenians heavily taxed themselves, conscripted many fighting men, and financed a wholesale expansion of their navy in making this effort.[32] As to the fulfillment of this promise, there seems to be no reason to disagree with Hammond. Tod believes that the Athenians were under some suspicion and were attempting to reassure the Mytilenaians, when they decreed in 369/8:

40

[ἀποκρί]νασθαι δὲ τοῖς πρέσβεσιν [τοῖ]-
[ς ἥκουσιν] ὅτ[ι] ᾽Αθηναῖοι ἐπολέμησαν [ὑπ]-
[ὲρ τῆς ἐλευθερία]ς τῶν ῾Ελλήνων· κα[ὶ ἐπε]-
[ιδὴ Λακεδαιμόν]ιοι ἐπεστράτευο[ν τοῖ]-
[ς ῞Ελλησιν παρὰ τ]οὺς ὅρκους καὶ τὰ[ς συν]-

45

[θήκας], κτλ.

The presbeis [who have come] are to be [answ]ered tha[t] (the) Athenians waged war [on behalf of the freedo]m of the Greeks; an[d when (the) Lakedaimon]ians attacke[d the Greeks in violation of t]he oaths and th[e agreements], etc.[33]

31. Euboia: Diod. 15.30.2 and 16.7.2; Dem. 23.14 (the expedition of 357 actually restored lost allies to the League). Thebes: Xen. *Hell.* 5.4.49. Zakynthos: *ib.* 6.2.2.; Diod. 15.45.2f. Akarnania: Xen. *Hell.* 6.2.37. Peparethos: Diod. 15.95.1f. Neapolis: *SV* 312; Polyain. 4.2.22. Non-League allies, and even some states which had seceded from the League, also received military assistance from Athens, e.g., Korkyra in 373 (Xen. *Hell.* 6.2.9–14 and 33–37; Diod. 15.46.3 and 47.4), Peloponnesian allies during the Theban invasions of 370–362 (Xen. *Hell.* 6 and 7, *passim*; Diod. 15.62–88), and states menaced by Philip (summary in Diod. 16.54.1f)—including secessionist League members Olynthos (Philoch. *FGrH* 328 F 49–51; Dem. 1–3, *passim*) and Byzantion (Diod. 16.77.2; Plut. *Phok.* 14; ?*IG* II², 233).

32. Hammond, *HG*² 489, with sources.

33. *IG* II², 107, lines 40–45 (brackets and underdotting as in Tod 131); Tod 131 comm.

Reassurance probably was the Athenian motive, but we need not infer that some misdeed of Athens had alarmed the Mytilenaians. Rather, they were probably being reassured about the implications of the recently concluded alliance between Athens and Sparta. The message appears to be that Athenian military activity continues to support Greek freedom, but that Sparta is no longer the chief menace to it: Athenian policy has not changed, only circumstances.

The Athenians, in fact, were entitled to complain of their allies' failure to meet their mutual military responsibilities—and they did so, according to Xenophon, when no help was offered after the Thebans seized the border town of Oropos in 366. Even this incident, however, is taken by some commentators as evidence of Athenian mistreatment of the League members. Marshall describes the event as the failure of Athens's new *Peloponnesian* allies to render aid, which may be correct. But he has no basis for describing this as suitable punishment for the Athenians' having compelled their island allies to let these states enter the League in 371: as shown in chapter 4, the Peloponnesians were *not* League allies. In any case, what Xenophon says is (my emphasis): "*None* of the allies gave aid to the Athenians." The Athenians reacted to this disappointment by accepting an alliance with the Arkadian league (chapter 5).[34]

Up to this point, Athenian performance in keeping the promises of the decree of Aristoteles looks quite impressive. The chief areas of controversy, however, remain to be discussed. By handling the respective guarantees in the sequence here adopted, I hope I have made it possible to approach the controversial issues with something like a clean slate.

---

34. Xen. *Hell.* 7.4.1f, translated passage in sec. 1 (τοῖς δ' Ἀθηναίοις οὐδεὶς τῶν συμμάχων ἐβοήθησεν); Marshall 81 and 89. Sealey, *City-Sts.* 428, seems to offer a similar interpretation.

9

KLERUCHIES, GARRISONS,
AND GOVERNORS

Disavowal of ownership of real property in allied territories is the most thoroughly spelled out promise of the decree of Aristoteles. First comes a renunciation of claims (lines 25–31):

For those maki[n]g alliance with (the) Athenians and their allies, the demos shall give up the possessions, however many there happen to be, either private or [p]ublic, of Athenians in the l[ands of those mak]ing the alliance, a[nd concerning these matters] give [as]surance. . . .

The next clause (lines 31–35), which empowers the boule at any future time to destroy stelai at Athens unfavorable to League members, may or may not (see chapter 8) be a continuation of one long, carefully worded guarantee about Athenian property ownership—depending on whether it refers specifically to treaties granting Athenians the right to hold landed property in allied states. In any case, this clause is followed immediately by another statement (lines 35–41) about property ownership:

From the archon[sh]ip of Nausinikos, it shall not be permitted to any Athenian, either privately or publ[i]cly, to possess in t[h]e territories of the allies either a house or an estate, neither by purchasing nor by mort[g]aging, nor by any other means.

The guarantee concludes with a detailed outline of enforcement procedures (lines 41–46), in which only the allies, not the Athenians, are to participate (chapter 7).

It is generally agreed that Diodoros is referring to these provisions when he says:

ἐψηφίσαντο δὲ καὶ τὰς γενομένας κληρουχίας ἀποκαταστῆσαι τοῖς πρότερον κυρίοις γεγονόσι, καὶ νόμον ἔθεντο μηδένα τῶν Ἀθηναίων γεωργεῖν ἐκτὸς τῆς Ἀττικῆς.

They also voted to restore the existing kleruchies to those who were formerly their owners, and established a law that none of the Athenians would cultivate land outside Attica.[1]

A kleruchy (κληρουχία) was technically "a community of Athenian citizens living abroad, enrolled in Athenian tribes and demes, who had to serve in the Athenian armed forces and pay Athenian taxes but who enjoyed some municipal self-government"—as contrasted with a regular colony (ἀποικία or ἐποικία), which was a newly established separate state

1. Diod. 15.29.8.

with its own citizenship. In the fifth century, certain kleruchies had been established in lands confiscated from rebellious Athenian allies, without compensation to the dispossessed landowners. These enclaves of Athenians were naturally much resented.[2]

Diodoros (or his source) has somewhat garbled his description of the decree's property ownership provisions, as several scholars point out. Athens had lost its overseas land holdings, public and private, as a consequence of being defeated in the Peloponnesian War. The few kleruchies that had been regained—those on Lemnos, Imbros, and Skyros —were permitted to remain in existence when the terms of the King's Peace recognized these islands as Athenian possessions, and their status continued unchanged throughout the history of the Second Athenian League.[3] Moreover, there was no pledge to abandon all Athenian holdings "outside Attica," only holdings within the territory of states joining the League. In examining the Athenians' compliance with their promises about landed property ownership, the phrasing of the decree of Aristoteles is relevant; the interpretation of Diodoros carries no comparable weight.[4]

Uncertainty exists whether any private property in Athenians' possession at the time the decree was passed was given up under its terms. Some scholars believe that lines 25–31 merely recognize as legally valid and irreversible the allied seizures of Athenian holdings that attended the dissolution of the Athenian Empire. Under this interpretation, no property would actually change hands; potential claims and litigation would simply be forestalled.[5] The clause could, however, refer to Athenian holdings under early fourth-century treaties (no longer extant) with current or prospective members of the League, perhaps inscribed on the stelai whose destruction is called for in lines 31–35.[6] The distinction

2. Definition of P. A. Brunt, "Athenian Settlements Abroad in the Fifth Century B.C.," in E. Badian (ed.), *Ancient Society and Institutions: Studies Presented to Victor Ehrenberg on His 75th Birthday* (New York 1967) 73. On the widespread resentment, see, e.g., Diod. 15.23.4.

3. General descriptions of these islands as Athenian possessions: [Dem.] 59.3; Ais. 2.72; Aristot. *Ath. Pol.* 62.2. Sources mentioning only Lemnos and Imbros: Dem. 4.34; Diod. 16.21.2. Epigraphic evidence for the kleruchies: Lemnos: *IG* II², 30 (see chapter 1 n. 4) and *IG* XII (8), 3, lines 4f; 4, lines 1f; 5, lines 7f; 6, lines 6f; 9, lines 1f; 10, line 1; 11, line 2; 12, line 2; and 26, lines 1f. Imbros: *IG* XII (8), 46, lines 1 and 3. Skyros: *IG* XII (8), 668, lines 1–5. (Delos was apparently also an Athenian possession, though not a kleruchy; see chapter 2).

4. See the comments of, e.g., A. H. M. Jones, *Athenian Democracy* (Oxford 1960) 167; Brunt (supra n. 2) 85f; Philippe Gauthier, "A propos des clérouquies athéniennes du Ve siècle," in M. I. Finley (ed.), *Problèmes de la terre en Grèce ancienne* (Paris 1973) 170–172.

5. Cawkwell, "Found." 48; Gauthier (supra n. 4) 170f, citing Ed. Meyer as the person first suggesting this interpretation.

6. Gauthier (supra n. 4) 170f rejects such interpretations only because he believes that "autonomous" states could not grant such a concession to Athens, but classical definitions

would, in any case, soon become unimportant: the wording of lines 25–31 would require abandonment of *both* actual possessions *and* ineffectively asserted claims. It is possible that Athenians with current holdings in allied territories (if such existed) were not immediately expropriated, but were given a brief grace period in which to dispose of their properties. This may be the import of the dating formula ⟨ἀ⟩πὸ δὲ Ν/αυσινίκο ἄρχον[τ]ος in lines 35f. If lines 25–46 constitute a single consistent statement of League policy on Athenian land ownership, the implication may be that the announced policy is to become enforceable at the end of the current archon year. On this issue also, different interpretations of the provision might lead to consequences which do not themselves differ greatly: Athenians, compelled to sell their properties between the seventh prytany (lines 4f) and the end of the ten-prytany Attic year, would face a buyer's market, and would probably have to sell at a loss.

Did the Athenians honor their promise? Within the received text of Demosthenes' oration *On the Crown* is a decree of the Byzantines and Perinthians, supposedly passed in gratitude for Athens's rescue of their cities from Philip in 340/39. Among the honors bestowed on the Athenians by this decree is the right to own land in the territory of Byzantion and Perinthos. These cities were listed among the members of the League (lines 83f), and the cited decree *could* fall within the period of the League's existence. But three problems exist in connection with this document: (1) it is generally believed to be spurious; (2) even if genuine, it could have been passed after the dissolution of the League in 338; and (3) even if genuine and of appropriate date, it was passed by cities that had seceded from the League, and whose current alliances with Athens were of non-League type (chapter 5).[7] This completely unreliable document is the entirety of the extant evidence for private Athenian property ownership in League members' territories. The remainder of my discussion of property ownership concerns kleruchies.

Beyond those on Lemnos, Skyros, and Imbros, several Athenian kleruchies are attested for the period of the League. The one sent to Samos, probably in 365 B.C., apparently was the earliest established, and is the best documented. Aristotle's citation of a passage from the orator Kydias indicates that there was opposition within Athens to the sending out of this kleruchy, though nothing implies that its establishment was viewed as a breach of any formal treaty obligation. It is probably

---

of "autonomy" were flexible (chapter 8). See also Brunt (supra n. 2) 82f, and literature cited there, on the relationship of Thuc. 3.50 and *IG* I², 60.

7. Dem. 18.91: ἔγκτασιν γᾶς. See intro. to Loeb ed., p. 17; cf. Gauthier (supra n. 4) 170. H. Wankel, "Zu P.Oxy.3009, P.Haun.5 und den Urkunden in der Kranzrede des Demosthenes," *ZPE* 16 (1975) 151–162 discusses problems connected with documents within this speech, but says nothing about this particular document.

reasonable to see Kydias as a representative of a faction opposed to the general Timotheos, who took the island away from Persian control. Certainly other Athenians praised Timotheos' action: Demosthenes says he "freed" Samos. Even though scholars generally agree that Samos was not a member of the Second Athenian League (chapter 2), it is common to see the establishment of the Samian kleruchy denounced in modern literature as some sort of decisive breach of the "spirit" of the decree of Aristoteles.[8] Poteidaia, another city captured by Timotheos (shortly after Samos), but apparently left self-governing, itself requested the dispatch of Athenian kleruchs to its territory, according to an inscribed Athenian decree of 362/1. Modern scholarship supplies the censure that is in this case entirely absent from extant sources, e.g., the statement of Tod: "In responding to this appeal Athens was transgressing the principles of her Second Confederacy . . . , though, since Potidaea was not one of its members, there was no technical infraction of its charter. . . ."[9] Other kleruchs were sent to the Chersonesos ca. 353/2. According to the *Hypothesis* to Demosthenes' oration *On the Chersonesos* (we cannot tell how reliably), their coming was welcomed by most of the peoples of the peninsula.[10] Other Athenian inscriptions of debated dates may refer to other kleruchies—including possibly the earliest of all—or may simply refer to one or more of those already mentioned. These documents are too fragmentary to provide any information about the actual location(s) of the settlement(s) they mention, or about contemporary attitudes toward the kleruchs.[11] Accame believes that another kleruchy was sent to Methone, and that Methone was a member of the League. But Methone is very unlikely to have been a League member (chapter 4),

8. Date: Diod. 18.18.9 (cf. Sch. Ais. 1.53). Other evidence of the kleruchy's existence: G. Klaffenbach, "Samische Inschriften," *MDAI(A)* 51 (1926) 36; *IG* II², 1437, lines 20f; Ais. 1.53; Philoch. *FGrH* 328 F 154; Aristot. *Rhet.* 1384b. E. Badian, "A Comma in the History of Samos," *ZPE* 23 (1976) reinterprets a Samian inscription published by Chr. Habicht in 1957, showing that it refers to Athenian kleruchs, not (as Habicht suggested) to *Samian* kleruchs; the context is in any case some years after the dissolution of the League. Positive views toward Timotheos' actions: Dem. 15.9 (ἠλευθέρωσε); Isok. 15.108 and 111 (consistent with hopes expressed as early as 380 B.C.: *id.* 4.163; Isok. was capable, however, even of praising the *fifth*-century kleruchies: *id.* 4.107 and 12.167, cf. 190); Dein. 1.14 and 3.17; Polyain. 3.10.9f; Nep. *Timoth.* 1.2. Among modern commentators see, e.g., Marshall 92; Beloch 3:1.194 and n. 3; Accame 61 and 183 and nn. 1f; Ryder, *KE* 84 and n. 1. See also general comments on all kleruchies, cited infra.

9. *IG* II², 114, lines 1 (date), 4–6 and 9–11 (Poteidaians' request), and 8f (sending of τὸς κληρόχος). The kleruchs are mentioned in Dem. 6.20 and [Dem.] 7.10. Timotheos' capture of the city is mentioned in Isok. 15.108 and 113; Dein. 1.14 and 3.17; and Diod. 15.81.6. Quotation from Tod 146 comm.

10. *Hyp.* Dem. 8; date from Diod. 16.34.4; existence attested by *IG* II², 228, lines 15f.

11. *IG* II², 1952, lines 1f, and 1609, line 89; see J. K. Davies, "The Date of *IG* ii².1609," *Historia* 18 (1969) 309–333, and the bibliography and brief summary of recent discussion in Sealey, *City-Sts.* 437 n. 3.

and the inscriptional evidence which Accame cites has been shown to be of fifth-century date and hence irrelevant.[12]

Despite the total lack of ancient evidence that kleruchies were established in the territories of League members and the indecisive evidence as to contemporary attitudes toward those established elsewhere, scholars have chosen to make the existence of the handful of attested kleruchies a major element in their critique of the Second Athenian League. The statement of Hammond will serve as a forceful example of this widespread attitude:

In promising to liberate the Greek states and to respect the autonomy of her allies, Athens had undertaken a clear and solemn obligation. It was a mere quibble to argue that, because Samos, Potidaea, Sestus, and Crithote were not already members of the Athenian alliance, Athens was entitled to subjugate them and seize their land for her own citizens to occupy as cleruchs. The imperialistic policy of Athens was now apparent to the Greek world, and her methods in diplomacy and in war were comparable to those of pirates.[13]

This entire "renewal of Empire" argument is, however, wrongheaded and misleading. So far as we can tell, the Athenians kept the promise they made about property ownership in allied territories. No one expected them to honor some nonexistent assurance which later historians (Diodoros and the moderns) have inferred. The Athenians were treating the members of their League as specially favored and protected states in making the promise not to own landed property in their territories. The kleruchies established in non-League territories apparently had justifiable purposes—protection of Athens's grain supply, prevention of Persian reconquest, outposts against the expansion of Philip, etc.—and there is no indication that the League allies found their existence alarming. During the Social War, the rebels who attacked Athenian kleruchies apparently attacked the loyal allies as well.[14]

The only guarantee of the decree of Aristoteles remaining to be discussed is the provision (lines 21–23) that states may enter the League

12. Accame 183 and n. 6; cf. B. D. Meritt, "Greek Inscriptions: 2. Aphytis and Poteidaia," *Hesperia* 13 (1944) 215, who shows that the inscription cited by Accame (a fragment joining *IG* II², 55), despite its fourth-century style of lettering, must be a fifth-century document (as must *IG* II², 55 as a whole), because it mentions οἱ Ἑλληνοταμί[αι---] (line 13)—a board of magistrates which existed only under the Athenian Empire.

13. Hammond, *HG*² 503; see also, e.g., A. R. Burn, *The Pelican History of Greece* 321; Bengtson, *G&P* 235f; Burnett, "Expans." 14. The very different position of Sealey, *City-Sts.* 432, represents a shift from the conventional position he took in "Transf." 99.

14. This seems to be the meaning of the statement of Diod. 16.21.2 that they ravaged Imbros, Lemnos, Samos, and "also many other islands which were subject to the Athenians" (πολλὰς δὲ καὶ ἄλλας νήσους οὔσας ὑπ᾽ Ἀθηναίους)—an interpretation whose likelihood is increased by the existence of inscriptional evidence that citizens of the allied island of Amorgos (DA, line 124) were captured and had to be ransomed: *IG* XII (7), 5, lines 15f (quoted infra).

"neither receiving a [garris]on nor ac[cep]ting a governor nor paying tribute." The entire clause, of course, recalls fifth-century imperial practices which potential allies would have been reluctant to see reinstituted. The dative participles of μή/τε [φρορ]ὰν εἰσδεχομένωι μήτε ἄρχοντα /ὑπο-[δεχ]ομένωι μήτε φόρον φέροντι do not seem to admit of exceptions under any circumstances. I believe that states joined the Second Athenian League on the understanding that they would never pay tribute and never have Athenian garrisons or governors in their territory. Any of these that may be discovered to have existed can only be justified—if at all—in spite of a guarantee that was originally unconditional.[15] Evidence for the Athenians' levying of tribute in the fourth century is nonexistent, implying that tribute in fact was never assessed or paid (chapters 7 and 8). Therefore, at this point, only discussion of garrisons and governors is relevant, and my comments are confined to these.

Garrisons and governors are linked not only in Aristoteles' phrase, but in both ancient and modern discussions of Athenian relations with the allies. Accordingly, I will treat the two as aspects of a single policy: justifications or condemnations of the presence in League territory of one will be taken as applying equally to the other. The meaning of "garrison" (φρουρά) is unambiguous: a group of soldiers continuously stationed at some particular place. Soldiers might, however, be at some location only temporarily—for a siege, on a campaign, or merely camping while passing through—so literary or epigraphic references to στρατιῶται at some place may or may not indicate that a garrison is stationed there. The term ἄρχων, in fifth-century sources, sometimes refers to a specific Athenian official in an allied state, having certain judicial powers, and "governor" is a reasonable translation for the title of such an official. But often the word is used generically (frequently in the plural, ἄρχοντες) to refer to any or all of several types of Athenian magistrates involved in controlling the states within the Empire—not only the "governors" proper, but also "overseers" (ἐπίσκοποι), garrison commanders (φρούραρχοι), and "heralds" (κήρυκες). Sometimes, particularly in fragmentary epigraphical sources, it is difficult or impossible to tell whether ἄρχων is being employed specifically or generically. This is far more of a problem with fifth-century sources than with those of the fourth century, however, for the obvious reason that some of these types of magistracies ceased to exist with the destruction of the Athenian Empire. The singular accusative ἄρχοντα of the decree of Aristoteles almost certainly refers to the specific official describable as a "governor." Presumably the commander of a fourth-century garrison (properly a φρούραρχος) could

15. The translation of WV 22 and the interpretations of, e.g., Tod 123 comm. and B&E 85, seem to dodge this problem; my interpretation is consistent with the translations of Pouilloux 27, Pfohl 103, and Adcock and Mosley, *Diplomacy in Ancient Greece* (London 1975) 260, and with the summary of Sealey, *City-Sts.* 411.

still be referred to, however, as an ἄρχων or magistrate. Whether used specifically or generically, the term ἄρχων as employed in the fourth century cannot be taken as precisely equivalent to the fifth-century term. At the very least, the fourth-century governor could have had no duties connected with tribute or with Athenian property ownership in League territories. The Spartans sometimes sent out an official called a "harmost" (ἁρμοστής, plural ἁρμοσταί), whose duties might be likened to those of an Athenian ἄρχων and/or φρούραρχος. A source referring to "governors" sent out by *both* powers presumably could employ either the Attic term or the Lakonian term without creating confusion among contemporary readers.[16]

Evidence for the existence of a few Athenian garrisons in the early years of the League may be discoverable in epigraphic sources. A much-damaged inscription regarding Athenian relations with Kephallenia, generally dated by commentators to some point in the 370s, may be restored so as to refer to [---τὰς φρ]/οράς αἵπερ εἰσὶν ἐν ταῖς νήσοις]. The restoration of "[gar]risons" seems safe enough, but it is impossible to tell whether the conjecturally restored "islands" (even if correct) are League members or not. Athenian functionaries (ἐπιμελη[τά]ς) of some type are being sent to Kephallenia, but most scholars currently reject Schweigert's bold further restoration of a reference to [---ἄρχοντ]/ες πέ[ντε---].[17] His inference that another largely restored phrase points to the presence on Kephallenia of an Athenian garrison is also tenuous (see discussion, infra). Since only one of the four cities of Kephallenia is listed among the members of the League (Pronnoi, lines 107f), the relevance of this fragmentary inscription for discussion of garrisons and governors in the territories of League allies is inherently questionable, at all events.

Dedications of crowns to Chabrias on the base of his statue in the Athenian agora appear to refer to the general's accomplishments during

---

16. See the full discussion of all these terms, with quotation of sources and bibliography, of J. M. Balcer, "Imperial Magistrates in the Athenian Empire," *Historia* 25 (1976) 257–287, on which much of this paragraph is based. I am grateful to Prof. Charles D. Hamilton for a pre-publication draft of an article scheduled to appear in *Traditio* in 1980, in which he offers the sensible suggestion that the guarantees of DA were intended also to draw a contrast between Athens's new League and the imperialistic recent practices of *Sparta*, notably the imposing of harmosts and garrisons.

17. *SV* 267, quotations from lines 16f, 18, and 12f, respectively; Schweigert, "Greek Inscriptions: 33. A New Fragment of the Treaty between Athens and Kephallenia," *Hesperia* 9 (1940) 321–324. The currently preferred date of ca. 372 is inferred from Xen. *Hell.* 6.2.33 and 38. Marshall, 62 and n. 6, posited a garrison on Kephallenia in 375 on the basis of Diod. 15.36.5 (the inscription had not yet been discovered); cf. Beloch 3:1.160 n. 1. Schweigert's restoration of a reference to five magistrates is rejected by Accame, 185 n. 5, and by Bengtson, who restores [---ἐπάναγκ]/ες· π[έμψαι---] instead, citing Wilhelm; Burnett, "Expans." 14 n. 20, seems inclined to accept Schweigert's version.

the 370s. Several of the crowns were awarded by groups of soldiers, including οἱ στρα[τιῶτ]αι οἱ ἐμ Μυτιλήνει and Δι[ό]τιμος καὶ οἱ στρατιῶται [οἱ] ἐξ[ν Σ]ύρωι οἱ ἐπὶ τῶν νεῶν. Mytilene, of course, was a listed League member (line 80), and Syros is quite likely to have been one of the lost names of the front face of the League stele (chapter 2). It is possible, then, that these soldiers were garrison troops (and Diotimos a garrison commander) in League members' territories within the first few years of the League's existence—though the modifying final phrase of the Syros group's dedication makes the supposition rather weak in its case. If the other groups of soldiers mentioned in the dedicatory passages on this monument were indeed garrisons, apparently they were established in non-League territories.[18] These, the garrison within a hostile Euboian city in 377, another in the territory of non-League ally Korinth in 366, and some garrisons and governors in other non-League territories at later dates, are essentially irrelevant to an evaluation of Athens' fulfillment of its promises to League members, and need not be discussed.[19]

The inscriptional evidence for the presence of garrisons and governors within the lands of the League allies prior to the Social War is, as has been shown, all doubtful or ambiguous. I see no reason, however, to reject the clear testimony of the literary sources, which say that garrisons and governors were dispatched in the very early days of the League. A garrison was set up at Abdera, a listed League member (line 99) in ca. 375 B.C. Establishment of Spartan governors and garrisons prior to the peace of 375/4 is attested, and these seem to have been countered by Athenian garrisons; a condition of the peace treaty was the removal of garrisons, and Diodoros says that agents were sent from state to state to supervise their evacuation. With the renewal of the war, garrisons and governors were employed again, and their removal was an element of the peace of Sparta of 371: Xenophon explicitly mentions the removal of Athenian garrisons, along with Spartan governors and garrisons.[20] In view of the fairly clear evidence cited thus far, and the even more defi-

---

18. See the argument of B&E 79–91 (quoted texts on pp. 79f). The statue is attested by Ais. 3.243; Aristot. *Rhet.* 1411b; Nep. *Chab.* 1.3; and Diod. 15.33.4. See also J. K. Anderson, "The Statue of Chabrias," *AJA* 67 (1963) 411–413, and Buckler, "A Second Look at the Monument of Chabrias," *Hesperia* 41 (1972) 466–474 and plates 115f.

19. Euboia: Diod. 15.30.5. Korinth: Xen. *Hell.* 7.4.4–7. Hellespont: *IG* II², 133, lines 23–25 (τὸν λι[μενόφρουρον? τὸν 'Α]/θηναίων ἐν Ἑλλησπόν[τωι καὶ τοὺς ἄρχ]/οντας τοὺς ἐν Ἑλλησπ[όντωι---]). Chersonesos: Dem. 23.159. Krithote: *ib.* 161. Accame, 185, treats virtually all of these areas as League members' territory. The garrison on Korkyra, commanded by Chares, which is mentioned in Ain. Takt. 11.13–15 presents special problems; see quotation and discussion in chapter 10.

20. Abdera: Diod. 15.36.4 (though incorrect elements exist within the narrative; cf. 16.7.3). Early Spartan establishments: Xen. *Hell.* 5.4.41 and 46; Isok. 4.117 and 14.13 and 18; Diod. 15.33.6 and 37.1; Plut. *Pelop.* 15.4 and 16.1f. Withdrawal after peace of 375/4: Diod. 15.38.2. Withdrawal after peace of 371: Xen. *Hell.* 6.3.18 and 4.1f.

nite and explicit evidence of the Social War period (infra), the conclusion is inescapable that this particular Athenian promise *was* breached. We must still ask how and why.

What apparently happened, the sources imply, is that both the Athenians and their allies realized at a very early date that adherence to the letter of this particular guarantee would prove disastrous—not only to Athens, but to the League members as well. The defense of the islanders against attack was the hegemon's primary obligation (lines 46-51). It must have soon become evident that in times of danger only a continuing Athenian military presence in certain critical or exposed areas could fulfill that obligation. The provision within the decree of Aristoteles probably was not formally abrogated—no Athenian politician would be likely to offer such a suggestion, since another clause of the decree (lines 51-63) could make him liable to the loss of his civic rights, his property, and even his life for so doing.[21] But somehow—and it would be idle to speculate exactly how, given the total absence of evidence—the understanding must have arisen that garrisons and governors might be sent out, *with the approval of the allied synedrion.*

A phrase in the League membership alliance treaty of Chalkis (377) may provide a clue for dating this development. The last few extant lines of the inscribed treaty, which describe the conditions of Chalkis' membership in the League, include a close paraphrase of the guarantees of the decree of Aristoteles—with one perhaps significant addition:

ἔχε[ν τὴ]ν ἑαυτῶν Χαλκιδέ[ας ἐλ]-
[ευθέρ]ος ὄντα[ς καὶ] αὐτονόμος καὶ αὐ[. . .]
[. . .6. . .]ς μήτε φρορὰν ὑποδεχομένος [παρ']
['Αθηναίων μ]ήτε φόρον φέροντας μήτε [ἄρχ]-
25   [οντα παραδ]εχομένος παρὰ τὰ δόγματ[α τῶ]-
[ν συμμάχων.]

(The) Chalkidi[ans are t]o hold their own (territory), bein[g fre]e [and] autonomous and . . . ., neither accepting a garrison [from (the) Athenians n]or paying tribute nor [admi]tting [a governor] contrary to the dogmat[a of the allies.][22]

The final quoted phrase, in which the presence of the technical term "dogmata" makes the restoration "of the allies" virtually certain, may indicate that the aforementioned understanding had already been reached, within the same archon year in which the decree of Aristoteles

---

21. The severity of this threat, incidentally, is another reason for supposing that the bold step of erasing lines 12-14 of the stele came comparatively late, rather than (as many believe) early in the history of the League. Ryder's suggestion, which I find most acceptable (chapters 2 and 10), fits a date more than a decade after the League's establishment.

22. *SV* 259, lines 21-26.

had been passed. It is difficult to account for the phrase otherwise. The decree of Aristoteles itself, an Athenian resolution, would not be cited among "the dogmata of the allies." The reference to garrison, tribute, or governor παρὰ τὰ δόγματα may imply the alternative possibility of garrison, tribute, or governor κατὰ τὰ δόγματα—i.e., those approved (presumably in advance) by the synedrion. Since there is no evidence that any tribute was ever collected, there is naturally no evidence of the synedrion's ever having approved it. But its acceptance of the establishment of certain garrisons and governors can be documented.

An inscription universally agreed to be of Social War date records a resolution (its main provisions are quoted, infra) of the boule and demos of a city (Arkesine) on the island of Amorgos, a League member (line 124), honoring the Athenian governor Androtion and making reference also to the garrison troops stationed there. The stele breaks off with the beginning of a new provision or amendment: υυ ἐπεὶ [οὖν / κ]αὶ [τοῖ]ς συμμάχοις ἔδοξε [....8..../....8... ὡ]σαύτως [---].[23] It seems inconceivable that this decree of an allied city would mention (favorably) an Athenian governor, a garrison, *and* an allied resolution (whatever its lost content) unless the governor and garrison had been approved by the synedrion. This impression is confirmed by an Athenian decree dated to 356 concerning League member Andros (line 112), in which it was resolved:

ὅπως [ἂ]ν Ἀνδ[ρο]-
[ς] ε[ἰ] σ[ᾶ] τῶι δ[ή]μωι τῶι Ἀθη[να]ίων [κα]-
[ὶ] τῶι δήμωι τῶι Ἀνδρίων καὶ ἔχ[ωσ]-
    10   ιν ο[ἱ] φρουροὶ οἱ ἐν Ἀ[νδρω]ι μισ[θὸ]-
ν ἐκ τῶν συντάξεων κ[α]τ[ὰ τ]ὰ δόγ[μα]-
[τ]α τ[ῶ]ν συμμάχων καὶ μὴ καταλύ[ητ]-
αι ἡ φυλακή, ἑλέσθαι στρ[α]τηγ[ὸν ἐ]-
κ τῶγ κεχειροτονημένων, [τ]ὸ[ν δὲ α]-
    15   [ἱ]ρ[ε]θέντα ἐπιμελεῖσθαι [Ἄνδρου].
εἰσπρᾶξαι δὲ καὶ τὰ ἐγ ν[ήσων χρή]-
ματα Ἀρχέδημον τὰ ὀφ[ειλόμενα τ]-
οῖς στρατιώταις το[ῖς ἐν Ἄνδρωι]
[κ]αὶ παραδοῦναι τῶ[ι ἄρχοντι τῶι]
    20   [ἐν] Ἄνδρωι, ὅπως [ἂν οἱ στρατιῶται]
[ἔχ]ωσι μισθ[όν---]

So th[a]t And[ros] may b[e] sa[fe] for the d[e]mos of (the) Athe[ni]ans [and] for the demos of (the) Andrians, and (that) th[e] garrison troops on A[ndro]s [may] have (their) p[a]y out of the syntaxeis ac[cord]in[g to t]he dog[mat]a of t[h]e allies,

---

23. *IG* XII (7), 5, lines 24–26 (brackets and underdotting as in Tod 152).

and (that) the guard [may] not be terminated, a ge[n]era[l] is to be chosen [ou]t
of those having been elected, [w]h[o], having been [cho]s[en], is to be in charge of
[Andros]. Archedemos is also to collect the
[mo]ney from (the) is[lands] which [is]
ow[ed] to [t]he soldiers [on Andros a]nd to
turn (it) over to th[e governor on] Andros,
so that [the soldiers] may [hav]e (their)
pa[y. . . .][24]

Here again, in connection with a garrison (lines 10, 13, 18, 20) and probably also with a governor (line 19), we find a citation of the resolutions
of the allies (lines 11f). The synedrion which had arranged for the garrison troops to be paid must necessarily also have given its approval to
the garrison's presence on the island.

Other evidence for the presence of Athenian garrisons and governors
in the territories of League members in this later period, though frequently cited, is all rather tenuous. An undated fragmentary inscription
from Ios, which may have been a League member (one of the lost names
of the stele of Aristoteles; see chapter 2), bestows honors on some Athenian (name lost) which resemble the honors voted to Androtion by
Arkesine. For this reason, it is generally inferred that the unnamed Athenian was also a governor, and that he, like Androtion, held this magistracy during the Social War period.[25] Another type of indirect evidence
involves extrapolation from a phrase within the Andros inscription
quoted supra, the introductory phrase beginning in line 7: "So that Andros may be safe, etc." Xenophon reports on a resolution employing a
similar phrase, in a passage relating to the Athenian garrison in the territory of non-League ally Korinth. Commentators consequently infer that
the phrase is a formula calling for the installation of a garrison. This
reasoning leads scholars to believe that an Athenian garrison was stationed on Keos: an inscription making no explicit mention of a garrison
there (nor is one attested in any other source) includes the phrase
[---ὅ]πως ἂν σᾶ ἦι Κέως τῶ[ι δήμωι τῶι 'Αθηναίων?---]. Similar phrasing
—almost totally restored—is accorded a similar implication in the fragmentary inscription concerning Athenian relations with Kephallenia,
cited supra.[26] But this entire chain of inference is suspect. The grammat-

24. *IG* II², 123, lines 7–21 (brackets and underdotting as in Tod 156). Though ἄρχοντι in
line 19 is entirely restored, Ais. 1.107f shows that there was at least one Athenian governor
on Andros during the period of the League (see n. 28, infra).

25. *IG* XII (5), 1000. See Paul Graindor, "Fouilles d'Ios: Inscriptions," *BCH* 28 (1904)
313; Accame, 185 and n. 3, appears to accept the argument.

26. Korinth: Xen. *Hell.* 7.4.4 (ὅπως καὶ Κόρινθος σῷα ἦ τῷ δήμῳ τῶν 'Αθηναίων); Keos: *IG*
II², 404, line 7 (Maier); Kephallenia: *SV* 267, lines 22f (ὅπω[ς ἂν ἦι σᾶ τοῖς τε 'Α]/θηναίοις καὶ
Κε[φαλλῆσιν---]). See Schweigert (supra n. 17), and WV 56 intro.

ical relationships among the clauses of the Andros inscription are clear. The stone does *not* say that a garrison is to be—or has been—sent out "so that Andros may be safe, etc." It says that a general is to be put in charge on Andros, with specified duties, "so that Andros may be safe" *and* the already established garrison may be paid, etc., etc. In other words, the phrase modifies the selection of the general, and has nothing directly to do with the garrison. In the cited Xenophon passage, also, the garrison is already present at Korinth; the next event reported by Xenophon is in fact its withdrawal, upon the Korinthians' request. The phrase as restored in the Kephallenia inscription modifies the sending out of three Athenian commissioners. There may have been Athenian garrisons on Kephallenia (part of which was not League territory) and/or on Keos (where the fragmentary state of the cited inscription makes the reference of the key phrase impossible to discover), but their existence is only one possible inference from phrasing which is ambiguous. The only absolutely identifiable garrisons or governors in League members' lands are those at Abdera in 375 and on Andros and Amorgos during the Social War period. Others apparently existed, both early and late, but evidence in each individual case is inferential, and must be used with caution.

Some conjectures about League members' attitudes toward the Athenian garrisons and governors may be ventured, however, in connection with the sources cited. On the base of Chabrias' statue, next to the dedication of οἱ στρα[τιῶτ]αι οἱ ἐμ Μυτιλήνει (the possible Athenian garrison), is another dedication from ὁ δῆμος ὁ Μ[υτιλ]ηναίων. The inscriptions' editors believe that this juxtaposition shows that "the garrison at Mytilene was popular enough."[27] This is an overstatement, but it is reasonable to infer that the Mytilenaians did not find the soldiers' presence intolerable. The clauses discussed above, saying "so that Andros, Keos, Kephallenia, etc., may be safe"—whatever their implication about the presence of Athenian garrisons—are in any case expressions of Athenian concern for the allies' welfare. Independent evidence seems to indicate that the people of Andros, at least, perceived this Athenian concern as genuine: the Andrians conferred a crown upon the Athenian demos in 348/7. If another inscription (very fragmentary) refers to the presence on the island of an Athenian garrison and general, as Accame and others believe, it provides further evidence—at least insofar as it is a resolution praising the persons tentatively identified as such. The epigraphic evidence for good Athenian-Andrian relations should be trusted more than the wild and unspecific remarks made by Aischines, in his desperate prosecution of Timarchos in 345, about the magistracy of the latter on

27. B&E 85; they go so far, in fact, as to conclude on this evidence that the guarantee of the decree of Aristoteles "did not mean that there were to be no Athenian garrisons, but that no garrison was to be forced on a city unwilling to receive it." See arguments opposing this interpretation, supra.

Andros—though some scholars have been willing to accept these remarks at face value.[28]

The resolution in honor of Androtion, being a well preserved decree of an allied city, not an Athenian document, should provide the best available evidence for allied attitudes toward Athenian garrisons and governors. The relevant lines say:

ἐ[π]ειδὴ Ἀνδροτίων ἀνὴρ
ἀγαθὸς γέγονε περὶ τὸν δῆμον τὸν Ἀρ-
κεσινέων, καὶ ἄρξας τῆς πόλεως οὐδέ-
5   να τῶν πολιτῶν οὐδὲ τῶν ξένων τῶν ἀφ-
ικνουμένων εἰς τὴν πόλιν ἐλύπησε, κ-
αὶ χρήματα δανείσας ἐγ καιρῶι τῆι π-
όλει τόκον οὐδένα λαβὲν ἠθέλησεν, κ-
αί, τὸν μισθὸν τοῖς φρουροῖς ἀπορού-
10   ⟨σ⟩ηι τῆι πόλει, παρ' ἑαυτὸ προαναλώσας, ἐ-
π' ἐξόδωι τοὐνιαυτὸ κομισάμενος οὐ-
δένα τόκον ἐπράξατο, καὶ τὴμ πόλιν ἐ-
λάττω χρήματα δαπανᾶν δώδεκα μναῖ-
ς παρὰ τὸν ἐνιαυτὸν ἕκαστον ἐποίησ-
15   ε, καὶ τῶν ἁλόντων εἰς τὸς πολεμίους
οἷς περιέτυχεν ἐλ[ύ]σατο.

Androtion is praised for doing no harm either to citizens or visitors in Arkesine (lines 4–6), for loaning money without interest to the city in a period of crisis (lines 7f), for advancing his own money to pay the garrison groops and charging the city no interest upon repaying him (lines 9–12), for saving the city twelve minas per year (lines 12–14), and for ransoming persons captured by the enemy (lines 15f).[29] The cited ser-

---

28. The records of the treasurers of Athena list the crown: IG II², 1441, lines 12f ([στέφ]ανος, ὧι Ἀνδρ[ιοι] ἐστεφ[άνωσαν τὸν / δῆμ]ον τὸν Ἀθηναίων); Tod 156 comm. says this dedication "suggests that at least down to that time the island remained loyal." Fragmentary honorary decree: IG XII (5), 714, lines 6–15; an early editor suggested that it referred to a third-century Macedonian garrison, but Theophil Sauciuc, "Zum Ehrendekret von Andros IG XII 5, 714," MDAI(A) 36 (1911) 1–20 argues that Antidotos, the chief honoree, was an Athenian general in command of a garrison on Andros in the Social War period; Accame, 184 and n. 5, finds this interpretation convincing. Timarchos' governorship: Ais. 1.107f says he bought the office so as to satisfy his lusts at the allies' expense, taking advantage of the wives of free men—none of whom, however, are to be called to testify; Marshall, 111 n. 3, says that this passage "shows us what misery an unscrupulous ἄρχων could inflict."

29. IG XII (7), 5, lines 2–16 (brackets and underdotting as in Tod 152). Note that Arkesine must pay its garrison, whereas the garrison on Andros is apparently paid from the syntaxeis of the entire League (IG II², 123, lines 9–12 and 16–21, quoted supra). The difference probably is insignificant. An improved system may have been developed through trial and error, or perhaps the relative size of the two garrisons led to different ways of paying them, or possibly the variable is that Arkesine requested its garrison while the League synedrion initiated the stationing of troops on Andros.

vices are concrete and of obvious value to the Arkesinians, so there is no reason to doubt the sincerity of the gratitude expressed. Demosthenes' oration *Against Androtion,* a scathing attack that nonetheless mentions no misdeeds of Androtion as governor, would provide support for this interpretation if given its traditional date of 355/4, but it has been plausibly suggested that a date prior to the Social War is defensible, which would make the speech irrelevant for Androtion's wartime governorship.[30]

A further observation about Athenian garrisons and governors emerges from this survey of the sources: no clear example exists of their establishment in the territory of rebel states forcibly returned to the League (though, as said supra, an ambiguous phrase in an inscription relating to Keos *may* imply the existence of a garrison there). The known garrisons and governors were, so far as we can tell, set up in the territory of loyal allies, or outside the lands of League members altogether. This would be a rather surprising state of affairs, if the purpose of the Athenian garrisons and governors was the suppression and control of the League allies. But it makes perfect sense if they were established—as the Athenians claimed—for the protection of the allies as well as of themselves.

Most scholars appear to shy away from discussing the garrisons and governors of the early days of the League. In dealing with the peace of 375/4, Marshall does not mention its provision for the removal of garrisons, whereas Accame takes it as applying only to Spartan garrisons. Another scholar takes Xenophon's use of the Lakonian term "harmosts" as a cue for seeing the provision for recalling governors in the peace of 371 as applying unilaterally to the Spartan side. When modern authors turn to discuss the garrisons and governors of the Social War period, however, they are both attentive and critical. Even though most commentators accept the strategic necessity of these later establishments (Andros could control the grain supply route around the tip of Euboia, while Amorgos was the loyal island closest to the main group of rebels), they agree almost unanimously that the sending out of garrisons and governors indicates a worsening in Athens's treatment of its League allies. But if the later examples represent a betrayal of the promises of the decree of Aristoteles, the early examples do also. The inconsistency is not in Athenian behavior, but in scholars' evaluations of this behavior.[31]

30. Dem. 22; see D. M. Lewis, "Notes on Attic Inscriptions: XIII. Androtion and the Temple Treasures," *ABSA* 49 (1954) 39–49, suggesting possibly an earlier date, but not a precise year; Sealey, "Dionysius of Halicarnassus and Some Demosthenic Dates," *REG* 68 (1955) 89–92 argues against Lewis and in favor of Dionysios' date of 355/4.

31. See the opinions, admissions, and omissions of, e.g., Marshall 42, 61, 65f, and 111; Beloch 3:1.154–160; Accame 89, 146, and 184f; Tod 152 comm. and 156 comm.; Ryder, *KE* 67; Meiggs, *AE* 403; and Phillip Harding, "Androtion's Political Career," *Historia* 25 (1976) 188f and 194f.

The explanation of this inconsistency is as obvious as the explanation of several other questionable interpretations that have been cited throughout the foregoing chapters: it follows from the common presupposition that the Athenians, at first benevolent leaders, later returned to the harsh practices of the fifth-century Empire. Though the sources on garrisons and governors are not as numerous or as clear as we might wish, they imply that Athenian policy in these matters was consistent —and non-oppressive—from the early days of the League's existence. In fact, this entire two-chapter-long survey of Athenian performance on the promises of the decree of Aristoteles—as applied to the states to whom they were addressed, and as understood in ways appropriate to their own times—shows that those promises were kept. The Athenians swore to abandon the imperialist policies of the fifth century, and they adhered to their word.

A nagging problem remains, however. Allies did secede from the Second Athenian League (some successfully and some restored to their allegiance by force), and the weakened League was unable to defeat the Macedonians. May not all this discussion of guarantees and their fulfillment be essentially legalistic quibbling? Do not the defections themselves (like the revolts that destroyed the fifth-century Empire after the Sicilian disaster crippled the Athenian fleet) show widespread allied resentment toward Athens, hostility engendered by oppression—whatever the apparent implication of the scanty sources available? These issues require direct treatment.

10

DEFECTIONS FROM THE LEAGUE

The Social War of 357–355 B.C. and the Macedonian conquest of 338 loom over the history of the Second Athenian League in much the same way that the Roman Civil War and the emergence of one-man rule dominate thinking about the late Republic. In retrospect of the fatal disruption and takeover, scholars scan the sources for clues to the "decline" which made the catastrophe inevitable. Ancient sources can be found that seem to support this common interpretation. But hindsight is sometimes deceptive. Certainty about what the general body of evidence "must" indicate may lead to a preference for bits of evidence that seem to have the desired implication over other bits whose implication is contrary or noncommittal. Even perfectly reliable information can be misinterpreted from the anachronistic perspective of hindsight.[1]

In discussing defections from the League, the same kind of questions must apply that have been asked throughout this entire study:

1. What do the sources say?

2. If the sources are incompatible, which are to be preferred?

3. Are modern treatments[2] responsive to the implications—and limitations—of the available data?

The logical procedure is to suspend any presupposition about "development" or "process" and to examine each attested defection from the League in turn, in chronological order. This practice must be observed with particular care for the years prior to the outbreak of the Social War —the period in which trends leading to that uprising must be discovered, if they are to be discovered at all. Athenian abuse of the members of the League during or after the war might be censurable, and might worsen an already bad situation; but it obviously could not be causative in the

---

1. As an example of a serious attempt to avoid the dangers of hindsight, see Erich S. Gruen, *The Last Generation of the Roman Republic* (Berkeley 1974), esp. 504f.

2. In a chapter of this length, constant citation of the standard modern treatments in agreement or disagreement on points associated with the various defections seems pointless. The rebellions can be associated with toponyms, and most of the books have indexes. The pages of frequently cited works relevant to this chapter's topic are: Busolt 783–866; Marshall 78–121; Beloch 3:1.172–254 and 474–515, and 3:2.238–303; Accame 159–225; Ryder, *KE* 58–101; Hammond, *HG²* 492–516 and 539–570; Bury/Meiggs, *History of Greece*⁴ (New York 1975) 366–383 and 414–441; Sealey, *City-Sts.* 423–494 (which greatly revises his position in "Transf."). These works will only be cited for direct quotations or particularly striking points of disagreement. See also the brief summary statements of Meiggs, *AE* 403, and G. D. Zinzerling, "The Transformation of the Second Athenian Confederacy into a Second *arkhe*," *VDI* 122 (1972) 133 (English summary).

same manner as prewar actions could be. Desperation might lead to many of the same practices that would arise from unprovoked arrogance, but the difference in motive is critical for those who would fairly judge the actors.

In the absence of more direct evidence, the mere fact that Athens attempted to compel defected League members to return to the alliance does not itself imply the existence of abuse or oppression on the Athenians' part. The Second Athenian League was organized as a permanent alliance, under the terms of which members did not have the right to secede. The permanent alliance was not a new thing in Greek diplomacy. A sixth-century agreement between Sybaris and the Serdaioi—apparently the oldest extant Greek alliance treaty of any type—describes its signatories as allies "forever." Similar phrasing appears in Athens's treaty of 433/2 with Rhegion, and possibly also in an alliance of the same year with Leontinoi, both of which may be renewals of the terms of earlier alliance treaties. An inscribed Athenian-Boiotian alliance dated by literary sources to 395 was sworn "[for all] time"; the same phrase is generally restored in an Athenian alliance with Lokris attributed to the same year, and is extant in the Athens-Korkyra alliance treaty (chapter 4). Moreover, the Peloponnesian League, the Delian League, and Philip's "League of Korinth" were all permanent multi-member alliances.[3] Evidence for the Second Athenian League is convincing, though indirect (we cannot legitimately rely upon Accame's restoration of a phrase meaning "forever" in the entirely erased line 13 of the decree of Aristoteles; see chapter 2). The Athenian treaty with Chios of 384 was an alliance "[for all t]ime," and editors generally restore in the Athenian-Byzantine treaty a clause to the effect that "the [alliance] is to [be for] them [just as for (the) Chians]." The decree of Aristoteles (lines 23–25) prescribes that all League members will become allies "on t[h]e same (terms), just like (the) Chians and Thebans an[d] the other allies." Since the Chian alliance was permanent, the other League members' alliances were also permanent, and it follows that the League was conceived as a permanent organization.[4] Secession is therefore *ipso facto* a breach of sworn treaty obligations, not to be countenanced if the power to oppose it exists.

3. Sybaris: SV 120, lines 4f (ἀε/ίδιον). Rhegion: SV 162, lines 12 ([---ἐς ἀί]διον) and 15 (same, entirely restored); Leontinoi: SV 163, line 26 ([---ἀίδιοι]). The latter two treaties are cited via the better texts of ML 63 and 64, which provide useful comm. and bibliography; Thuc. 3.86.3 suggests the antiquity of these alliances. Boiotia: SV 223, lines 2f ([ἐς τὸ/ν ἀεὶ] χρόνον). Lokris: SV 224, lines 3f. Korkyra: SV 263, lines 1f. Leagues: Larsen, *Rep. Govt.* 47–50 and sources in 207–210 nn. 1–9.

4. Chios: SV 248, line 36 ([ἐς τὸν ἄπαντα χ]ρόνο[ν]). Byzantion: SV 256, lines 6f (τὴν [δὲ συμμαχίαν ἒ]/ναι αὐτ[οῖς καθάπερ Χίοις]). The Second Athenian League is among the permanent alliances discussed by Larsen (preceding note); no one seriously opposes its inclusion in the category.

Dismissing speculation about the supposed "expulsion" of the supposed League member Jason of Pherai (chapters 2 and 5), the first defection from the Second Athenian League for which any evidence exists is that of Paros (DA, line 89), probably in 373/2. Accame provides the most useful text of a fragmentary inscription including the end of an Athenian decree and the (dated) beginning of a resolution of the synedrion, both apparently concerned with Paros' restoration to the League (see chapter 7). In the Athenian decree, the Parians are required to bring an ox and panoply to the Panathenaic festival and an ox and phallos to the Dionysia, "since the[y h]appen t[o be] colonists of [t]he demos of (the) Athenians." This provision at first sight recalls language within some of the harsher legislation of the Athenian Empire, namely Kleinias' decree (?447 B.C.), which tightened up tribute payment, and the reassessment decree of 425/4, which proclaimed that all states paying tribute had to bring an ox and panoply "[just like colo]n[ists]." But the obligation placed upon the Parians—whom the Athenians, ancient evidence indicates, genuinely regarded as their colonists—probably reminded them only of their traditional relation with Athens, not any imperial "subject" status. Accame, who reports all the evidence in detail, implies that the attitude shown by the Athenians in this decree was mild and unvindictive.[5]

It seems clear that Accame's interpretation is correct from the terms of the allied decree which immediately follows:

[μ]ηδ[έν]ᾳ οἴκω[ν] ἢ κλ[ῆρο] ἐ[ξελάσ]αι καὶ μη-
δὲν [πρᾶ]ξαι βίαιο[ν] παρ[ὰ] τάδε· ἐ[ά]ν τις ἀ-
ποκ[τείν]ηι, [τ]εθ[ν]ά[ν]αι καὶ τ[ὸ]ς α[ἰ]τίος τ-
20 ô θα[νάτ]ου κρ[ῖ]ναι [δῆ]μον καὶ [βο]λὴν κατ-
ὰ τὸς [θ]εσμός· ἐ[ὰν] δ[έ] τις [ἐξελ]αύ[ν]ηι ἢ φυ-
γαδε[ύ]ηι [τιν]ὰ παρὰ τὸ[ς θεσ]μὸς καὶ τὸ [ψ]-
[ή]φι[σμα τ]ό[δ'] ἄ[τιμ]ος [ἔ]σ[τω---]

[N]o o[n]e [is] to be e[xpelled] from hous[es]
or pr[operty] and nothing violen[t] is to be

---

5. SV 268 (text of Accame 230), lines 3–6 (translation from lines 5f: ἐπειδὴ [τ]υγχάνοσ/[ι] ἄποικοι ὅ[ντες τ]οῦ δήμου τὸ Ἀθηναίων); full discussion and citation of relevant sources in Accame 231 and 238–240. Kleinias' decree: IG I², 66 (ML 46), lines 41f ([ἐ]άν τις περὶ τὲν ἀπα[γογὲ]ν τὲς βοὸς ἒ [τὲς πανhοπλία]ς ἀδικἐι, κτλ). Reassessment decree: IG I², 63 (ML 69), lines 55–58 (hοπόσ/[εσι πό]λεσι φόρος [ἐτάχ]θ[ε ἐπὶ τ]ὲς [βολὲς ἑι Πλεισί]ας πρότος [ἐγρα]μμάτευε ἐπὶ Στρατοκ/[λέος] ἄρχοντος βō[ν καὶ πανhοπ]λίαν ἀπάγεν ἐς Παναθ]ένaια τὰ με[γάλα] hαπάσας· πεμπόντον / δ[ὲ ἐν] τὲι πομπὲι [καθάπερ ἄποι]κ[οι---]). See also the regulations for Erythrai (before 450?), probably regarded as an Athenian colony: SV 134 (ML 40), lines 2f ([---Ἐρ/υθραῖ]ος ἀπάγεν σ[ῖ]το[ν ἐς] Παναθέναια τὰ μεγά[λα ἄ]χσ[ιον---]); and the decree establishing the colony at Brea: IG I², 45 (ML 49), lines 11–13 (βοῦν δὲ καὶ π[ανhοπλ/ίαν ἀπά]γεν ἐς Παναθέναια τὰ μεγάλ[α καὶ ἐς Δ/ιονύσι]α φαλλόν).

[don]e, contra[ry] to the following (resolution): If anyone kil[l]s (someone), (the)
[de]mos and [bou]le are to jud[g]e that t[h]e
c[ul]prits are also to [s]u[f]f[e]r their de[at]h,
according to the [l]aws. A[nd] i[f] anyone
[exp]e[l]s or exil[e]s [someo]ne contrary to
th[e la]ws and [t]hi[s re]sol[ution, he is to b]e
without [civic rig]hts. . . .

While this does not appear to be a grant of amnesty for past offenses, it
is certainly a requirement that punishment for various crimes shall only
be meted out according to traditional laws, not arbitrarily. Accame is
probably right in inferring that the laws and the demos and boule mentioned in this allied decree are those of Paros, not of Athens.[6] No evidence exists for the establishment of any Athenian military presence on
Paros after the suppression of the revolt, or of Paros having joined in
any later rebellion. For that matter, we know nothing of the causes of
Paros' attempt at secession. Even the most ardent advocates of the "second Empire" thesis, however, do not suggest that the Parian rebellion,
occurring at such an early date in the history of the League, was caused
by Athenian oppression.

The first attested successful withdrawal from the League was that of
Thebes. Ancient evidence certainly does not indicate—and no scholar
has been so bold as to assert—that the Thebans were driven away by
Athenian oppression. Clearly the leaders of Thebes were motivated by a
desire for their own state's aggrandizement, a wish for it to assume its
"natural" position as leader of a united Boiotia and a major power in
Greece. Thebes was never an enthusiastic participant in the Athenian
League: it joined to gain Athenian support in the impending war with
Sparta, shirked its League obligations, and began reconstituting the
Boiotian confederacy as soon as it dared (chapter 3). The Athenians,
though alarmed, were forbearing. Even the Theban destruction of Plataia, whose survivors fled to Athens for shelter (373), did not terminate
cordiality in Athenian relations with Thebes: when the allied resolution
(quoted supra) was passed, a Theban was presiding in the synedrion. At
the peace conference of Sparta in 371, an Athenian envoy said to the
Spartans (in the strongest language Xenophon reports in three speeches):
"It is clear that some of the allies are not acting toward us in a pleasing
manner, or pleasing toward you." Criticism of the Thebans could hardly
be more delicate. When Agesilaos' refusal to allow the Theban representatives to take the oath of the peace on behalf of all the Boiotians led

6. *SV* 268 (text of Accame 230), lines 17–23; see discussion of Accame 241 and 243; WV
31 intro. agrees with the interpretation cited. WV and I connect τεθνάναι with the clause
which follows it; equally possible is connection with the preceding clause.

them to walk out of the meeting, the conflict that ensued (culminating in the battle of Leuktra) did not involve the Athenians. Doubtless they would have been content to see their upstart ally chastised—or, better yet, fight the Spartans to an exhausting draw. The Thebans certainly did not treat the Athenians' attitude as openly hostile. Just before the battle they voted to remove their wives and children to Athens for safety, and after their surprising victory, they sent a herald to Athens to announce it and to ask for Athenian aid in gaining revenge on Sparta. Athens, however, had finally become fearful of its dangerous ally. The herald was given no answer on his request for aid against Sparta, and he was not even invited to the customary hospitality accorded foreign guests of the city. Soon (still in 371) the Athenians called another peace conference, one in which Sparta participated and Thebes did not. The representatives at the conference took an oath to give aid to any signatory that might be attacked—this time not (as at Sparta) a voluntary provision, but a compulsory one. The signing of the peace of Athens of 371 marks Thebes' definitive separation from the Second Athenian League. There was no "expulsion" of Thebes, nor any declaration of war upon the Thebans, only a clear warning that war would be an expected result of certain types of behavior. Direct Athenian-Theban armed conflict was generally rather minimal. The Thebans' name was not erased from the stele of the allies (line 79).[7]

The spate of rebellions, successful and unsuccessful, which afflicted the Athenian League in the next few years can be attributed mostly to the aggressiveness of Thebes, under the assertive leadership of Epameinondas and Pelopidas. Joining the Theban invasion of the Peloponnesos in 370 were (among others) Athenian League members from Euboia and Akarnania. The Boiotian coalition continued to add members during the next few years, mostly Peloponnesians falling away from the steadily weakening hold of Sparta. The Theban position was further strengthened through Pelopidas' stunning diplomatic success in 367: he persuaded the Persian King to abandon his traditional support for Sparta (at this time allied with Athens) and switch to a position in favor of the hegemony of Thebes. The rescript suggested by Pelopidas and adopted by the King not only specified that Sparta must recognize the independence of Messene (reestablished by the invading Thebans as a

---

7. Destruction of Plataia: Isok. 14; Xen. *Hell.* 6.3.1f; Diod. 15.46.4–6; Paus. 9.1.8. Conference at Sparta: Xen. *Hell.* 6.3.1–4.6 (quotation from 6.3.13: εὔδηλον ὅτι εἰ τῶν συμμάχων τινὲς οὐκ ἀρεστὰ πράττουσιν ἡμῖν ἢ ὑμῖν ἀρεστά); Diod. 15.50.4–51.4; Nep. *Epam.* 6.4; Plut. *Ages.* 27.3–28.5. Leuktra and related events: Xen. *Hell.* 6.4.19f and 5.1–3; Diod. 15.52.1. Conference at Athens: chapter 4, esp. nn. 27–29. See Ryder, "Athenian Foreign Policy and the Peace-Conference at Sparta in 371 B.c.," *CQ* 57 (1963) 237–241; Mosley, "Theban Diplomacy in 371 B.c.," *REG* 85 (1972) 312–318; and Cawkwell, "Epaminondas and Thebes," *CQ* 22 (1972) 260 and 264f.

separate state), but that Athens should remove its ships from the water. Though unable to persuade the other Greeks to accept the rescript as the basis for a new Theban-dominated common peace, the Boiotian power had scored a major propaganda victory, and one it continued to exploit. Acquiring the disputed Attic-Boiotian border town of Oropos by deception in 366, the Thebans simply held onto it, and the frustrated Athenians were forced to allow the seizure to stand. No ancient source suggests that Athens's losses to Thebes in the late 370s and early 360s were caused by Athenian mistreatment of the League allies. The states known to have been drawn from the Athenian League into the Boiotian alliance in these few years were neighbors of Boiotia who had as much or more to fear from the Boiotian army as from the Athenian fleet. Like insecure small states of all eras, they knew the vital importance of being on the winning side; the Thebans were the assertive and aggressive Greek power of the period.[8]

Many scholars believe that increasing Athenian military involvement in the northern and eastern Aegean in the 360s led to defections of League members during the same period. The sources on these developments bear reexamination. Aischines cites a vote by the Greeks, in which a representative of Amyntas of Macedon joined, which pledged aid to Athens in recovering Amphipolis on the River Strymon, near the Thracian coast. Since Amyntas died in 370/69 (see chapter 5 on his relations with Athens in general), it is therefore certain that the Athenians were asserting territorial claims in the northern Aegean area by some point in 369. The pressing of its claim to Amphipolis is frequently taken as evidence of a change toward a more imperialistic policy on Athens's part. But the claim (however unrealistic) was already of long standing, as Aischines himself says. Its assertion in 369 may have had no special significance at all. The representatives of both the Athenian League and the Peloponnesian League were assembled, and perhaps of other states

8. Euboians and Akarnanians (DA, lines 80–83, 88f, and 114; 106): Xen. *Hell.* 6.5.23 (ἠκολούθουν δ' αὐτοῖς ... καὶ Εὐβοεῖς ἀπὸ πασῶν τῶν πόλεων ... καὶ ᾿Ακαρνᾶνες); *Ages.* 2.24. Two Akarnanian cities, Alyzeia and Anaktorion, made contributions in 355–351 to the Theban (and anti-Athenian) side in the Third Sacred War: *IG* VII, 2418, lines 5–7 and 16–18. Ryder, *KE* 77 n. 2, suggests that the Euboians may have been following Theban leadership in joining the Athenian League in 377. Conference at the Persian court and/or subsequent events: Xen. *Hell.* 7.1.33–40; Dem. 19.31, 137, and 191; ?Diod. 15.76.3; Plut. *Pelop.* 30 and *Artax.* 22. Buckler, "Plutarch and the Fate of Antalkidas," *GRBS* 18 (1977) 139–145 takes issue with the general belief that the suicide of the Spartan architect of the King's Peace, described in Plut. *Artax.* 22.4, was a reaction to this conference. Seizure of Oropos: Xen. *Hell.* 7.4.1; Isok. 5.53; Ais. 2.164 and 3.85 and Sch.; Dem. 18.99 and Sch.; Sch. Dem. 21.64; Diod. 15.76.1. Buckler, "On Agatharchides *F. GR. HIST.* 86 F 8," *CQ* 27 (1977) 333f suggests connecting another rarely cited source with this event. Theban propaganda position: Plut. *Pelop.* 31.4; cf. Isok. 8.58f. Incentive for small states to follow an aggressive power's lead: Xen. *Hell.* 7.1.4.

as well; it was therefore an excellent opportunity to solicit a vote that would tend to lend "legitimacy" to the traditional claim. There is no basis for believing that the Greeks' votes were coerced; the only attested fact is the vote itself, and it was favorable.[9] Athens had never renounced all territorial ambitions, only property ownership in the territory of members of the League (chapter 9).

It is also clear from Aischines' narrative that Amphipolis was a long-time bone of contention between Athens and Macedon, and that the Thebans injected themselves into the conflict. Amyntas, friendly to Athens, had accepted Athens's claim. But the regent Ptolemaios, who came to power shortly after Amyntas' death,

ὑπὲρ Ἀμφιπόλεως ἀντέπραττε τῇ πόλει, καὶ πρὸς Θηβαίους διαφερομένων Ἀθηναίων συμμαχίαν ἐποιήσατο, καὶ πάλιν ὡς Περδίκκας εἰς τὴν ἀρχὴν καταστὰς ὑπὲρ Ἀμφιπόλεως ἐπολέμησε τῇ πόλει.

in the matter of Amphipolis worked against the city (Athens), and made an alliance with the Thebans, (who were then) at odds with the Athenians; and again, as Perdikkas was becoming established in his rule, he made war against the city over Amphipolis.

Philip himself would later court Athenian friendship with deceptive promises about recognizing Athens's claim to the coastal city. Therefore, the fact that Athens began seriously to act upon its long-standing claim by sending out Iphikrates with a fleet in 368 probably reflects only a changed situation, not any change in Athenian policy. The new elements are the unsettled condition of Macedon after the death of Amyntas and the involvement of Thebes.[10]

With the Persian King's conversion in 367 to support of Thebes, the Athenians were beset by enemies on all sides. This situation of crisis can easily explain the ensuing period of Athenian assertiveness, without resort to hypotheses of any (wholly unattested) mistreatment of the League allies. The demos reacted to the King's change of sides with a resoluteness to which Athenian orators later pointed with pride. The envoy who had acquiesced in Pelopidas' terms was executed upon his return home from the conference with the King. If a further Athenian claim to the Chersonesos had not yet been asserted (no source mentions it up to this point), that claim was now added to the claim of Amphipolis, and the King was ultimately compelled to accede to both.[11] The

9. Ais. 2.31f (key passage quoted in chapter 5; see discussion in n. 8 there); see also Dem. 19.253.
   10. Ais. 2.26–30 describes the developments (quotation from sec. 29); see also Plut. *Pelop.* 27.2f. For Philip's intrigues, see Dem. 23.116 and [Dem.] 7.27f.
   11. Xen. *Hell.* 7.1.38; Dem. 9.16 and 19.137 and 253; [Dem.] 7.27–29; Plut. *Pelop.* 30.6 and *Artax.* 22.5f. Cawkwell, "Agesilaus and Sparta," *CQ* 26 (1976) 71, suggests that the King's change of policy also led to renewed hostility from Sparta.

aftermath of the conference at the Persian court, and/or the abortive Theban attempt to impose a Theban-dominated common peace with the King's support in 366, provides an ideal context for the erasure from the text of the decree of Aristoteles of the provision (lines 12–14) dedicating the Athenian League to the preservation of the King's Peace (see chapters 1 and 2).

Apparently in 366, Timotheos besieged Samos, which had been occupied by a Persian garrison. He expelled the garrison and, in 365, the Athenians established a kleruchy on the island to prevent Persian recapture (chapter 9). Following his victory at Samos, Timotheos was sent to replace Iphikrates in command in the northern Aegean, where he recorded other victories, several of them at Persian expense. In the same region and during this same period, Timotheos also captured cities that had been under the control of the Chalkidian league, led by Olynthos. This confederacy had once been a member of the Athenian League (DA, lines 101f), though it is impossible to tell whether it consisted of precisely the same cities in each period. Demosthenes, who tells of Timotheos' replacing Iphikrates in this command, refers also to Ὀλυνθίοις τοῖς ὑμετέροις ἐχθροῖς καὶ τοῖς ἔχουσιν Ἀμφίπολιν κατ᾽ ἐκεῖνον τὸν χρόνον. Whether "your enemies the Olynthians" were "those holding Amphipolis at that time," or the latter phrase refers instead to the Amphipolitan government itself, to which the Olynthians were allied, it is in any case clear that all the people thus described were at war with Athens. When and why had the Olynthians become Athenian enemies? Marshall, Beloch, and Accame all treat their secession from the League as a consequence of Athens's assertion of its claim to Amphipolis. No ancient source makes this connection, nor even indicates that they are in revolt at any point earlier than the appointment of Timotheos in 365. Consequently, their defection could have occurred at any prior time, and for their motives we have no evidence, but only modern speculations. My own speculation is that the Olynthians seceded at some point after the Thebans began to be involved in northern Aegean affairs ca. 369, the move being encouraged by the fact that Athens had its hands full dealing with Thebes and Macedon. As for motive, I suggest that the Olynthians were *rivals* of Athens for control of Amphipolis: their interest in controlling that city is also documented—as is their capacity for involvement in Machiavellian intrigues. But the simple truth is that we do not know either the date or the motive of the Chalkidians' defection.[12]

12. Dem. 23.149f (quotation from sec. 150); Isok. 15.108 and 112f (including the overstatement that Χαλκιδέας ἅπαντας κατεπολέμησεν, in sec. 113); Dein. 1.14 and 3.17; Nep. *Timoth.* 1.2. See Marshall 82f; Beloch 3:1.194f; and Accame 178f. Accame's suspicion that certain smaller Thracian states, e.g., Dion (DA, lines 128f), followed the Chalkidians in seceding from the Athenian League may be correct, though chapter 2 argues the doubtfulness of his putting Arethousa (line 82) in this category. At some point in the 350s, Athens was said to have lost all the cities in Thrace (Isok. 7.9), but the exact reference of this statement is unclear. For Olynthian intrigues with Philip, v. infra.

Meanwhile the hostility of Thebes continued and intensified. In his narrative for 364/3, Diodoros records a harangue by Epameinondas in the Theban assembly, urging his compatriots to seek supremacy on the sea. Byzantion asserted its separation from Athens about this time; independent evidence exists for its interference with Athenian grain ships in 362/1. It is believable that Byzantion's detachment from the Athenian League was prompted by Theban influence (Byzantine synedroi within the Boiotian alliance are attested in the 350s). Diodoros may be overstating the Thebans' success, however, when he says that they also detached Rhodos and Chios. His description of these states' rebellion in the 360s may be a doublet of their well-documented involvement in the Social War of the 350s; contemporary sources do not require the belief that they also rebelled earlier. Byzantion's defection is understandable, whether inspired by Thebes or not. The city's commanding position on the Bosphoros would be enough to make its leaders desire a free hand, unrestricted by ties to League allies or a hegemon; the profit to be extorted from Athens's grain trade alone would be a sufficient motive. Byzantion was apparently able to maintain its separation; the Byzantines later lent support to the Social War rebels.[13]

No ancient evidence specifically connects the Theban naval enterprise with the epigraphically attested revolt of one or more cities of Keos from the Athenian League. Presumably because the inscribed treaty specifying the terms of the readmission of Ioulis (DA, line 120) is dated to 362, some modern commentators make the connection, which is not unreasonable. But in reality we know nothing whatever about the motives prompting the Kean rebellion. What we do know, with certainty, is that the settlement imposed upon these unsuccessful rebels was quite mild (chapter 8). Some have inferred the stationing of an Athenian garrison on Keos after the crushing of this revolt, but the inference is probably unwarranted (chapter 9). In any case, there is no reason to suppose that any of the Keans joined in later revolts.[14]

Certain states were detached from the League through their seizure by Alexander of Pherai. This tyrant—himself once an Athenian ally (chapter 5)—had captured Tenos (DA, line 113) by some point in 362, we are told in a speech by Apollodoros. Probably the narrative Diodoros sets in 361/0 refers to the same campaign; he says that Alexander attacked "the Cyclades islands" in general and Peparethos (DA, line 85) in particular. An Athenian force under Leosthenes, sent to relieve Peparethos, was severely defeated, leading the angry demos to condemn the general.

13. Effects of Theban offensive: Diod. 15.78.4–79.1; cf. Isok. 5.53 and Dem. 9.23. Definite Byzantine separation from Athens: [Dem.] 50.6; ?Nep. *Timoth.* 1.2; *IG* VII, 2418, lines 11 and 20–25. See discussions of, e.g., Ryder, *KE* 84; Cawkwell (supra n. 7) 273; and Sealey, *City-Sts.* 433f. On Byzantine involvement in the Social War, v. infra.

14. *SV* 289 *passim* (Theban connection inferred by, e.g., Tod 142 comm.); *IG* II², 404, line 6 (text of Maier, *SEG* XIX, 50).

Polyainos tells us that after his success at Peparethos Alexander was sufficiently emboldened to attack the Peiraieus itself. Athens and its League made a treaty of alliance with other Thessalian cities against Alexander in 361/0 (chapter 4). The preserved dates within Apollodoros' speech and this inscribed treaty make it quite certain that Alexander was the aggressor, whereas Athens and the League allies were the aggrieved parties. It is eminently possible, furthermore, that the tyrant of Pherai was cooperating with the Thebans in launching these attacks: he apparently had been compelled to become a Boiotian ally in 364.[15]

Maroneia on the Thracian coast, another League member (DA, line 87), was in 361 forced by Athenian naval intervention to arbitrate a territorial dispute with Thasos (DA, line 100). If this recalcitrance by the Maroneians constituted a rebellion, as some believe, it seems to have been abortive. Despite Philip's later self-serving criticism of the Athenians for compelling the two League members to arbitrate their claims, this action seems perfectly appropriate for the hegemon, and without selfish implication. In any case, Maroneia's quarrel was with Thasos, not with Athens.[16]

Every attested defection (successful or unsuccessful) of states listed on the stele of the allies which occurred prior to the outbreak of the Social War of 357–355 has now been discussed. The only possible exceptions are Byzantion's detachment of Selymbria (DA, line 125) and the secession of another nearby city, Perinthos (line 84)—both of which are more likely to have happened during the Social War (v. infra).[17] Athenian mistreatment as a cause of *any* of these revolts is not a necessary, or even probable, inference from the sources describing the rebellions. In some cases, no opinion at all is justified, because of the paucity or ambiguity of evidence. In other cases, revolts or forcible detachments seem likely to have been the products of efforts by earlier successful rebels or outside powers.

In strict fairness, we should examine the sources not only for specific attested rebellions, but also for any pattern(s) of Athenian behavior that may have created a climate favorable for revolt. Scholars' arguments relating to various "denials of autonomy" have been discussed and re-

15. [Dem.] 50.4 includes the report ὅτι Τῆνος μὲν καταληφθεῖσα ὑπ' Ἀλεχάνδρου ἐξηνδραποδίσθη among crises discussed at a meeting during the second month of 362/1; the Kyzikenes had also attacked Prokonnesos, probably a bilateral Athenian ally (chapter 5). Other sources for Alexander's aggression: Diod. 15.95.1–3 (more on sec. 3, infra); Polyain. 6.2.1f; SV 293. His Boiotian connection: Diod. 15.80.6; Plut. Pelop. 35.2 (date certain because of solar eclipse during the campaign).

16. [Dem.] 50.20–22 (date from secs. 4 and 23); [Dem.] 12.17. Accame, 180, describes the event as a revolt; some of the sources of his n. 1 (Dem. 23.183 and Polyain. 4.2.22) apply not to this controversy itself but to Philip's eventual capture of the city.

17. Dem. 23.165 shows Athenian ships using the harbor of Perinthos as late as ca. 359, which indicates that the city was loyal at least to that point.

jected elsewhere (chapter 8). Another element of Athenian behavior that may repay examination is the treatment of the allies by Athenian generals in command of naval squadrons, both on wartime campaigns and while collecting syntaxeis. Accounts of pre-Social War misbehavior by such generals in late ancient sources and modern commentaries are confused and unconvincing. Plutarch increases the magnanimity of Phokion toward the League allies by implying that Chabrias used harsher methods in collecting their syntaxeis, but Chabrias' cordial relations with the allies are documented in fourth-century sources.[18]

J. K. Davies argues that Timotheos' "unprovoked aggression on Samos" and his ownership of property on Lesbos (whose cities were League members) are "safer evidence of his attitude towards Aegean states in and outside the league than the tinsel phrases of Isokrates. . . ." Actually, however, in a period of intense conflict with the Persians (v. supra), Samos was seized from Persian control—which itself had been a violation of treaty relations with the Greeks; and no source says that Timotheos owned property on Lesbos, only that he sometimes lived there; at another period he lived on Euboia. It is obvious (consider Athens's own resident alien class) that a person need not own property to dwell at a given place. It is also perhaps worth mentioning that we know of no Athenian garrisons or kleruchs in the places where Timotheos took up residence. In contrast to such preferred "evidence," the aforementioned "tinsel phrases of Isokrates" are unquestionably relevant, precisely to the point, consistent, and uncontradicted in other ancient sources. Shortly after Timotheos' death, Isokrates praised the general for having made his conquests without imposing burdens on the allies, and noted specifically that the siege of Samos was conducted without allied money, and that Timotheos used only his own funds and the Thracians' syntaxeis in taking Poteidaia. His attitude toward the allies was favorably contrasted with that of unnamed rival generals (Chares is meant; v. infra). He wished no city to fear him, says Isokrates, realized that Athens's strength rested on the allies' friendship, gave advance notice when collecting syntaxeis so as not to cause alarm, and was mild toward states he defeated in battle; in summary, he had gained Athens much goodwill among the Greeks. Apollodoros, even while prosecuting Timotheos and saying much in criticism of his character, does not seem to imply that mistreatment of the allies was among the general's faults. He notes the support given to Timotheos by allies Alketas (DA, line 109), Jason, and Amyntas, and the help that he had given to the Boiotian trierarchs with the League's fleet.[19] The record on Iphikrates, the re-

18. Plut. *Phok.* 7.1; cf. Dem. 20.76f and 81, and 24.180; inscription of B&E 85 (quoted in chapter 9). On the career of Phokion, see Hans-Joachim Gehrke, *Phokion* (München 1976).

19. Davies, *Athenian Propertied Families* (Oxford 1971) 510, citing Theopomp. *FGrH*

maining important pre-Social War general, is less clear-cut,[20] but does not alter the general truth of the statement that contemporary evidence for Athenian generals' abuse of League members in the years prior to the Social War is conspicuous for its absence.

One incident, in fact, is virtually the only specific evidence routinely cited in support of the general belief that Athens showed a pattern of oppression leading up to the Social War. In his narrative for 361/0, immediately following the condemnation of Leosthenes for failure in aiding Peparethos (supra), Diodoros says:

... ἑλόμενοι δὲ στρατηγὸν Χάρητα καὶ ναυτικὴν δύναμιν δόντες ἐξέπεμψαν. οὗτος δὲ τοὺς μὲν πολεμίους εὐλαβούμενος, τοὺς δὲ συμμάχους ἀδικῶν διετέλει. καταπλεύσας γὰρ εἰς Κόρκυραν συμμαχίδα πόλιν, στάσεις ἐν αὐτῇ μεγάλας ἐκίνησεν, ἐξ ὧν συνέπεσε γενέσθαι σφαγὰς πολλὰς καὶ ἁρπαγάς, δι' ἃς συνέβη τὸν δῆμον τῶν 'Αθηναίων διαβληθῆναι παρὰ τοῖς συμμάχοις. ὁ μὲν οὖν Χάρης καὶ ἕτερα τοιαῦτα παρανομῶν ἀγαθὸν μὲν οὐδὲν διεπράξατο, τῇ δὲ πατρίδι διαβολάς.

... And choosing Chares general and giving (him) a naval force, they sent (him) out. But he continued avoiding the enemy and injuring the allies, for, putting into port at Korkyra, an allied city, he stirred up great disturbances in it, out of which it followed that much slaughter and pillage occurred, because of which it happened that the demos of the Athenians was calumniated by the allies. Now Chares also performed other such acts of illegality, discredits to his country, but nothing good.[21]

The earliest extant account of Chares' misbehavior on Korkyra is one of Aineias Taktikos' examples under the rubric of "Conspiracies":

ἐν Κορκύρᾳ δὲ ἐπανάστασιν δέον γενέσθαι ἐκ τῶν πλουσίων καὶ ὀλιγαρχικῶν τῷ δήμῳ (ἐπεδήμει δὲ καὶ Χάρης 'Αθηναῖος φρουρὰν ἔχων, ὅσπερ συνήθελεν τῇ ἐπαναστάσει) ἐτεχνάσθη τοιόνδε. τῶν τῆς φρουρᾶς τινες ἄρχοντες σικύας προσβαλόμενοι καὶ τομὰς ἐν τῷ σώματι ποιησάμενοι καὶ αἱματωθέντες ἐξέδραμον εἰς τὴν ἀγορὰν ὡς πληγὰς ἔχοντες, ἅμα δ' αὐτοῖς εὐθὺς προπαρεσκευασμένοι οἵ τε ἄλλοι στρατιῶται τὰ ὅπλα ἐξηνέγκαντο καὶ τῶν Κορκυραίων οἱ ἐπιβουλεύοντες. τῶν δ' ἄλλων ἀγνοούντων τὸ πρᾶγμα καὶ εἰς ἐκκλησίαν παρακληθέντων συνελαμβάνοντο οἱ προστάται τοῦ δήμου, ὡς ἐπαναστάσεως γενομένης ἐξ αὐτῶν, καὶ τὰ ἄλλα μεθίστασαν πρὸς τὸ συμφέρον αὐτοῖς.

In Korkyra an uprising (the party) of the rich and oligarchic wished to accom-

---

115 F 105 and Nep. *Chab.* 3.4 against Isok. 15.108 and 124f. Sealey, "Athens After the Social War," *JHS* 75 (1955) 76f offers similar remarks, as does Phillip Harding, "Androtion's Political Career," *Historia* 25 (1976) 188f and 195. Euboian residence: Nep. *Timoth.* 3.5. Isokrates is paraphrased from Isok. 15.108, 111, 113, 116, and 121–127; see also sec. 303. Apollodoros' position: [Dem.] 49.10, 14f, 26, and 49 (the vague innuendos of sec. 65 affect this picture below). Further indirect evidence for Timotheos' general attitude is Xen. *Hell.* 5.4.64 (quoted in chapter 4).

20. Virtually nothing about Iphikrates' attitude toward the allies is said. The Kephallenians from whom he collected money ἀκόντων (Xen. *Hell.* 6.2.38) may not have been League members; possibly they were hostile states (see chapter 4).

21. Diod. 15.95.3.

plish against the demos—Chares the Athenian was staying there, having a garrison, who assisted in the uprising—was contrived as follows. Some of the leaders of the garrison, attaching cupping-glasses and making cuts in their bodies and bleeding, ran into the marketplace as if having suffered wounds. At the same time as this, immediately, the other soldiers, being prepared in advance, took up their arms, (as did) also the conspirators among the Korkyraians. The others not knowing what was happening and having been called to an assembly, they rounded up the leaders of the demos, on the ground that the uprising had been staged by them. They also arranged other things to their own advantage.[22]

Several observations must be made about these passages and the relation between them. To begin with, Korkyra, though an Athenian ally (chapter 4), was apparently not a member of the League, so the event discussed in both sources is not strictly relevant for evaluating Athenian relations with its League allies.

Additionally, there is much that is suspicious about Diodoros' date and context for the incident. Aineias Taktikos is probably Diodoros' ultimate source, but nothing in the earlier author's passage suggests a chronological setting: the incident is the last "conspiracy" he describes, following an example from the far-distant past, after another example of unknown date. Diodoros' use of the word "continued" (διετέλει) seems to imply consultation of some source which mentioned several misdeeds of Chares (it is the first discussed by Diodoros and the only mention of Chares by Aineias). Perhaps this intervening source, of unknown date, gave Diodoros his basis for putting the incident in 361/0, but it certainly fits his narrative very poorly. The conflict with Alexander of Pherai at Peparethos, for which Diodoros' date is comparatively accurate (supra), was part of a continuing crisis in the Aegean during the late 360s. It is possible (though otherwise unsubstantiated) that Chares was chosen to succeed the condemned Leosthenes.[23] But it is *not* believable that a general chosen in response to a situation taken so seriously by the demos could cavalierly disregard the Aegean crisis and sail halfway to Italy to stir up trouble in Korkyra. W. K. Pritchett has shown that fourth-century generals were not in fact the independently operating "condottieri" one encounters in modern treatments of the period, but were generally subject to control and discipline by their states (an observation he applies specifically to Chares, among others).[24] In Aineias' account, moreover, Chares does not sail up as a general in command of a naval force,

---

22. Ain. Takt. 11.13–15.

23. [Dem.] 51.8f and 16 says that Aristophon prosecuted trierarchs serving in this campaign under Leosthenes. This politician's cooperation with Chares is well attested: see sources and discussion in Sealey (supra n. 19) 74.

24. Pritchett, *The Greek State at War* II (Berkeley 1974) 59–116, esp. 77–85; Pritchett accepts Diodoros' date for the incident, but notes that the item is unusual in that no effort by the home authorities to assert control over the general is mentioned (pp. 56–58).

but is already stationed on Korkyra as commander of a garrison. Dio-doros' date and context, then, carry no weight, and it is legitimate to inquire whether some different situation might be more likely.

During what period could Chares have stirred up an oligarchic revolt on Korkyra and have avoided condemnation by the Athenian demos? Beloch may implicitly redate the incident to the time of the Social War. Such a period of crisis might provide a reasonable occasion. But Chares' whereabouts immediately before and during the war are pretty well known, and he is invariably found in the Aegean area.[25] The oligarchic character of the Social War revolts (infra) also militates against believing that an Athenian general would cooperate with an anti-democratic movement at this time—or would survive if he had. Even more attractive would be some period after the war, when Athenian control over its generals in the field seems in fact to have been weakened. Chares was, after all, active—and controversial—until well into the reign of Alexander of Macedon. But two problems exist in suggesting such a late date for the incident: whatever revolution occurred on Korkyra seems already to have taken place by some point before mid-353, i.e., not very long after the end of the war; and Aineias is generally believed to have written his manual during the period of the war itself.[26]

It may be ultimately more reasonable—though perhaps surprising—to suggest a date *earlier* than Diodoros'. Chares first enters our sources, in a datable context, in 366, at the time of the third Theban invasion of the Peloponnesos, apparently already holding the rank of general. It is noteworthy that another commander involved in the same campaign, Αἰνέας Στυμφάλιος, στρατηγὸς τῶν Ἀρκάδων, is generally identified as none other than Aineias Taktikos. During this year, Xenophon tells us, the Korinthians (non-League Athenian allies) requested the removal of an Athenian garrison from their territory. Shortly afterward, Chares arrived with a fleet and "said that, having heard there was plotting against the city, he was there to give aid." The Korinthians politely but firmly de-

25. Beloch 3:1.244f allows this inference, but does not require it. Dem. 23.173 has Chares on Euboia in 357, shortly before the war begins; for his wartime activities, v. infra.

26. Pritchett (supra n. 24) 56 and 115 systematically excludes the statements of orators as unreliable, but Ais. 2.73 seems to refer to an actual resolution, in which it is indicated that the Athenian demos had no idea of where Chares and his forces were. See Dem. 23 *passim* on Charidemos and Dem. 8 *passim* on Diopeithes. Chares' latest attestation: [Dem.] *Lett.* 3.31; [Plut.] *Mor.* 848E. The terminal date for the Korkyraian coup is a reasonable, though not absolutely necessary, inference from the reference (probably in summer of 353) in Dem. 24.202 to τῶν γὰρ ὑμετέρων ἐχθρῶν ἑνί, Κερκυραίῳ τινὶ τῶν νῦν ἐχόντων τὴν πόλιν; Dem. 18.234 deals with too late a period to provide any clarification. On Aineias' date of composition, see W. A. Oldfather, Loeb intro. (1948) 5–7, accepted by Pritchett (supra n. 24) 57 and n. 107. See also A. Dain, Budé intro. (1967) viii–ix and comms. *ad loc.* on passages cited there. All editors agree that many incidents described in the book are undatable.

clined his offer, asking him to leave, and the garrison was withdrawn. How very reasonable their suspicion would be if, for instance, Chares had already commanded a garrison in another non-League allied city, in whose government a revolution had occurred. Command of a garrison also would seem to be a logical steppingstone to one's first generalship.[27]

Athenian garrisons in the territories of western allies—apparently both League and non-League types—were commonplace in the struggle with Sparta that lasted down to 371 (chapter 9). In the years of Theban aggressiveness that followed, they may have been established anew. Akarnania, which is known to have cooperated with Korkyra in the 370s, was an early accession to the Boiotian alliance (supra). It would have been reasonable for the Athenians to fear that Korkyra might soon follow. This would explain why a garrison might be established on the island in the early 360s. Athenian willingness to countenance Chares' support of an oligarchic coup would also be explicable on this hypothesis. Theban propaganda was democratic, and it used the new Athenian connection with the hated Spartans to good advantage. In this changed situation, the Athenians may have felt that a democratic Korkyra was more likely to go over to Thebes than an oligarchic Korkyra. In this area, far away and difficult of access, the Athenians may have been more concerned with security than with their public role as champions of democracy. Modern parallels are painfully easy to invoke. Anyway, the Athenian garrison's support of the oligarchs was apparently intended to be secret, and it only became scandalous, we may suspect, because it was revealed (again, modern parallels abound). It is even possible that the revelation of Chares' involvement in the plot *was* harmful to him. He is known to have been prosecuted (though our source does not say when, and though he was acquitted). If the revelation of his complicity in the coup occurred just after his appearance at Korinth, such a development might tend to explain why he then disappears from the sources for almost a decade. He may have been in disfavor at Athens, possibly even living abroad out of concern for his own safety.[28] If Athens followed such a policy on Korkyra, it was ultimately a failure: enemies of Athens—perhaps the very oligarchs Chares had supported—were in

27. Chares' activities in 366: Xen. *Hell.* 7.2.18–22 and 7.4.1 and 4f (quotation from 7.4.5: ἔλεξεν ὅτι ἀκούσας ἐπιβουλεύεσθαι τῇ πόλει βοηθῶν παρείη); Diod. 15.75.3. Davies, "The Date of *IG* ii².1609," *Historia* 18 (1969) 310 infers that Chares was general in or immediately after his being mentioned in *IG* II², 1609, line 116, but the inscription itself is of debated date, and Chares is not described in it as a general. "Aineas the Stymphalian" is mentioned in Xen. *Hell.* 7.3.1; the eds. of the Loeb (p. 7) and Budé (p. xii) texts agree on the identification.

28. Akarnanian and Korkyraian cooperation: *SV* 262. Theban propaganda: Plut. *Pelop.* 31.4. Chares' trials and acquittals: Dem. 19.332. His dwelling abroad: Nep. *Chab.* 3.4.

control there by sometime in 353 (supra), and Athens only belatedly recovered the island's allegiance (chapter 5).

However discredited the policy followed on Korkyra, it nonetheless remains true that that policy essentially tells us nothing about Athenian relations with members of the League. The sources on the event described are obviously beset with too many uncertainties to warrant modern authors' confident citation of them as revealing a primary cause of the Social War. Even if Diodoros' account be accepted as literally true, the causal connection between Korkyraian events of 361/0 and the outbreak of conflict in the Aegean in 357 has never been—and cannot be —established. The incident might add some small weight if it were only one item in a series of events showing a pattern of pre-Social War Athenian abuses. But when the incident supplies, as it generally does, virtually the totality of that "pattern" (because, as shown supra, no other such events seem to be recorded in our sources), the argument cannot be taken seriously. It is no more helpful in explaining the coming of the war than the statement within the late, fictionalized *Hypothesis* to Isokrates' oration *On the Peace*, to the effect that the war began when Chares,

μᾶλλον βουλόμενος τὴν ἀρχαίαν δύναμιν περιποιῆσαι τοῖς ᾽Αθηναίοις, ἐπεχείρησε Χίοις καὶ ῾Ροδίοις καὶ τοῖς λοιποῖς συμμάχοις.

wishing rather to acquire their ancient power for the Athenians, attacked the Chians and Rhodians and the remaining allies.

That speech itself, delivered at the end of the war, after Athens had been forced to open negotiations with the rebel allies, is almost universally characterized as a just and unanswerable indictment of what the Second Athenian League had become.[29] I share this viewpoint, within limits; but what is usually meant (as if this were the same thing) is that the speech condemns a *process of degeneration* of the free League of 378 into a steadily more coercive second Empire, against which this revolt

---

29. A strikingly different view is expressed by Phillip Harding, "The Purpose of Isokrates' *Archidamos* and *On the Peace*," *CSCA* 6 (1973) 147, who argues that Isok. 8 is an epideictic exercise written as an antilogy to Isok. 6 (he therefore also redates the latter from its "dramatic date" of 366 to the same time as Isok. 8, i.e., after 355/4). I cannot agree. Whatever its flaws in effectiveness, style, or quality of thought, *On the Peace* is not lacking in *seriousness*. The situation faced by Athens was serious: the general and politician whom Isokrates most abhorred (Chares and Aristophon) were in control of Athenian policy, and already they had conspired to discredit his own most admired pupil (Timotheos), to lose several battles with the rebels, and to provoke the King's ultimatum. In comparison, the Spartan dilemma about whether or not to fight resolutely to recover Messene in 366 could be treated by an Athenian author much more easily as a topic for a rhetorical exercise. Erika Rummel, "Isocrates' Ideal of Rhetoric: Criteria of Evaluation," *CJ* 75 (1979) 25ff refers in passing both to Isokrates' non-serious works and to works in which he offers serious instruction, mentioning specifically *On the Peace, Areopagitikos*, and *Antidosis* within the latter category (p. 32).

was natural and inevitable. The content of the oration is, however, strikingly at variance with this common interpretation. There are many certain and probable references to the abuses of the fifth-century Athenian Empire; also to be found are many certain and probable citations of Athenian misdeeds and destructive attitudes during the Social War itself; references to imperialist fourth-century behavior by Sparta and Thebes are fairly numerous, as well as statements about benevolent Athenian actions in both the fifth and the fourth centuries. A handful of vague references exist to the effect that some current Athenian abuse has been going on for a long time (generally matters of attitude). *But the speech does not provide a single specific example of imperialistic Athenian behavior between the end of the Peloponnesian War and the outbreak of the Social War.* Such an omission cannot possibly have been accidental. Scholars are correct in believing that Isokrates in this speech condemns "the Empire of the sea" and accuses his fellow citizens of having sought it. But they have ignored the implication of his choice of supporting evidence: he is saying that *during the Social War*, under the leadership of certain despicable characters, the Athenians have returned to this discredited fifth-century orientation. Unlike modern commentators, Isokrates does not equate the Second Athenian League, or Athenian hegemony *per se*, with "the Empire of the sea." A benevolent Athenian hegemony, he consistently holds, is a good thing for the Greeks, but during the war it has been perverted into Empire. It is the war, he explicitly says, that has gained Athens the enmity of the Hellenes.[30]

Modern presuppositions about Isokrates' viewpoint have caused us, I believe, to overlook a strong laudation of the fourth-century League near the end of the oration. His advanced age, says Isokrates, prevents him from saying everything that he might,

πλὴν ὅτι καλόν ἐστιν ἐν ταῖς τῶν ἄλλων ἀδικίαις καὶ μανίαις πρώτους εὖ φρονήσαντας προστῆναι τῆς τῶν Ἑλλήνων ἐλευθερίας, καὶ σωτῆρας, ἀλλὰ μὴ λυμεῶνας αὐτῶν κληθῆναι, καὶ περιβλέπτους ἐπ' ἀρετῇ γενομένους τὴν δόξαν τὴν τῶν προγόνων ἀναλαβεῖν.

30. Sections of Isok. 8 mentioning fifth-century Athenian abuses: 13, 30, 47, 51, 69, 75, 78–88, 91f, 104f, 108, 116, and 121–123. Social War Athenian abuses: 19, 26, 29, 36f, 42, 44, 46, 48, 50, 52–56, 64, 66, 75, 114f, 121–125, 127–131, 134, and 142. Spartan misdeeds: 95–105, 107f, and 116. Theban misconduct: 17 and 58f. Benevolent Athenian actions: (a) fifth century: 8, 47, 54, 75f, 90, 104, 123, and 126; (b) fourth century: 16, 67–69, 105, 107, and 141 (see discussion, infra); (c) apparently applied to both centuries: 30. Vague statements about continuing abuses: 25, 30, 36, 61, and 142. Athenian hegemony characterized as desirable: 21–24, 134–140, and 144. The war as the problem: 19. Isokrates' other major speeches from the period of the war, *Areopagitikos* (Isok. 7) and *Antidosis* (Isok. 15), are consistent with the viewpoint here attributed to *On the Peace*. His usage in the *Address to Philip* of 346 B.C. contributes, ever so slightly, to the same impression, in that the magic appeal of the word "freedom" is said to have destroyed the Empire of Athens and of Sparta—in that order (Isok. 5.104). For a succinct statement of the more widely held opinion, see Cawkwell, "Eubulus," *JHS* 83 (1963) 52.

The Loeb editor interprets this passage as a suggestion for present and future policy (which of course it is, at least), and translates the emphasized participles and infinitives with present-tense forms; the French of the Budé edition appears to follow the same interpretation. Yet all these Greek forms are aorists, and *can* be taken as referring to events in the past. I suggest that the passage also may responsibly be translated as follows:

except that it is good, among the injustices and insanities of the others, having thought sensibly, first to have championed the freedom of the Greeks, and to have been acclaimed as their saviors and not their destroyers, and, having become illustrious for virtue, to have regained the fair fame of our ancestors.

Understood thus, the passage becomes an encomium upon the Second Athenian League in the period prior to the war.[31]

By a long and sometimes circuitous route, we have now examined all relevant evidence for Athenian treatment of the League allies, including those who successfully or unsuccessfully rebelled, down to the eve of the Social War. Strict attention to the sources (in this chapter and in those preceding) has revealed a fact that contradicts the position of almost everyone who has discussed the League in modern times: the sources simply do not provide credible evidence for Athenian mistreatment of the League members as a cause of the outbreak of the Social War. Like so many other aspects of the "second Empire" position, the removal of the presupposition undermines the conclusion that has routinely been drawn. We must look elsewhere for the cause(s) of the war.

A definite fourth-century statement on the causes of the war does exist. Demosthenes (ca. 351 B.C.), says:

ἠτιάσαντο μὲν γὰρ ἡμᾶς ἐπιβουλεύειν αὐτοῖς Χῖοι καὶ Βυζάντιοι καὶ ʽΡόδιοι, καὶ διὰ ταῦτα συνέστησαν ἐφ' ἡμᾶς τὸν τελευταῖον τουτονὶ πόλεμον. . . .

For the Chians and Byzantines and Rhodians accused us of plotting against them, and because of this they concerted this last war against us. . . .

Demosthenes implicitly dismisses this suspicion as baseless, by mentioning in his very next clause

ὁ μὲν πρυτανεύσας ταῦτα καὶ πείσας Μαύσωλος

the one taking the lead and persuading in this matter, Mausolos

—adding that he has since betrayed those he misled. This contemporary characterization of the satrap of Karia as fomenter of the Social War generally has been dismissed in modern treatments, though Diodoros confirms the satrap's support of the rebels, and Demosthenes in a different context mentions a postwar Athenian embassy to Mausolos, one

31. Isok. 8.141; a similar viewpoint seems to be expressed by Dein. 1.75f.

of whose members was Androtion, wartime governor of Arkesine on Amorgos (chapter 9).[32] The oligarchic character of the Social War revolts may also be significant. Though permitting oligarchic states to be members of its League, Athens's traditional stance was pro-democratic (chapter 8; cf. the suggestions about Korkyra, supra). Perhaps the accusations of Athenian "plotting," dismissed by Demosthenes, were merely the unfounded suspicions of new oligarchic regimes in the rebel states.[33]

The Social War as a whole can reasonably be seen as less a struggle of Athens against its discontented allies than as the struggle of Athens and the loyal League members against Thebes, the Persians, Philip of Macedon, and a small number of rebellious allies and former allies following their lead or pursuing ambitions of their own. The prelude to the war was a round of conflict between Athenian and Theban partisans on Euboia (swiftly decided in Athens's favor; v. infra). About a year after the conclusion of the war, Isokrates, making a general statement about powers hostile to Athens, refers to Θηβαίοις μὲν καὶ τοῖς ἄλλοις ἐχθροῖς.[34] Mausolos may have been acting on his own initiative as a quasi-independent despot, but the undeclared hostility of the Persian King himself is also a reasonable inference. Little had happened to mollify Athenian-Persian conflict since Artaxerxes' switch to support of Thebes, followed by Timotheos' strikes against Persian-held territory (supra). It is to be noted that the King was not invited to share in the Greek common peace of 362/1, of which Athens was a signatory (chapter 1). Chabrias, though not serving on state orders, was permitted to aid Egyptian rebels shortly afterward. If relations between Athens and the King had not been strained, Chares presumably would not have accepted service with the rebel satrap Artabazos in 355, bringing on the ultimatum which ended the war. We are told by Diodoros that the Athenian demos approved Chares' taking this command. The reestablishment of cordial relations between Athens and the King at the end of the war may explain the Thebans' willingness to send Pammenes to take service with Artabazos' continuing revolt.[35]

Philip's activities during and just after the Social War were directed against Athenian possessions and allies of all types, League and otherwise. He besieged Amphipolis (claimed by Athens) in 357 and captured

32. Dem. 15.3 (see also sec. 27); Diod. 16.7.3; the embassy (purpose unknown) is mentioned in passing by Dem. 24.12. Sealey, City-Sts. 440 is unusual in taking Demosthenes' statement about Mausolos seriously.

33. The oligarchic character of these rebellions is mentioned by Marshall 110 and Hammond, HG² 515f. See Dem. 15.19; Aristot. Pol. 1304B; and ?Ain. Takt. 11.3–6.

34. Isok. 15.248.

35. Greek common peace: SV 292. Chabrias in Egypt: Diod. 15.92.3; Nep. Chab. 2.1–3.1; Plut. Ages. 37.1–4. Chares and Artabazos: Diod. 16.22.1f. Reestablishment of friendly relations: ?Dem. 24.11f. Pammenes: Diod. 16.34.1f.

it, thereby initiating a state of war with Athens that persisted, at least technically, until 346. After Amphipolis, Philip captured Pydna (one of the cities taken by Timotheos in the 360s), then made an alliance with the Olynthians and handed Poteidaia (captured probably in 356) over to them—allowing the Athenian kleruchs there to go home, however. Soon afterward, he defeated certain kings, Athenian allies (chapter 5), and captured the city of Krenides, valuable for its control of gold mines, renaming it Philippoi. He then besieged Methone (another city formerly captured by Timotheos), which surrendered ca. 354. Within another year or so, Philip attacked League member Maroneia (DA, line 87). Athenian struggles to control the Chersonesos in the years during and after the Social War were influenced by Philip's shifting relations with the region's despot, Kersobleptes. The conflict between Philip and Athens was not terminated by the ending of the Social War, but it began during that war, and Philip's position was strengthened by Athens's involvement in the Aegean-wide struggle. His successes during the war, e.g., the securing of access to the sea and to gold reserves, were crucially important for the great expansion of his power and influence which soon followed. In a real sense, then, Philip's threat to Athens was a product of the Social War, and Athenian conflict with him was one of several aspects of that war.[36]

Among the rebellious former allies pursuing their own interests during the Social War were the Chalkidians led by Olynthos. At times (supra) they worked in cooperation with Philip. Later betrayed by Philip, the Olynthians would make peace and then a new alliance (chapter 5) with Athens—too late, as Philip besieged and took their city before effective Athenian help could arrive.[37] Byzantion, apparently separated from the Athenian League since the late 360s (supra), actively assisted the Social War rebels. It was probably at this time that the neighboring cities of Selymbria and Perinthos were drawn into the movement by the Byzantines. The implication of a rhetorical question asked of the Athenian demos by Demosthenes a few years after the war is that Selymbria's detachment from the Athenian alliance was involuntary:

. . . τί δήποτ' ἐν Βυζαντίῳ οὐδείς ἐσθ' ὁ διδάξων ἐκείνους μὴ καταλαμβάνειν . . . Σηλυμβρίαν, πόλιν ὑμετέραν ποτὲ σύμμαχον οὖσαν, ὡς αὑτοὺς συντελῆ ποιεῖν καὶ Βυζαντίων ὁρίζειν τὴν τούτων χώραν παρὰ τοὺς ὅρκους καὶ τὰς συνθήκας, ἐν αἷς αὐτονόμους τὰς πόλεις εἶναι γέγραπται;

. . . Why is there no one at any time in Byzantion to tell them not to seize . . . Selymbria, a city being formerly your ally, so as to make it tributary to

36. This summary of early Athenian struggles with Philip largely reflects Sealey, *City-Sts.* 442f and 449 (see 462 nn. 2 and 4 for sources). See also J.R. Ellis, "Philip's Thracian Campaign of 352–351," *CPh* 72 (1977) 32–39.

37. *SV* 308 (including literary sources); Dem. 1–3 *passim*; Philoch. *FGrH* 328 F 49–51.

themselves, and including its territory within that of Byzantion, contrary to the oaths and the agreements, in which it is written that the states are to be autonomous?

It is apparent from Diodoros' account and from contemporary inscriptional evidence (chapter 9) that the rebels attacked loyal League members as well as Athenian possessions.[38]

Chares led Athenian forces from disaster to disaster during the war. The battle of Chios cost Athens the valuable services of Chabrias, slain there serving (apparently) as a trierarch under Chares. The latter's rashness led to a further defeat near Embata, on the coast of Asia Minor, blame for which he managed (with the help of Aristophon) to foist mainly upon Timotheos and Iphikrates. Finally, Chares' support of Artabazos led the King to threaten direct naval retaliation and forced Athens to make peace with the rebels.[39] Whereas the ancient tradition of the greatness of the three old generals (and the benevolence of at least Chabrias and Timotheos) has been largely disregarded by scholars depicting the supposed continuous growth of Athenian imperialism (supra), the generalizations of scholarship have had the effect of improving Chares' reputation. For most modern commentators, he was just another imperialist Athenian general, no worse—or not much worse—than the others. In the judgment of his contemporaries and of later ancient authors, however, he was uniquely brutal and lawless among generals of his time, and he was specifically blamed for Athens's failure in the Social War.[40] It is believable that the Athenians engaged in some excesses during this struggle for the survival of their alliance; this is indeed the whole point of Isokrates' condemnation of the policy of imperialism in *On the Peace*. Many of the allies remained loyal, however,

38. Dem. 15.26 (on Perinthos' defection, see Plut. *Dem.* 17.2); cf. Hammond, *HG²* 515f, who says laconically that Byzantion was "joined by" Perinthos and Selymbria, and generalizes about the rebels as follows: "In their hatred of democracy they foolishly attacked some islands which might otherwise have joined in the revolt. . . ."

39. Chabrias' status at Chios: Diod. 16.7.3f says he was a general, but Nep. *Chab.* 4 describes him as *privatus*; Dem. 20.80f and Plut. *Phok.* 6.1 are consistent with either interpretation; debate about why his name was erased from *SV* 304, line 20, does not enlighten. Trials after Embata: Isok. 15.159; Dein. 1.14 and 3.17; Polyain. 3.9.39; Nep. *Timoth.* 3.3–5 and *Iphic.* 3.3; Diod. 16.21.4. Service with Artabazos and King's reaction: Dem. 4.24; Sch. Dem. 3.31; Sch. Dem. 4.19; Diod. 16.22.1f; Plut. *Arat.* 16.3; papyrus fragment quoted in Pritchett (supra n. 24) 80.

40. He and Aristophon are the unnamed objects of wrath in Isok. 8, which would be expected from Isokrates' connection with Timotheos (see [Plut.] *Mor.* 837C) and was in fact generally recognized (Aristot. *Rhet.* 1418a). On Chares' disastrous war record, see esp. Ais. 2.70–73 (cf. the very weak rejoinder of Dem. 19.332–334). Condemnations of Chares' behavior in general are numerous (see, e.g., Plut. *Phok.* 14.2–4). The attitude of Cornelius Nepos is typical: having said something about Konon, Iphikrates, Timotheos, and Chares, he adds apologetically: *dissimilis quidem Chares horum et factis et moribus* (*Chab.* 3.4; see also *Timoth.* 4.4).

and evidence exists that some were even grateful to the Athenian commanders who aided in their defense (chapter 9). In any case, it is obviously illegitimate to interpret wartime excesses as *causes* of the war in which they occur.

There is a rather interesting ambiguity in the sources as to the exact nature of the settlement ending the war. Diodoros says only that peace was made. Isokrates, writing apparently while peace negotiations were going on but not yet finalized, advocates—seemingly as a more generous settlement than the one currently being offered by Athens—the type of understanding reached in 375/4 and 371, i.e., essentially a restatement of the King's Peace, with mutual withdrawal of garrisons. Demosthenes in 349 says of certain Athenian politicians that "these men have lost in peacetime allies which we gained in the war." A scholiast connects this passage with the settlement ending the Social War, but Sealey is surely correct in denying all authority to the opinion expressed by the scholiast. It is obvious that no allies were *gained* by Athens during that war. The war referred to must be, as Sealey says, the war with Sparta from 378 through 371, during which most of the members of the League were added. The allies lost "in peacetime" were probably those taken by Philip during undeclared hostilities in the northern Aegean area (the speech, one of the *Olynthiac* orations, generally refers to events in that region).[41] Modern authors usually assert that by agreeing to the peace treaty Athens gave *de jure* recognition to the rebels' separation from the League—a concept generally simply equated with Athenian recognition at this time of their "autonomy." But Athens had of course always recognized the League members' autonomy (chapter 8), and this key provision of the King's Peace had been restated in every Hellenic peace settlement since the King's rescript had first imposed it on the Greeks in 386 (chapter 1). What may very well have happened in 355 is that the Athenians were obliged only to swear to recognize the rebels' "autonomy," i.e., to express their agreement *de jure* to a simple reaffirmation of the King's Peace, but both sides recognized *de facto* that the "autonomous" rebels were now out of the League.[42]

---

41. Diod. 16.22.2; Isok. 8.16; Dem. 3.28 (οὓς δ' ἐν τῷ πολέμῳ συμμάχους ἐκτησάμεθα, εἰρήνης οὔσης ἀπολωλέκασιν οὗτοι). See discussion of Sealey (supra n. 19) 75f, including quotation of scholion.

42. Even *de facto* Athenian recognition of the loss of the Social War rebels seems at odds with some statements of Isokrates, however. In *Antidosis*, published a year or so after the war, he cites his own words in *On the Peace* as "having shown that it was to the advantage of the city (Athens) to end the war," and adds that Athens "because of the hatred (of the allies) barely avoided falling victim to the most extreme fate" (Isok. 15.64 and 122). If the peace settlement had in fact cost Athens many allies, it is hard to see why Isokrates states in retrospect that ending the war was to Athens's "advantage," or that disaster had been avoided, even "barely." The problem cannot be escaped by adopting the position of some scholars that Isokrates was now so disenchanted with Athenian "imperialism" that he had ceased to believe that Athens should play a leading part in Hellenic

Whatever these allies' official status, their definitive actual separation from the Athenian League occurred soon, as Mausolos and his widow and successor Artemisia sent in garrisons and took them over by sometime in 351. The ambiguity and fluidity of the settlement with Chios, Rhodos, and Kos, the apparent lack of any Athenian success in restoring Byzantion and its neighbors to functioning League membership, and Philip's continuing takeover of League members, other allies, and Athenian possessions in the north easily could have led writers of later antiquity to equate the *de facto* and *de jure* positions of Athens vis-à-vis the rebels. I believe, rather, that Athens had never up to this point recognized the legality of any ally's separation from the League. Seceded allies were regarded officially as being in a temporary state of separation, to be restored to participation in the confederacy whenever they could be enticed or compelled to agree (the obvious analogy is President Lincoln's theory of the constitutional position of the seceded southern states). The Euboians in fact had renewed their League membership in 357, and the Mytilenaians (who seceded at some point after the Social War) would do so in 346, as inscriptional evidence shows. If such was the Athenian legal position, this might help explain why states that had no treaty relationship with Athens (according to most theories) were in later years to ask the Athenians for military assistance against powerful aggressors, frequently getting a favorable response.[43]

Indeed, the mistaken focus on Athens's "driving away" of its allies tends to conceal the existence of a notable countermovement toward renewed friendly relations with Athens on the part of states that had renounced their Athenian alliances. The policy of readmitting states to the

---

affairs. His high praise, in this very speech, for Timotheos—chief architect of the Athenian League and also conqueror of much non-League territory—belies this opinion, not to mention Isokrates' passionate praise of Athenian leadership in the much later oration *Panathenaikos* (Isok. 12, 342 B.C.). I have omitted *Areopagitikos* from this discussion because of uncertainty about its date. If its traditional date of shortly after the war is correct (see arguments for this position, and literature, in Ryder, *KE* 93 n. 1), the magnitude of the problem is increased by this oration's failure to mention any specific losses of allies beyond whatever is meant by the phrase ἁπάσας μὲν τὰς πόλεις τὰς ἐπὶ Θρᾴκης, even though the Athenians are said to have πρὸς δὲ τοὺς Ἕλληνας διαβεβλημένοι καὶ τῷ βαρβάρῳ πολέμιοι γεγονότες, ἔτι δὲ τοὺς μὲν Θηβαίων φίλους σώζειν ἠναγκασμένοι, τοὺς δ' ἡμετέρους αὐτῶν συμμάχους ἀπολωλεκότες (Isok. 7.9f; the context of the final quoted phrase is clearly Peloponnesian: Athens had certainly never "saved" any Aegean allies of Thebes). W. Jaeger, "The Date of Isocrates' *Areopagiticus* and the Athenian Opposition," in *Athenian Studies Presented to William Scott Ferguson* (Cambridge, Mass. 1940) 409–450 uses the absence of concrete statements about the loss of known Social War rebels as conclusive evidence for dating the speech earlier—to 357, just before the outbreak of the war. The date he suggests is perfectly possible, and may be preferable to the traditional postwar date, but the inference on which his argument is founded may be baseless. Certainly Jaeger's constant refrain of renewed "empire" is.

43. Dem. 15.3, ?19, and 27 and 5.24f; Vitruvius, *De Architectura* 2.8.14f; *SV* 304 and 328.

League finally seems to have been supplanted, in these later years, by the making of completely new (usually bilateral) alliances with such states—probably because states becoming Athenian allies for the first time during this period also were doing so through bilateral agreements (chapter 5). Akarnania, which had been detached from the League by the Thebans in 370 (v. supra), reappears in congenial relations with Athens in the 340s: an inscribed treaty (dated to 349/8) between Athens and the Akarnanian city of Echinos seems to include a commendation of the Akarnanian confederacy, and evidence exists for Athenian military cooperation with the Akarnanians in 343/2 and ca. 340; certain Akarnanians fought on the Athenian side at Chaironeia, and they and their cities were later commended by the demos. The one constant in the fluctuating loyalties of the Euboian cities was the Athenians' concern to keep the states of the island happy and well disposed; they succeeded intermittently, but ultimately failed in the bidding against Philip (chapter 4). The new Olynthian-Athenian alliance of 349, also unsuccessful against Philip, is mentioned supra. Demosthenes was unable to persuade the demos to aid the repentant Rhodians in 351, but was more successful on behalf of the Byzantines a decade later. Byzantion, though having become an ally of Philip, began at last to fear him much more than its erstwhile hegemon, and apparently a new alliance with the Athenians was sworn. Aid from Athens, from the Persian King, and possibly from Chios, Kos, and Rhodos, among others, forced Philip to abandon his siege of Byzantion and Perinthos in 339. Athenian involvement in this campaign led to what amounted to Philip's declaration of war on Athens. Finally, the crowning glory of Demosthenes' attempt to unite the Greeks against Philip was a renewed Theban-Athenian alliance, sworn in 339, shortly before the defeat at Chaironeia (338).[44]

It remains true that the Social War was a disaster for the Second Athenian League. Even if not accepted *de jure*, the *de facto* separation of key allies was a direct consequence—whether immediately or soon afterward—of the weakened state of the alliance and its hegemon. In this matter, the bleak picture of Isokrates' *On the Peace* is confirmed by Xenophon's equally bleak *Poroi*. The League allies' syntaxeis had never been used—as were the fifth-century tributes—to enrich Athens at the allies' expense, but they were necessary for the maintenance of the League's navy. With fewer contributors, the burden undoubtedly became heavier on those still expected to pay, probably creating a greater

---

44. Akarnania: SV 325, lines 2 (date) and 12f (commendation); [Dem.] 48.24–26; Ais. 3.97f; IG II², 237, lines 11–15, 22–24, and 33–35. Rhodos: Dem. 15 *passim*. Byzantion (and Perinthos): Dem. 8.14–16; ?9.34: and 18.87, 230, and 302: Plut. *Phok.* 14.2–5; Diod. 16.74–77 (though Dem. 18.234 may create a problem); Theopomp. *FGrH* 115 F 292; Philoch. *FGrH* 328 F 162; ?IG II², 233, lines 6–10 (see discussion, infra); [Dem.] 12.2, 16, and 23; [Dem.] 11.5f and 20 (see Sealey, *City-Sts.* 493 n. 4). Thebes: SV 345 (several literary sources).

reluctance to contribute, and producing in turn a less patient attitude on the part of Athenian generals assigned to collect the money. Athenian forces were increasingly sent out virtually without promise of wages, being expected to live on booty taken from enemy territory. "Contributions," sometimes called "goodwill offerings," were extorted from nonallies. Generals with attitudes similar to those of Chares became the norm, while Chares himself continued his unsavory career. It is not necessary to trace this sad and desperate period in detail. In summary, the power and influence of Philip increased while that of Athens—despite the herculean efforts of Demosthenes and others—declined. When Philip's invasion of central Greece led to the fateful battle of Chaironeia, his forces were superior to those of the Athenians, Thebans, and other Greeks drawn up against them. The Macedonian victory ended Hellenic independence and the existence of the Second Athenian League.[45]

The important fact for this study, however, is not that Athens and its allies ultimately lost. It is rather that Athens remained, to the end, the rallying point for the Greeks who wished to preserve their own liberty. Any source-supported "imperialism" on Athens's part was late, limited, and a product—not a cause—of Athens's weakened and desperate situation. Moreover, there is virtually no evidence for Athenian abuse of current members of its League even in these latest and darkest years. On the contrary, the synedrion continued to be consulted on policy, and allies of unswerving loyalty were consistently praised and rewarded. The involvement of the allies in negotiations leading to the short-lived peace of Philokrates of 346 has been mentioned in several contexts (see, e.g., chapters 4 and 7). Elaious, the only attested League member (DA, line 123) in the critically important Chersonesos, was commended by the Athenians in 357/6 and again in 340, and the Elaiousians may eventually have been given Athenian citizenship.[46] Tenedos (line 79) was not only praised for loyalty in 339 (apparently for helping in the relief of Byzantion), but also received tangible financial benefits: a period of exemption from syntaxeis and other exactions (chapter 7). The announcement of

45. Even though he insists that the home authorities were firmly in control of Athenian generals throughout this period, Pritchett (supra n. 24) 116 concludes: "We should look not so much to the moral decline of Athens but to the military power of Makedonia to explain Chaironeia." See Carl Roebuck, "The Settlements of Philip II with the Greek States in 338 B.C.," CPh 43 (1948) 73–92, now repr. in C. G. Thomas (ed.), Economy and Society in the Early Greek World: Collected Essays of Carl Roebuck (Chicago 1979) 131–150; E. D. Frolov, "The Congress of Corinth in 338/7 B.C. and the Unification of Hellas," VDI 127 (1974) 63 (English summary); Ryder, "Demosthenes and Philip's Peace of 338/7 B.C.," CQ 6 (1976) 85–87; and Sealey, City-Sts. 490f.

46. Schweigert, "Greek Inscriptions: 4. A Decree Concerning Elaious, 357/6 B.C.," Hesperia 8 (1939) 14, lines 15–17 ([---ἐπ/ε]ιδὴ Ἐλαιόσ[ι]οί εἰσιν ἄνδρες ἀγαθ/οὶ περὶ τὸ[ν δ]ῆμο[ν τὸν Ἀθηναίων---]); IG II², 228, lines 8–18 (citizenship is the inference of, e.g., Tod 174 comm. from the Elaiousians' invitation to δεῖπνον rather than ξένια, line 17). In 347/6 the Elaiousians bestowed a crown upon the Athenian demos (IG II², 1443, lines 93–95).

the reward is followed by a statement of the Athenian demos' reason for granting it:

---ὅ[πω]ς ἂν καὶ εἰς τὸν λοιπὸν [χρόνον εἰδῶσιν]
οἵ τε σύμμαχοι καὶ ἄλλος ὅστ[ις ἂν εὔνους ἦι τῶι]
20 δήμωι τῶι 'Αθ⟨η⟩ναίων ὅτι ὁ δῆμ[ος ὁ 'Αθηναίων ἐπι]-
μελε[ῖ]ται δικαίως τοῖς πρ[άττουσιν τῶν συμμά]-
χων τὰ συμφέροντα τῶι δή[μωι τῶι 'Αθηναίων καὶ]
τοῖς συμμάχοις.

. . . s[o th]at also in the future [time], both the allies
and who[ever] else [is well disposed toward the]
demos of (the) Athenians [shall see] that the dem[os
of (the) Athenians] justly [lo]oks [af]ter those [of the
all]ies d[oing] things beneficial to the de[mos of (the)
Athenians and] the allies.

Marshall is compelled to grant that "This inscription, which gives the last direct notice of the Second Athenian Confederacy, sheds a gleam of brightness upon its close."[47]

A reading of the sources without presuppositions would, in fact, shed this gleam of brightness over the entire period of the Second Athenian League, with regard to Athens's treatment of the League's member states. The Athenians offered membership in a free alliance with the publication of the decree of Aristoteles in 377, specifying safeguards to assure that it would not become another Athenian Empire. Contrary to the consensus of modern scholarship, it never did. The League lost strength because some of its members came into the orbits of aggressive powers and some sought their own advantage through secession. Many of these came to realize, too late, that the Athenian alliance offered the best available protection for their freedom. After Chaironeia, Philip organized the Greek states, for his purposes, into the so-called League of Korinth. Its structure parodied many features of the Athenian League, as legislative bodies in modern dictatorships parody those of free governments. A synedrion with representatives from all the Greek states had to approve the policies of this new league's hegemon, the Macedonian king. But Macedonian garrisons were placed at strategic locations around Greece, and no one asked for Greek approval of their establishment. Athens had restored rebels from its League to full, equal membership. When (in 335) Thebes rebelled from the League of Korinth, Alexander terrified other potential dissidents by levelling the city to the

47. *IG* II², 233, lines 18–23 (brackets of Tod 175, in which these are lines 30–35); Marshall 120. It may also have been a mark of honor that a Tenedian, Aglaokreon, was taken as the synedrion's representative with the Athenian embassy negotiating the peace of Philokrates (Ais. 2.20, 97, and 126).

ground. So much for structural similarities between the Leagues of Philip and Athens.

By organizing its League and generally adhering to the principles upon which it was founded, Athens emerged in the first half of the fourth century B.C. as the most powerful and respected state in Greece. The League was the cornerstone of Athens's system of alliances, directed first against Spartan aggressiveness, then against the expansionism of the Thebans, Persians, and Macedonians. The fact that Demosthenes and other Athenians were proud of their city's tradition of Hellenic leadership and exaggerated its benevolence should not blind the honest historian to Athens's greatness, nor to the *comparative* truth of its claim of benevolence. When the Thebans, in pursuit of their own glory, undermined Athens's leadership, they undermined the survival of Greece as an independent entity. Nor should we overlook the significance of the unique individual. Philip of Macedon, antagonist and admirer of Athens, is given short shrift by those who believe that he essentially only "mopped up" a ruined, degenerate Greece. His genius deserves greater credit than this traditional viewpoint allows. Conversely, the excessive praise of his character and generosity and the concomitant denigration of those of his chief Hellenic opponents (most notably Demosthenes), which have also become scholarly commonplaces, have equally little factual basis.[48] In the absence of Philip's military and diplomatic skill—and his good fortune at escaping several brushes with violent death—the likelihood is that *Athens* would have emerged as the unchallenged leader of fourth-century Greece.

It is possible to speculate about what might have happened if the Athenian alliance had not been debilitated and Philip had been stopped at or prior to Chaironeia. Athens was the least agressive of the Hellenic powers of the fourth century. It might have been able to preside over a Greece of independent states, bound by treaties of nonaggression and defensive alliance, for decades—perhaps even until the development of a genuine Greek federal state. Historians today might study not the Roman Empire but the Greek Federation—which would have been more democratic, intellectual, and creative, we might wager, and perhaps consequently more enduring.[49]

My purpose in this study, however, is not to offer speculations. Nor, as I said in the Introduction, is it to write a full-scale history of the

48. See the severe review of Cawkwell, *Philip of Macedon* (London 1978) by Phillip Harding, *Phoenix* 33 (1979) 173–178, and the still sensible statements of A. W. Gomme, *Essays in Greek History and Literature* (Oxford 1937, repr. Freeport, N.Y. 1967) 225–233.

49. See the interesting related speculations of A. R. Burn, in E. N. Borza (ed.), *The Impact of Alexander the Great* (Hinsdale, Ill. 1974) 147f. Generally moderate and sensible descriptions of fourth-century Athenians' attitudes are to be found in S. Perlman, "Panhellenism, the Polis and Imperialism," *Historia* 25 (1976) 1–30.

League or its period. I have reexamined the sources on the League, particularly the inscriptions, in a way that I believe clarifies their content and their limitations. I feel that the last half-century of Hellenic independence is ripe for a major revision in historical treatment. Freeing investigators of the period from the constraints imposed by the "second Empire" interpretation of the Second Athenian League which permeates modern treatments should help pave the way for that revision. My research has convinced me that the "second Empire" hypothesis is not true. I hope that any open-minded reader of these pages will at least have to concede that it *need not* be true—and will accordingly make the effort to hold the presupposition firmly in abeyance when approaching topics and problems within the period.

SUMMARY HISTORY OF THE
SECOND ATHENIAN LEAGUE (378–338 B.C.)

Any contribution this work might make to historical scholarship on the fourth century B.C. has been made in its carefully documented chapters 1–10. So many commonly held interpretations are questioned within those chapters that almost any informed reader may find there both something which appears new and useful and something with which to disagree strongly. No one is likely to write a detailed historical account that accepts every revised interpretation I have suggested. Nor is this a task I have set for myself. Nonetheless it may be useful to offer a very sketchy outline of the type of chronological history of the Second Athenian League that might be written from the new perspective I have tried to suggest and defend.

Sparta, having won the Peloponnesian War and having deprived Athens of virtually all its fifth-century allies, emerged as hegemon of Greece as the fourth century began. The Lakedaimonians' behavior, however, was such that the previous Athenian domination soon came to appear less frightful to the Greeks, and the Persian King—allied to Sparta in the closing years of the Peloponnesian War, but now also subject to Spartan attack—helped Athens, Thebes, and other Greek states weaken the Spartan position (Korinthian War, 395–387 B.C.). Athens—or at least a powerful faction of Athenians—dreamed for a time of a renewed Empire, but the end result of this long period of turmoil was stalemate all around, and the imposition upon Greece of the King's Peace (386).

This settlement, which recognized Persian control of the Asian Greeks, proclaimed in general the autonomy of other Hellenic states, and (implicitly) supported Spartan hegemony on the Greek mainland, became the fundamental shibboleth of Greek politics for the next several decades. The role of the King himself in enforcing it was sometimes minimized, sometimes reasserted, and the term "common peace" also came to be used, with meanings that overlapped those of "King's Peace." Sparta interpreted its self-appointed role of enforcing the peace as justifying the breakup of all confederacies that might be threatening to Sparta, and were weak enough to yield. The occupation of the Kadmeia (382) as part of the process of dissolving the Theban-dominated Boiotian confederacy was a decisive act of Spartan aggressiveness, causing shock and anger throughout Hellas.

Athens began forming defensive alliances as early as 384, when a permanent pact with Chios was signed, its terms carefully conforming to the provisions of the King's Peace. Several other such bilateral treaties soon followed. In 378 the Athenians converted this collection of alliances into a League in which an allied synedrion, sitting at Athens, would share authority with Athens as hegemon. This fledgling League apparently made an alliance (also in 378) with Thebes, which in 379 had freed itself from the occupying Spartan garrison, drawing on a debatable amount of Athenian assistance. War loomed between Sparta and Thebes, into which Athens and its League might expect to be drawn, and became virtually inevitable when the Spartan commander Sphodrias staged an abortive raid on the port of Athens and his deed was allowed to go unpunished by a Spartan court.

Now *Athens* could pose as the defender of the King's Peace and declare Sparta in violation of it, now Thebes felt sufficiently threatened to become one of six equal members of Athens's League, and now (377) Athens offered something to its island allies (and prospective allies) to make the membership of Thebes and the likelihood of war with Sparta palatable: the publication of the decree of Aristoteles. This proclamation described guarantees and protections which the Athenians promised to states that would accept Athens's hegemony and join its League: defense against attack, freedom and autonomy, self-government under any constitution desired, no collection of tribute, no imposition of Athenian garrisons and governors, and prohibition of Athenian property ownership in the territories of all member states. The publication of this decree amounted to a thorough renunciation of the hated practices of the fifth-century Athenian Empire. Sanctions made the promises believable: Athenian property owners could be expropriated by a process in which Athens did not even participate; punishment of Athenians who might suggest altering the terms of the decree would involve allied participation as well as Athenian.

States flocked to join this Second Athenian League, beginning on Euboia and the Aegean islands and shorelines (excluding Asia, which was recognized as being under the King's power). The decisive naval victory of Chabrias at Naxos (376) further weakened Sparta's position and brought in more Athenian allies. Chabrias and Timotheos recruited members in the Aegean and in the waters off northwest Greece (375) —though agreements made with Korkyra and some Kephallenian cities apparently were not consummated in League membership. The states that joined were of all types: Ionians, Dorians, other Greek stocks, "barbarians"; democracies, oligarchies, kingdoms; single cities and regional confederacies. After further losses in the west, Sparta was forced to make peace (375/4), recognizing Athens (at least implicitly) as joint hegemon of Greece. But the Athenians made the mistake of pushing Sparta too far, according recognition and League membership to democratic factions in states oligarchically governed and friendly to Sparta,

Zakynthos and (probably) Thera (ca. 374). This led to renewed war, and ultimately to stalemate and the peace of Sparta of 371. Athens made no more alliances with factions, and in fact ceased to make additions to its League.

All the states joining the Athenian League had their names inscribed on the stele bearing the decree of Aristoteles, exhibited prominently beside the statue of Zeus Eleutherios in the Athenian agora. Joining involved several stages: recruitment, often through a visit from an Athenian general and fleet; sending of presbeis to Athens, who swore oaths of alliance and in turn received the oaths of Athenian and League officials; then the sending of a committee to receive ratifying oaths from the new member's magistrates at home. When all this was completed, the name of the new ally would be inscribed and its representative(s) in the synedrion (the mode of choosing whom is unknown) would be seated. Athens was not a member of the synedrion, nor did an Athenian preside. Each member state, regardless of size (or number of synedroi), cast one vote in this council: the alliances were officially "equal," and patterned after those of Chios and Thebes. The vote of the majority of the synedroi had equal authority with the vote of the Athenian demos, and the establishment of any League policy required the approval of both; each could, in effect, "veto" the other. Athenian hegemony consisted of holding this half of the voting power, providing the actual commanding officers who led expeditions and collected and spent money for the League's purposes, and being recognized by all concerned as the most powerful state within the alliance and the one providing the largest share of the League navy's ships and crews.

Athens and the League were highly successful in their struggle with Sparta (378–371), and the members had reason to be pleased with Athenian leadership: evidence exists of allied goodwill toward Timotheos and Chabrias especially. Late in 371, a peace agreement signed at Athens would exalt the Athenians and their League to virtually the position Sparta had occupied under the original King's Peace. Though recruitment of new League members had ceased, Greek cities continued to ally themselves with the League (Korkyra and probably others seem to have done so in the 370s). Certain kings and tyrants apparently made bilateral alliances with Athens during the same period (e.g., probably Jason of Pherai and/or Amyntas of Macedon). The making of both these types of alliance would persist through the 360s. But trouble was brewing within the League from the ambitious Thebans, led by Epameinondas and Pelopidas.

The Thebans reconstituted the Boiotian confederacy, shirked League military and financial responsibilities, and razed the resisting Boiotian town of Plataia, despite expressions of opposition from Plataia's longtime supporter Athens (373). At the Spartan peace conference of 371 things came to a head, as the Theban demand to be allowed to take the peace oaths on behalf of all "the Boiotians" was rejected by King Agesilaos. As Athens and the other League allies passively looked on, no doubt hoping to see Theban aggressiveness chastened, the Spartan army marched into Boiotia—only to suffer a surprising, humiliating, and epoch-making defeat at Leuktra (371). The peace signed at Athens shortly afterward tacitly recognized Thebes' withdrawal from the League, and its terms required military action against future aggression. A series of Theban-led invasions of the Peloponnesos (370–362) tested the seriousness of this threat, and found it rather ineffective. Allies were won away from both the Spartan and Athenian Leagues by the triumphant Thebans (from Athens's orbit were lost those nearest Boiotia—the Euboians and Akarnanians). The essentially maritime Athenian League could do little in this prolonged continental warfare, despite the alliance it signed with the Peloponnesian League in 369. Sparta, the fertile lands of Messenia having been detached by these invasions, would never again emerge as a major power in Greece. When a peace of exhaustion (both Pelopidas and Epameinondas now being dead) was signed after the battle of Mantineia (362), Sparta refused to participate because the treaty recognized Messenia's independence. This effectively terminated the Peloponnesian League's alliance with the Athenian League and led certain Peloponnesian states, heretofore Athenian allies by virtue of their connection with Sparta, to make their own renewed Athenian alliance.

Athens also had troubles in the Aegean within the 360s. Theban assertiveness won Persian approval at a conference at Susa in 367, awakening the Athenians to a renewed Persian menace. Quite possibly at this time an expression of adherence to the King's Peace was chiseled away from the text of the decree of Aristoteles. Athens pressed long-standing claims to Amphipolis and the Chersonesos, and the King was forced to accede to them. Probably in 365, in reaction to Persian involvement there, an Athenian kleruchy was sent to the island of Samos. Others were later dispatched to Poteidaia, to the Chersonesos, and perhaps to other places (but not to any League members' territories). In the late 370s and throughout the 360s certain Athenian allies were moved to revolt, i.e., to attempt to secede from the permanent League alliance. Theban sponsorship is attested or reasonably inferred in connection with several of these revolts. Alexander of Pherai, himself a disloyal Athenian bilateral ally, seized other League cities. Successful rebel states included Byzantion and the Chalkidian confederacy led by Olynthos. Decisive but temperate Athenian action succeeded in restoring some rebels to the League, and the terms of readmission, judging from an inscribed treaty with a city on Keos, were mild and reassuring. In particular, there is no firm evidence that an Athenian garrison or governor was established in the territory of any forcibly restored rebel.

Garrisons and governors by this time, however, had already long been employed in the lands of loyal members, and of non-League allies. The various peaces signed with Sparta during the 370s provided for the mutual withdrawal of them by the hegemones, and inscriptional evidence attests to the existence of several. The sources nowhere indicate that these installations gave offense to the members of the League. It must have been agreed, quite early in the history of the confederacy, that protection from enemy attack took precedence over the letter of the Athenian pledge of 377 against sending garrisons and governors. Inscriptions which mention similar establishments within the 350s show the synedrion's participation in such matters as paying the garrison troops, so it seems clear that the sending out of garrisons and governors was common League policy, not an Athenian imposition upon unwilling allies. The crisis that led to the dispatch of the best attested examples occurred in 357–355.

In 357, strife arose within the Euboian cities that in 370 had been detached from the League by Thebes. Factions called in both the Thebans and the Athenians, and a month of skirmishing went in the Athenian partisans' favor. The result was the restoration of at least several Euboian cities to the League. Forces elsewhere, however, were working to tear the League asunder; in that same year began the momentous Social War. The secessionists were states far from Athens and particularly subject to Persian influence. Demosthenes later blamed the satrap Mausolos of Karia for instigating the entire movement; at least it is clear that he assisted the rebels. Many authors have viewed this war as the logical consequence of increasing Athenian harshness toward the allies, the return of fifth-century style imperialism. The wartime behavior of the Athenian general Chares, unanimously condemned in the ancient sources, lends credence to this opinion (though some of his brutalities may be misdated in late sources), as does the tone of profound pessimism and exhaustion of Isokrates' *On the Peace* and Xenophon's *Poroi*, both apparently written around the end of the war. The existence of wartime garrisons and governors is also frequently cited as evidence for Athenian mistreatment of the allies.

This traditional interpretation, however, does less than justice to the sources. The use of garrisons and governors was long-standing League policy in times of crisis, not an innovation at the time of the Social War. Increasing Athenian "imperialism" also lacks ancient evidence: upon examination of the sources, arguments for Athenian breaches of the promises of the decree of Aristoteles turn out to be decidedly ill supported, whereas evidence for generous Athenian treatment of the allies is plentiful. Arguments based on the existence of kleruchies are particularly wide of the mark, since the Athenians' promise to avoid property ownership *in League members' territories* admittedly was kept to the letter. The Social War was in fact an Aegean-wide war of which the secession of certain allies was only one aspect. In addition to the activities of

Mausolos and the continuing hostility of former League members such as Thebes and Byzantion, Philip II of Macedon (having become king in 359) also was busily detaching cities from Athenian leadership along the shores of the northern Aegean.

Due largely to the bumbling and vindictive leadership of Chares, the Athenians suffered defeat after defeat. The mere necessity to pay his troops at length led him to take service (with the approval of the demos) under a Persian satrap in rebellion against the King. This in turn prompted the King to address an ultimatum to the Athenians, who agreed to make peace with the rebels and promised to recognize their autonomy. It is generally assumed that this amounted to accepting *de jure* their secession from the League, though it is striking that the sources omit saying so. In any case, their *de facto* separation must have been recognized, and several of the rebel states soon were taken over by their erstwhile ally Mausolos, or by his widow and successor Artemisia. Philip continued to conquer cities, and Byzantion absorbed certain nearby League members. The maritime League, then, was severely crippled by the events of the mid-350s. It continued in existence, but Athenian attentions were increasingly concentrated on the Greek mainland and the steady advance of Philip.

Athens, influenced by the fiery orations of Demosthenes, formed alliances of whatever type was possible against Macedonian expansion, generally bilateral. Thracian kings, former League members who did not want the responsibilities of renewed member status (Athens was in no position now to insist), and others became Athenian allies through their fear of Philip. Many Athenians, however, did not greatly fear him. These regarded his interest in Greek hegemony as essentially friendly, saw him as a possible leader in a panhellenic war against Persia (Isokrates came to hold this position), or were simply bought by his ample gold (Philokrates seems to fit this category). Even leaders who agreed on the principle of opposing Philip (e.g., Demosthenes and Euboulos) differed, sometimes bitterly, on methods and on where to take a stand. Aischines, the inveterate personal foe of Demosthenes, is difficult to classify, and one's choice of his category can influence one's opinion of the reliability of his orations as evidence—and the reliability, in turn, of the Demosthenic speeches they contradict. In 346 Philokrates sponsored a peace and alliance between Philip and the Athenian League, an agreement that proved to be a prelude to further hostilities. Rival politicians later claimed to have realized this would happen at the time, and argued that their personal roles in making the treaty were either minimal or reluctantly assumed from military necessity. The rancorous *post factum* debate over the circumstances of the signing of this peace and alliance provides several clues for the mechanism of dividing authority between Athens and the League synedrion.

Philip's power by this time was approaching unassailability. Another peace treaty, also signed in 346, ended the decade-long Sacred War associated with the Phokian seizure of Delphoi. Philip the Macedonian had become a member of the ancient Greek Delphic amphictyony and general of its army, and had established a precedent for his interference in Hellenic affairs. Some years later, an invitation from the amphictyony—in which Aischines played a decisive role—would bring him and his army through the pass of Thermopylai into central Greece for the beginning of the fateful campaign of Chaironeia. Demosthenes desperately negotiated alliances against Philip wherever he could find them. Even Byzantion finally decided that Philip was more to be feared than Athens, and Athenian and allied help succeeded in breaking Philip's siege of that important city in 339. But he seized many cities along the northern Aegean coast—Athenian possessions, League allies, non-League allies, no distinction being made between them—and worked his way inexorably down the mainland. Euboia had fallen under his influence sometime during the 340s. As the decisive conflict loomed, allies who had previously abandoned Athens voluntarily returned to join the last defender of Greek liberty: Akarnanians fought at Chaironeia, and Demosthenes was even able to negotiate a renewed Theban alliance in 339. Philip, ably assisted by his nineteen-year-old son Alexander as cavalry commander, won decisively at Chaironeia in Boiotia in 338. As part of the peace settlement he dictated, the Second Athenian League was dissolved, after some forty years of existence.

During these years Athens seems generally to have kept the promises made to prospective members in 377, and allied outcries against Athenian abuses are difficult to discover in contemporary sources. The states that rebelled, successfully or not, appear to have done so usually under the influence of their own ambitions (e.g., Thebes, Olynthos, Byzantion) or external pressure (e.g., from these successful rebels, Alexander of Pherai, Persian satraps, or Philip). Many allies remained loyal throughout; several who unsuccessfully rebelled in the early years of the League did not rise up in response to later movements toward revolt. Since no evidence indicates they were held to loyalty by any Athenian military presence, and since Athenian preoccupation with conflicts all over the Aegean should have provided many opportunities, it seems reasonable to believe such states (e.g., Paros and the Kean cities) were content with the settlements that had been made with them. Loyal allies (e.g., Tenedos and Elaious) were honored by the Athenians in both word and deed, and even disloyal allies were frequently given Athenian help when they belatedly sought it. Members' monetary contributions (syntaxeis) to the League were not high, and were levied in cooperation with the allied representatives. Though some signs of desperation during and after the Social War exist, and the destructive personal effect of

Chares is well attested, there is no reason to believe that the Second Athenian League ever became—or tried to become—another Athenian Empire. Isokrates' *On the Peace*, which is generally seen as a lament that such a development had occurred, is in reality an attack on wartime abuses, chiefly those of Chares.

It is reasonable to suppose that a panhellenic hegemony of the great democracy, acknowledged cultural and intellectual leader of the Greeks, limited moreover by explicit treaty commitments recognizing allies' autonomy, would have been very different from that of the foreign conqueror. The tradition that Chaironeia marks the watershed between the "classical" and "Hellenistic" ages is not an arbitrary one. When Athenian hegemony was finally broken, Greece became a political appanage of Macedon, and subsequently passed under the domination of Rome. Nothing can change these facts, but it is possible to reconsider the meaning of the development. Deterministic historical thinking has given us a fourth century of renewed Athenian imperialism, general Greek degeneracy, and inevitable Macedonian takeover. If Athens did not renew its fifth-century imperialism, the whole neat sequence breaks down. Any responsible treatment of the fourth century must begin with a reexamination of the behavior of Athens, and of the League that was central to its policy. And this reexamination must begin without presuppositions about where it must "inevitably" lead.

COMPARATIO NUMERORUM

The following table includes every inscription cited in the notes. The farthest left column in which an entry appears in the table is the collection by whose number the inscription is cited. *SV* entries which appear in the notes but not in the table are exclusively literary sources. *SV* numbers marked by an asterisk in the table are entries which include bibliography and commentary, but no text. Only such inscriptions, my own text of DA (chapter 2), and inscriptions that appear in neither *SV* nor *IG* are given entries in the "Other" column of the table, though the notes frequently refer to more than one version of a text. Inscriptions are never primarily cited by their numbers in Tod (or ML's revision of his vol. I) or WV, but cross-references to these handy selections are added.

SV	*IG* II²	Other *IG*	Other	Tod	WV
120				(ML 10)	
134		I² 10 + 12f		(ML 40)	
		I² 45		(ML 49)	
162		I² 51		(ML 63)	
163		I² 52		(ML 64)	
		I² 63		(ML 69)	
		I² 66		(ML 46)	
		I² 118		(ML 90)	
	1			97	1
223	14			101	5
224	15			102	6
229	16			103	7
232					
235*			Woodhead *Hesp.* 26 (1957) no. 85		
	1398				
	30				
		XII(8) 3f, 6, 9– 12, 26, 46, 668			
248	34 + 35			118	17
250	36			119	

SV	IG II²	Other IG	Other	Tod	WV
255	40				21
256	41			121	19
257	43 + 883		DA (chapter 2)	123	22
258	42			122	20
259	44			124	23
			SEG XXI 230		
	1604				
	55				
	1635				24
262	96			126	25
	5224				
			Stroud Hesp. 48 (1974) 157-9		
			Burnett and Edmonson Hesp. 30 (1961) 79f		
263	97			127	26
		XII(3) Supp. p. 280 no. 1289			
264	102			129	29
	1609				30
267	98				
	103			133	
268*			Accame, p. 230		31
278	104			134	
279*			Woodhead Hesp. 26 (1957) no. 84		
280	105 + 523			136	38
			Schweigert Hesp. 8 (1939) no. 3		
287		XII(5) 594		141	
			Klaffenbach MDAI(A) 51 (1926) 36		41
	110			143	45
289	111			142	44
290	112			144	46
292		IV 556		145	47
	114			146	48
293	116 + 175			147	49
294					
			Syll.³ 188	148	
		XII(7) 5		152	54
296					
	1952				
	122				

SV	IG II²	Other IG	Other	Tod	WV
	123			156	55
	125			154	53
			Schweigert *Hesp.* 8 (1939) no. 4		
303	126			151	51
304	124			153	52
	404				56
308				158	58
309	127			157	57
	133				
	141			139	
311	148				
312	128			159	59
		VII 2418		160	
		XII(5) 714			
		XII(5) 1000			
	155				
	1437				
320	1128			162	61
321	179				
			*Syll.*³ 209–211		
			*Syll.*³ 212	163	62
324	207				
325	208				
	211			166	
	212			167	65
	1441				
	1443				
328	213			168	66
			*Syll.*³ 213f + 216	171	
			*Syll.*³ 217–219		
337	225				
	226			173	71
	228			174	
340	230				
	232				
	233			175	72
(III) 403a	236			177	
	237			178	
	242				
	284			170	
	653				
		XII(5) 444		205	
		XII(5) 526f			

INDEX OF SOURCES CITED

Ancient sources cited in the notes are often discussed and/or quoted in the accompanying text, q.v. Textual discussions of sources which lack footnotes are entered here by their text page numbers. Asterisk indicates quotation (in note or text) of some or all of the Greek (or Latin) original. See "Abbreviations" (pp. xiii–xvii) and "Comparatio Numerorum" (pp. 197–199) for clarification of form of references. For brevity, epigraphical references here omit the word "line(s)" (thus *SV* 120.4f, e.g., means *SV* 120, lines 4f).

INDEX OF NAMES AND TOPONYMS

References here are to pages of the text; see accompanying notes for possible additional discussion. References are made to the notes only when names or toponyms are mentioned there and *not* on the same pages of the text. Entries for ancient authors refer to mentions in which no specific work is cited; in general see "Index of Sources Cited." Names of modern writers are not indexed. References to ethnics and adjectives related to a toponym are listed with references to the toponym itself. Entries are supplied for the Delian League/Athenian Empire and Philip's "League of Korinth"; for other confederacies, see appropriate toponyms, e.g., Boiotia and Peloponnesos. The King's Peace and the Peloponnesian, Korinthian, Social, and Sacred Wars are also given entries. No references are listed, however, for Athens, Attica, Athenian demes, months (etc.), the Second Athenian League, Greece, or Hellas.

Designer:	George Mackie
Compositor:	Freedmen's Organization
Printer:	Braun-Brumfield
Binder:	Braun-Brumfield
Text:	Palatino
Display:	Palatino